Poverty, Famine and Economic Development

The Selected Essays of Meghnad Desai
Volume II

Meghnad Desai

Professor of Economics and Director
Centre for the Study of Global Governance
London School of Economics

ECONOMISTS OF THE TWENTIETH CENTURY

Edward Elgar

Published by
Edward Elgar Publishing Limited
Gower House
Croft Road
Aldershot
Hants GU11 3HR
England

Edward Elgar Publishing Company
Old Post Road
Brookfield
Vermont 05036
USA

British Library Cataloguing in Publication Data
Desai, Meghnad
    Selected Essays of Meghnad Desai. –
Vol. 2: Poverty, Famine and Economic
Development. – (Economists of the Twentieth
Century Series)
I. Title II. Series
338.9

Library of Congress Cataloguing in Publication Data
Desai, Meghnad
    The selected essays of Meghnad Desai / Meghnad Desai.
        p.   cm. — (Economists of the twentieth century)
    Contents: v. 1. Macroeconomics and monetary theory —
v. 2. Poverty, famine, and economic development.
    1. Macroeconomics. 2. Monetary policy. 3. Economic development.
4. Poverty. 5. Famines. I. Title. II. Series.
HB172.5.D48   1994
339—dc20   94–33660
                                                                            CIP

ISBN   1 85278 689 2 (Volume I)
        1 85278 690 6 (Volume II)
        1 85898 095 X (2 volume set)

Printed and bound in Great Britain by
Hartnolls Limited, Bodmin, Cornwall

Contents

v

Acknowledgements

The publishers wish to thank the following for giving permission for the use of copyright material.

Allen and Unwin for article: 'Economic Alternatives for Labour, 1984–9' in J. Griffith (ed.), *Socialism in a Cold Climate*, 1983, pp. 37–64.

Arab Researcher for article: 'Is State Control Necessary for Economic Development in the Third World?', *Arab Researcher*, March 1985, reset.

Basil Blackwell for articles: with Dipak Mazumdar, 'A Test of the Hypothesis of Disguised Unemployment', *Economica*, February 1970, pp. 39–53; 'Story-telling and Formalism in Economics: The Instance of Famine', *International Social Science Journal*, August 1987, pp. 387–400.

Child Poverty Action Group for article: 'Drawing the Line: On Defining the Poverty Threshold' in Peter Golding (ed.), *Excluding the Poor*, 1986, pp. 1–20.

Elsevier Science Publishers B.V. for article: 'Rice and Fish: Asymmetric Preferences and Entitlement Failures in Food Growing Economics with Non-Food Producers', *European Journal of Political Economy*, 1990, pp. 429–40.

Indian Economic Review for articles: 'The Role of Exchange and Market Relationships in the Economics of the Transition Period: Lenin on the Tax in Kind', **XI** (1), April 1976, pp. 61–8; 'A General Theory of Poverty? A Review Article', **XIX** (2), 1984, pp. 157–69.

Oxford University Press for articles: with Anup Shah 'An Econometric Approach to the Measurement of Poverty', *Oxford Economic Papers*, **40** (3), September 1988, pp. 505–22; 'The Economics of Famine' in G.A. Harrison (ed.), *Famine*, 1988, pp. 107–38.

Tavistock Publications for article: 'Consumption and Pollution' in I.R.C. Hirst and W.D. Reekie (eds), *The Consumer Society*, 1976, pp. 23–36, reset.

Third World Quarterly for article: 'Homilies of a Victorian Sage: A Review Article on Peter Bauer', **4** (2), April 1982, pp. 291–7.

Preface

The essays collected together in these two volumes span my academic life up to 1991. I came to study Economics for negative reasons. I hated mathematics at school; what little talent I may have had for it was knocked out by bad teaching. So when I finished school and had my choice of what degree to pursue, I spurned science, medicine or engineering (the more sought after courses) and chose Arts. But even in Arts, I was not to have my choice of specializing in Sanskrit or History. I was strongly advised by my family that if I wanted to find employment upon graduation, I should study Economics. So I took Economics rather than my first love History (it wouldn't do to marry one's first love anyway!).

Upon getting my BA from the University of Bombay, I once again thought of escape and fancied specializing at the MA level in Political Science, then a comparatively new offering at Bombay. I was dissuaded from this course when, on my way to the University, I met a former student of my undergraduate college who was two years my senior. He had just completed his MA in Economics and had been rewarded with a management trainee position in a bank! That clinched it; I wanted such a glamorous job so, to the relief of my family, I once again plumped for Economics.

Studying Economics in Bombay both at the undergraduate and the graduate levels was a great experience. Libraries were very well stocked and our lectures being in the morning (7.30 am to 12.00 noon), I spent all my afternoons in the Library exploring all sorts of subjects. I was encouraged to read widely both by my family and, until they thought I was getting too big headed, by my teachers. The grounding I had in economic history in my BA was especially good as it has kept me interested in that subject ever since.

I studied for my MA at the Postgraduate Department of Economics, patterned on the LSE but much smaller. Bombay's strength was in applied economics with Professor D.T. Lakdawala in Public Finance and Professor M.L. Dantwala in Agricultural Economics. But our constant companion and delight as students was Professor P.R. Brahmanand. Anyone who met or corresponded with Brahmanand will remember him. As a bachelor and a very hard-working person he was forever on the Department premises, his large office at the end of the corridor on the first floor always open to students. Brahmanand was a Marshallian, and Pigouvian welfare economics was his favourite topic. He was largely self-taught and, at least while I was there (1958–61), innocent of mathematics. But he gave what I consider one of the best expositions I have ever heard of the General Theory. His efforts to make me respect Marshall fell however on stony ground.

It was during my MA that I deepened my understanding of economics, reading for example the entire controversy about 'empty economic boxes' from Clapham's classic paper through all the *EJ*s of the 1920s and early 1930s. I wrote a 60 page paper on Hayek's theory of the cycle; and ever since Hayek has been one of the economists I have kept up with, despite strong political disagreement with his views.

India in the 1950s was a battleground of the cold war, with the rival superpowers trying to win the 'hearts and minds' of Indians, especially educated youth, to their side. You could buy Marx's *Capital* for one rupee (even in those days worth 1s.3d or 6p in today's coin) on the pavements of downtown Bombay. The US Information Service retaliated with cheap editions of Mark Twain and J. Stuart Mill. It was as part of some such deep strategy that the Ford Foundation endowed a chair in Money and Banking at Bombay which for five years was filled by distinguished American economists, Alvin Hansen being the first. I remember as a 16-year old undergraduate going to listen to him speaking on Keynes, along with hundreds of others. I doubt if Alvin Hansen ever had a larger audience in his life.

It was as part of this scheme that Professor Charles Whittlesey of the University of Pennsylvania was visiting during 1959–60, my senior MA year. He encouraged me to apply to American universities and to take the Graduate Record Examination for this purpose. I was meant by my family to sit for the much-coveted Indian Administrative Service (IAS) examination and become a civil servant. But luck was on my side; one had to be 21 before one could sit the examination. Upon getting my MA I had yet another year to go before I would be 21, so I entered the PhD programme at Bombay. The Bombay regime was easy-going. As a PhD student I had a small fellowship and library borrowing privileges as well as a desk. I didn't do much work in my first year; I was not expected to by anyone except my supervisor Miss Kanta Ranadive who had just joined Bombay and not got used to local habits! I had a marvellous time reading, taking part in amateur dramatics (too long a story to tell here) and sitting in coffee houses. I had chosen a topic – International Commodity Agreements – but little else. It was this choice that was to prove crucial.

I did reasonably well in my GRE and got a fellowship to the University of Pennsylvania, thus saving me from the Civil Service. I was to join Penn as a Research Assistant and pursue graduate work. It was at this point that my long escape from mathematics ended. I arrived at Penn in pristine ignorance of maths and stats; it was taken as a stylized fact in the US that all Indians were good statisticians – I was the exception. But since I was supposed to know something about commodity agreements, I was assigned to work with Professor Lawrence Klein who wanted to build commodity models.

This was my lucky break. Starting from September 1961, I benefited from weekly meetings with Lawrence Klein. In fact these were meetings to report the progress I had made on building a model of the world tin economy. I was so eager for Klein to teach me that I concentrated on the model to the relative neglect of my course work. It was a sort of conspiracy between the two of us. I was too afraid to tell him how ignorant I was and he always gave me just that little bit of extra work to cope with, since he knew how ignorant I was but didn't say so to my face. It worked. Within two years of my arrival I had completed my comprehensives and submitted my PhD on 'An Econometric Model of the World Tin Economy'. I could not have done that without Klein's understanding or without the help of many colleagues and friends, among them Gerry Adams, Paul Taubman and K. Krishnamurty.

Another formative influence at Penn was Sidney Weintraub. Learning economics from Sidney Weintraub cures you for all time of faith in any textbook. He had himself written an extremely innovative and hence completely neglected textbook on Price

Theory. But it was his teaching of Keynes that was memorable. We were all made to read the *General Theory* and to hold in complete contempt all compromises, be they from Hicks, Samuelson, Patinkin, Tobin or Friedman. Weintraub is still relatively unknown, but that is because his power does not come through in his written work. I have never been enamoured of the neo-Keynesian or the new Keynesian interpretation of Keynes. When Axel Leijonhufvud's book came out in 1968, I was less impressed than many because Sidney warned us long ago that most people had got Keynes wrong. My subsequent writing on macroeconomics has always been unconventional because I could never take the IS–LM stuff seriously.

Keynes tried to theorize about a monetary economy. Neither the Walrasian nor the neo-Walrasian theory can handle this problem. Even the monetarists and their spiritual heirs, the new classical economists, treat money as a veil and wish the economy was a barter one. Before Keynes wrote his *General Theory*, only Myrdal in his *Monetary Equilibrium* and some later rare economists such as Hyman Minsky and Victoria Chick have made progress along that path. Even classical political economy, especially Ricardo, has essentially a non-monetary view. The homogeneity postulate is in my opinion the greatest obstacle to decent theorizing about a monetary economy.

From Penn I went to Berkeley for two years to work in the Agricultural Economics Department. I spent those years deepening my econometric knowledge and having a good time. For work, I was engaged on a massive computer simulation study of the California Dairy Industry. The idea was to measure the price distortion caused by the peculiar market structure which operated there. The work was in a way technically satisfying, but I itched to give up commodity modelling and get back to some proper economics.

Berkeley also rejuvenated me in a radical direction. The Civil Rights struggle led to the Free Speech Movement in Berkeley and then Vietnam became an issue. Since staying in the US was problematical as I would be eligible for the draft, I left and arrived at the LSE in October 1965. It was the hectic but convivial atmosphere at the LSE which give me my real boost. Although I was hired as an applied econometrician, no one questioned if I drifted into economic history, macroeconomics and development. My interests were in understanding the UK economy, which led to my work on the Phillips curve and the Goodwin model. It also led to teaching Marxian Economics as a result of the 1968 student rebellion. When the students demanded that they be taught Marx, I was happy to oblige.

The 1970s were thus occupied by my work on the Phillips curve and by macroeconomics, by Marxian economics and by applied econometrics. It was only towards the end of the 1970s that I turned to a critique of monetarism. I wanted to examine monetarism as an economic theory as much as for its econometric pretensions. This was to some extent the coming together of my various interests in econometric modelling, in Keynesian monetary theory and in political economy.

The 1980s saw my interests move much towards political economy. Inspired by Amartya Sen's work, I got interested in poverty, famine and human development. I went on monitoring the UK economy and succeeded, with the help of my student and colleague Guglielmo Weber, in building a 'proper' Keynesian model of the UK economy. But I am still not satisfied that I have even the rudiments of a proper theory of a monetary economy.

As I get older my interests proliferate rather than get narrower. But in the 1990s they will be in political economy, Keynes, Marx, macroeconomics, development, economic history and econometrics. Who knows? I may even succeed in getting some articles published!

Introduction

Many of the essays included in this volume were written during the 1980s. I had always been interested in the problems of economic development. After all, my early economics education was in Bombay at a time when names like Ragnar Nurkse, Arthur Lewis, Albert Hirschman and Harvey Leibenstein were creating the new subject area of economic development. Balanced *vs* unbalanced growth, the Big Push and surplus labour were major issues.

For my dissertation I had worked on an econometric model of the World Tin Economy. This was indirectly a way of linking consumers of the tin-developed countries with producers of tin-underdeveloped countries. Thus I came to development via econometrics. Chapter 1 in this collection is an example of this. The notion of surplus labour or disguised unemployment had been around for a long time, but it had been neither properly formulated nor rigorously tested. To test the hypothesis properly required microeconomic data; to be consistent with microeconomic theory, for surplus labour to exist at all it must be in family labour rather than hired labour. With the help of Dipak Mazumdar, who had done some pioneering work in this area, we set about testing the hypothesis. The results are fairly dramatic as readers will be able to see. Some of the simplicities of development economics had to be reexamined.

The bulk of other papers are a result of the influence of Amartya Sen. I read his article on Bengal famine in the *Cambridge Journal of Economics* in an early draft while I was visiting CORE during 1976–77. Then when his book *Poverty and Famine* appeared, I realized that this was exactly the sort of (development) economics I wanted to pursue (see Sen (1977), (1981)).

My first foray into 'SENsible' economics was the review article on Poverty and Famine which appears here as Chapter 11. This lays out in some pedagogic detail Sen's theory of famine. The picture is further elaborated and developed in Chapters 5 and 7. There is unfortunately some overlap between these two papers which is unavoidable in a collection of this sort. Perhaps the distinctive contribution in these essays is the systems modelling of entitlement failure. This way of presenting entitlement failure in terms of interacting subsystems is useful for policy modelling, as I was able to show in my work on early warning systems (Desai (1990) in Dreze and Sen (1990)).

In the famine area, it is my essay 'Rice and Fish', reprinted here as Chapter 8, which is perhaps somewhat original and takes the argument beyond Sen's own work. This paper appeals to my conviction that eventually there is no escape from a rigorous analytical formulation of any problem. Thus I formulate the Sen problem in terms of a two-person two-commodity general equilibrium framework. There are special assumptions about asymmetry of preferences and complete specialization in production, but these are explicitly made. The paper offers two examples where maximizing behaviour by individuals still leads to famine, but without having to invoke market failure. Behaviour is constrained by tastes and technology. Thus although parameter restrictions are required to bring the result about, it proves the possibility of such an outcome with market clearing.

There are four related papers on poverty (Chapters 2, 6, 13 and 14). Of these, Chapters 2 and 6 relate to UK poverty and are inspired by the work of Peter Townsend. Again in Essay 2 (written jointly with Anup Shah), the emphasis is on a rigorous formulation of Townsend's concept of relative deprivation. It is an attempt to formulate the notion of social and economic distance covering both the objective facts of deprivation and the subjective feeling of isolation. There is an attempt at econometric implementation of the new measure. Chapter 6 was written for a more popular but more concerned audience and defends the notion of a poverty level based on the earlier paper.

In logical terms, it is Chapter 14 which follows Chapter 2. Here I compare attempts to measure poverty in absolute terms which is more popular among policy makers. This paper came out of some work I did for the Latin America Regional Office of the UK Development Programme. My interest at that time was in examining the two alternative methods of measuring poverty that were used in Latin America.

It is this series of papers as well as Amartya Sen's work on capabilities which led to 'Poverty and Capability' (Chapter 13). This paper, like Chapter 14, has not been published before. It is an ambitious attempt to propose an empirical implementation of Sen's notion of capabilities. Sen's work is a continuation of his Geary lecture, of 'Poor, Relatively Speaking' and the debate with Townsend in the pages of the *Oxford Economic Papers*. He then took up the notion of capabilities in his *Commodities and Capabilities* and later in 'The Standard of Living' (all these references are in Chapter 13).

My concern in Chapter 13 is to try and render the capability-based notion of poverty econometrically implementable. Once again I exploit the Linear Expenditure System (LES) which I use in Chapter 8 for a different purpose. I regret that the actual implementation was never carried out as there were some difficulties in obtaining access to ECLAC data. But it remains my hope that someone may implement it one day.

The other five papers (3, 4, 9, 10 and 12) relate to broader theories in development. Nowadays the role of the market is much extolled in the development literature and the role of the state played down. Chapter 3 discusses an article of Lenin's which was at the basis of the New Economic Policy – the first attempt at 'market socialism' in the Soviet Union during the 1920s. Although it was written during my stay at the Delhi School of Economics during 1970–71 and appeared in the Delhi School Journal four years later, the themes it explores are much more alive today.

Chapters 9 and 10 take up the related theme of the state *vs* market. Peter (now Lord) Bauer was a colleague with whom I much disagreed but for whom I have much admiration. My review article of his book *Equality, the Third World and Economic Delusion* appeared at the beginning of the decade during which there was a sea change in the debate about state *vs* market. Chapter 10 marks the shift in my own thinking in this respect.

Chapter 12 is an early attempt to integrate pollution calculations in an input-output framework. Again the emphasis is on a conceptual scheme which is empirically implementable. The idea is that pollution is an integral part of economic activity and must be taken into account as the mirror image (dual) of consumption. There was an attempt to implement my scheme during the 1970s by my friend Peter Sadler which demonstrated the feasibility of the notion. Perhaps the time has come to look at it again with new data.

Last but not least is Chapter 4 which is an example of my activity as an economist on the political front. It was during the early 1980s that a group of LSE academics came together and started thinking about what the Labour Party would do when in office. The title of the collection, *Socialism in a Cold Climate*, conveys that as early as 1983 we were feeling the chill winds of exile from office. Since then I have written many such programmatic essays, but the hope of return to power still remains to be rewarded by actual experience. The essay however outlines structural problems of the UK economy which I do believe still persist even after ten years; hence although it is dated, it is by no means outdated.

Issues of poverty and development in rich as well as poor countries remain at the heart of my work nowadays. The selection offered here marks the beginning, but by no means the end, of my interest in these issues of political economy.

References

Dreze, J. and A. Sen (eds) (1990), *The Political Economy of Hunger*, Vol. 2 (Oxford: OUP).

Sen, A. (1977), 'Starvation and Exchange Entitlement: A General Approach and its Application to the Great Bengal Famine', *Cambridge Journal of Economics*, **1** (1).

Sen, A. (1981), *Poverty and Famine: An Essay on Entitlement and Deprivation*, Oxford: Clarendon Press.

[1]

A Test of the Hypothesis of Disguised Unemployment

By Meghnad Desai and Dipak Mazumdar

I

The literature on disguised unemployment in "under-developed" countries contains numerous attempts to measure the volume of surplus labour.[1] Although these attempts differ in the amount of detailed information used, and vary in degrees of refinement, most of them have one methodological point in common. They commonly use a method of estimating the difference between the total availability of labour time in a particular region and the total requirement of labour time in that region based on technological information about farm operations. As such, these studies suffer from three major conceptual weaknesses.

(a) The concept of the "availability" of labour is a non-economic notion, in so far as it completely ignores the notion of a supply curve of labour. The supply of labour forthcoming in a farm or a group of farms is not a fixed quantity, but is a flow varying with the returns per unit of effort as well as with the level of alternative sources of income in off-farm work.

(b) Similarly, the concept of the "requirement" of labour also is a technological concept and does not allow for the obvious possibility of varying factor proportions in agriculture with changing conditions.

(c) The exercise implicitly assumes the idea of an "average" farm whose labour requirement is being calculated, and to which all farms in the region tend to conform. The experience in most agricultural regions of under-developed countries suggests that there is such a wide divergence in farming practices among groups of farms with different economic characteristics that very little can be gained from attempts at measuring a theoretical surplus of labour by means of the implicit projection of the experience of a typical average farm. An altogether more fruitful approach would seem to be to shift the focus of research to the micro-level, i.e. to the feasible enquiry of identifying the existence of surplus labour on specific groups of farms in a region. The problem then is not one of "measuring" surplus labour, but of devising a satisfactory test of the existence of a pool of surplus labour.

Indeed, such a test exists in the literature: it derives from the testable notion of the zero marginal product of labour. As an example we can

[1] See, for example, the bibliography in C. H. C. Kao *et al.*, "Disguised Unemployment in Agriculture: A Survey", in C. K. Eicher and L. W. Witt (eds.), *Agriculture in Economic Development*, New York, 1964.

39

refer to the widely-quoted article by Mellor and Stevens reporting work on a group of rice farms in Thailand which seemed to suggest that the marginal product of labour on these farms was zero.[1] However the conclusion of this particular study is unacceptable. The authors measured labour in "stock" terms (i.e., in units of "bodies" of workers) rather than in flow terms (i.e., in units of hours of work actually performed). Again, the type of analysis employed ignores the notion of a supply curve of labour. The Mellor–Stevens finding, even if it were valid statistically, would mean merely that farms having a higher man–land ratio did not have a higher output per acre. This may reflect no more than that the man-hours per acre were no higher because the effort supplied *per worker* was less on a farm with a higher man–land ratio—a possibility strongly suggested by the notion of an upward-sloping supply curve of labour. (With diminishing returns the marginal returns to a unit of effort supplied by an individual worker is lower on a farm with a higher man–land ratio; and hence the supply of effort which equates the marginal disutility of effort to the individual worker with the marginal return to his effort is also less.) This is not the same as saying that farms with a higher man–land ratio *cannot have* more man-hours per acre; but a positive relationship between a higher man–land ratio and more man-hours per acre is a separate proposition whose validity has to be clearly demonstrated and not implicitly assumed. Without such a demonstration the Mellor–Stevens finding of a zero marginal product of labour, measuring labour in stock terms, is compatible with a positive marginal product of labour, measuring labour in flow terms.

Let us set out a model which recognizes explicitly a supply curve of effort for an individual worker, and which will help us test whether there is disguised unemployment on specific groups of farms. The disguised-employment theory asserts that with the removal of a certain number of workers from the farm sector the output of the sector will nevertheless be maintained. We are looking for a test that will indicate such a possibility. Consider the case of an individual farm with several workers. In the absence of any empirical sociological evidence to the contrary, we make the plausible assumption that the workers on the farm share the work equally among themselves. The normal equilibrium for an individual worker will then be as portrayed in Figure 1. The supply curve (SS) of labour is assumed to be the same for each worker. The marginal revenue product curve (MRP) is derived by dividing the marginal revenue functions for the farm by the number of workers on the farm. (The assumptions are of equal-work-sharing and of homogeneous labour.) The initial equilibrium is at A. This is the case where individual members of the family farms are treated "as if" they are hired workers—the correct assumption where landlords

[1] J. W. Mellor and R. D. Stevens, "The Average and Marginal Product of Farm Labour in Underdeveloped Economies", *Journal of Farm Economics*, vol. 38 (1956), pp. 780–91.

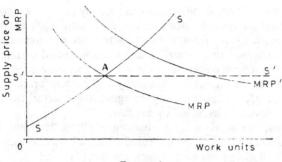

FIGURE 1.

expropriate the entire rent. If, however, some of the economic rent is retained by the family farm, the equilibrium will be established somewhat to the right of *A*, according to a schedule which lies above the *MR* curve to an extent determined by the retained rent.[1] But this alternative case (which is referred to again below) does not affect our subsequent argument.

The withdrawal of a worker from the farm shifts the marginal revenue curve (*MRP'*) facing the worker to the right (as the worker–land ratio falls). With a normal upward-sloping supply curve of labour, each worker contributes more effort; but the increase in total effort is not sufficient to make up for the loss due to the withdrawal of the worker. The marginal revenue product of workers remaining on the farm increases, i.e., total output falls.

If, however, the supply curve of labour is assumed to be horizontal (the line *S'S'*), then the marginal revenue product in the new situation will be the same as before the withdrawal of the worker. Output on the farm will be the same as before; the loss of labour hours due to the withdrawal of one worker will be made up exactly by the increased effort of those remaining on the farm. It is thus apparent that the validity of the "surplus labour" hypothesis depends upon the presence of a 'horizontal supply curve of labour in the region of observation. As is evident from the figure, the hypothesis is compatible with a positive marginal product of labour (labour being measured in "flow" terms). A zero marginal product of labour is *not* a necessary condition for the existence of surplus labour.

It might be asked, however, whether the horizontal supply curve of labour with a positive but constant supply price is an economically justified proposition to make for a family worker. Such a supply curve exists classically for hired labour whose supply price is determined by institutional factors, e.g., trade union in an industrial environment, or possibly social convention in a traditional society. But as far as family labour is concerned—the supply of labour by a member of

---

[1] This is subject to the proviso that the marginal revenue product of work units cannot fall below zero, if farmers are at all rational.

the family to his own family farm—the supply curve is determined by the individual's choice between leisure and farm work as well as by alternative earnings for farm workers. With a normal preference map— and the assumption that leisure is an economic good as implied by a positive supply price of labour—we would expect the supply curve of labour to slope upwards. This tendency will be reinforced by the fact that, with transfer of labour from the agricultural sector, the income in off-farm work can be expected to increase.

How, then, can we visualize a situation in which "surplus" labour in the normal definition can be expected to exist? In our view the only conceivable situation is one in which the worker–land ratio is so high that leisure is in such abundant supply that it can be considered a free good. Only after the worker–land ratio has been reduced significantly will leisure cease to be a free good, and the supply price of labour will then be positive.

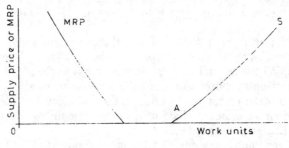

FIGURE 2.

The supply curve of labour for a member of a family will then be as shown in Figure 2. Up to the level of effort represented by point *A*, the supply price of labour is zero; only after *A* does leisure becomes an economic good, and the supply curve of labour becomes upward-sloping.

If, then, the marginal revenue product for the individual worker on the farm in both the initial and ultimate situations—i.e., both before and after the withdrawal of a worker from the farm—cuts the axis to the left of *A*, we can expect that, despite the withdrawal of a worker, output will be maintained on the farm. The test of such a "surplus labour" situation is, then, that the marginal product of labour (in flow terms) is zero. It must be noted, however, that although we have been able to conclude that while the zero marginal product test is a necessary test, it is not a sufficient test for the existence of surplus labour. This is so because the evidence of zero marginal product of labour in the initial situation might mean merely that the individual worker on the farm is in the region of point *A*. After the withdrawal of a worker the marginal revenue product curve might cut the supply curve of labour in the upward-sloping part—in which case output will fall.

In our study of the materials for a district of West Bengal collected for the Farm Management Survey of the Government of India, we confine ourselves to discovering whether the *necessary* condition for surplus labour exists for a group of farms. In an earlier article by one of the authors[1] it was pointed out that in the districts of the state of Uttar Pradesh covered by the Farm Management Survey, all the farms surveyed made use of some hired labour on a casual day-to-day basis. It is obvious that when *any* hired labour is used on a farm, the marginal product of labour on that farm cannot be zero and there cannot be any "surplus labour" in the usual sense (although there might be considerable seasonal unemployment). This was, indeed, borne out by other evidence presented in the article. In West Bengal the situation was found to be rather different. There were two groups of farms, those which used some hired labour, and those which made no use of hired labour. We decided to investigate whether the marginal product of labour was significantly different in the two groups of farms, and more specifically whether the marginal product of labour in the group without hired labour was zero, because surplus labour, if it existed, could be present only on this group of farms.

II

Our data relate to 99 farms of the 24 Paraganas district of West Bengal surveyed by the cost-accounting method as a part of the Farm Management Survey.[2] The survey relates to the year 1956–57. These 99 farms are from 10 villages. We had to omit one observation because the farm family produced only dairy products, whereas most of the other farms were rice and/or jute producers. Total value of output is divided into value of crop, value of by-products and value of dairy products.

The district is predominantly food-growing. Rice accounts for 90 per cent. of the area cultivated; and jute for 6·78 per cent. Other crops are: gram (2·24 per cent.), wheat, sugar-cane, oilseeds, til and tobacco (all under 1 per cent.). Irrigation is not important for the district, about 5 per cent. of the net sown area being irrigated. Implements form about 2 per cent. of total investment on all farms, their importance increasing with size.[3]

The farms are divided into two groups to test the possibility of the prevalence of "disguised unemployment". Farms employing hired labour form one group (Group A), and farms not employing hired labour the other group (Group B). Our approach is to fit a production

---

[1] Dipak Mazumdar, "Size of Farm and Productivity: A Problem of Indian Peasant Agriculture", *Economica*, vol. XXXII (1965), pp. 161–74.
[2] The data were extracted from the files of the Farm Management Survey through the courtesy of the Agriculture Price Commission, Government of India.
[3] For details on methods of measurement and list of variables, see Government of India, Ministry of Food and Agriculture, Department of Agriculture, *Studies in Economics of Farm Management of West Bengal: Results for 1954–55 to 1956–57*.

function with identical specification for each of the two groups (sub-samples). We use linear as well as loglinear production functions. The dependent variable is alternately total output and output per acre. The form of the dependent variable also dictates the form of the independent variables. Thus when the dependent variable is output per acre, all the independent variables, except acreage, are on a per-acre basis. This has given us twelve different production functions to fit for the two sub-samples. The specifications tried are the following:

Notation

q	= value of total output
h	= man-days of hired labour
f	= man-days of family labour
$h+f=l$	= total labour input
I	= value of major and minor implements
G	= gross cropped acreage
b	= hours of bullock labour
A	= size of the cultivating unit in number of acres.

(1–2)	$q/A = F^1[(l/A), (I/A), (b/A)]$	linear and double-log
(3–4)	$q/A = F^2[(l/A), (I/A), (b/A), A]$	linear and double-log
(5)	$q/A = F^3[(l/A), (I/A), (G/A)]$	double-log
(6)	$q/A = F^4[(l/A), (I/A), (G/A), A]$	double-log
(7–8)	$q = F^5[l, I, b]$	linear and double-log
(9–10)	$q = F^6[l, I, b, A]$	linear and double-log
(11)	$q = F^7[l, I, G]$	linear
(12)	$q/A = F^8[(l/A), (I/A), (b/A), (G/A)]$	linear

It seems desirable that the dependent as well as the independent variable should be normalized as this reduces multicollinearity among the independent variables and should eliminate heteroscedasticity. Thus Eqs. (1–6) as well as (12) are much less likely to involve these statistical problems than Eqs. (7–11). We tried a quadratic production function with q as dependent variable for group B, and for the same sub-sample we tried replacing the labour input in flow terms by family size, a stock variable. The latter procedure was impossible for group A.

We are interested only in the coefficients of the labour input term in each of the equations. The coefficient estimates are listed separately in Table 2 for both sub-samples. (All tables are in the Appendix.) Full results are given in Tables 5A and 5B. If there is zero marginal productivity of labour on our family farms, we would expect our sub-sample of families not employing hired labour (group B) to have a zero coefficient and the other sub-sample to have a positive coefficient. Our results in this respect are quite striking. Of the twelve cases for group B, the coefficient of the labour variable is not significantly different from zero in eight cases and in the remaining four it is significant but negative. Thus in four out of twelve cases we can reject the hypothesis of positive marginal product of labour on these farms. Of the other eight cases six coefficients are negative but not significant. This result means that the probability of a positive marginal product on these farms is much lower than the probability of a zero or negative marginal product.

Exactly the opposite seems to be true for group A. In nine cases out of twelve the coefficient of labour is positive and significant. In the remaining three cases, the coefficient is positive but not significant. In these three equations, the over-all R^2 is also non-significant. Our result is also not dependent on particular assumptions about the form of the production function, since in the Cobb–Douglas as well as the linear case we obtain similar results.

We believe this is an important result. Separating farms on only one criterion—the employment of hired labour—has been sufficient to obtain separate estimates of the productivity of labour, and the results quite strongly support the hypothesis of a lower, and zero, marginal productivity of labour on farms not employing hired labour. Our results are free of a number of statistical problems encountered in this field of enquiry such as the use of grouped data with unequal observations, insufficient input specification, and lack of homogeneity among observations due to geographical differences.

We can now examine whether there are any other systematic differences between the two sub-samples which may explain the differences in labour productivity. In Tables 3 and 4 we have listed the mean and standard deviations of a number of important economic characteristics of the two sub-samples expressed both in natural units and also in logarithms of natural units. For each variable we perform a test for differences between the means of the sub-samples. Our null hypothesis in each case is that there is no difference between the means. The results of this test are included in the tables.

We indicate first the characteristics which are not significantly different for the two types of farms. This will help us to reject some fairly obvious explanations of differences between farms with zero and with positive marginal products of labour, respectively. Thus it has been suggested that the former type of farm will be that on which the pressure of population on land resources is higher.[1] The indicators relating to this factor in Table 3 show that this is not so. Compared with farms in group A, farms in group B are not necessarily of smaller size with a larger family size per acre, or even with a larger stock of family labour per acre. Again, it might be suggested that the difference in observed marginal products of labour might be due to the fact that the flow of family labour out of a stock of the same size is different in the two groups due to differences in leisure preference. Farms with zero marginal product of labour might be those which utilize a greater flow of family labour input than farms in group A; the difference in marginal products of labour reflect the difference in the marginal supply-price of family labour and hired labour. The information in Table 3 refutes

[1] Cf. Asoka Mathur, "The Anatomy of Disguised Unemployment", *Oxford Economic Papers*, vol. 16 (1964).

this hypothesis. There is no significant difference between the two groups not only with respect to the stock of family labour per acre, but also with respect to labour flow per unit of family labour (see items 4, 5 and 6).

The real difference in the economic characteristics of the two groups seems to lie in the fact that the group of farms with a positive marginal product of labour has a significantly higher input of all labour per acre (i.e. family labour *plus* hired labour), and this difference is associated with differences in the intensity of cultivation and in the availability of complementary factors of production such as implements. The sub-sample using hired labour has a demand-for-labour schedule very much to the right of the demand schedule for labour of the other sub-sample, and this is due mainly to there being more land (by double cropping) and more implements.

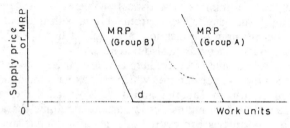

FIGURE 3.

At this stage we must consider the supply curve of labour. As we have shown in Figure 2, the supply curve of labour for group B should be along the x-axis up to a point, which is beyond point *d* in Figure 3. The supply curve of labour for group *A* does not have to satisfy this restriction. In order to check this assertion, we plotted man-hours of family labour per family member (f/F) against output per family member (q/F) for the two sub-samples. Output per family member (q/F) is not entirely adequate as a measure of supply price of family labour, but it is the best measure available. Because of the difficulty of identifying "earners" in the family economy, we have studied the variations in man-hours of family labour with respect both to "earners" as defined in the Survey and the total number of adults in the family.

Bearing the above qualifications in mind, we consider the results of regressing family man-hour input per earner (f/E) and per adult (f/T) on output per family member (q/F). The results, below, are equally striking here. There is no relationship between (f/E) or (f/T) and (q/F) for group B, but there is for the other group.

Group A

$$1 \text{ (A)} \quad f/E = 37 \cdot 70 + 0 \cdot 1819 \, (q + q')/F \qquad R^2 = 0 \cdot 156$$
$$(0 \cdot 0541) \qquad\qquad\quad S^2 = 2368$$

1 (B) $f/T = 13\cdot09 + 0\cdot0928\ (q+q')/F$ $R^2 = 0\cdot301$
                   $(0\cdot0181)$ $S^2 = 265$

Group B

2 (A) $f/E = 29\cdot84 + 0\cdot1674\ (q+q')/F$ $R^2 = 0\cdot0392$
                   $(0\cdot1487)$ $S^2 = 1559$

2 (B) $f/T = 14\cdot23 + 0\cdot0880\ (q+q')/F$ $R^2 = 0\cdot0415$
                   $(0\cdot0760)$ $S^2 = 406$

where E = number of earners; T = number of adults; q = agricultural output; q' = by-products and dairy products; and F = family size.

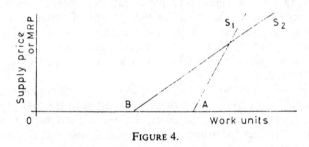

FIGURE 4.

The two supply curves show clear differences. The supply curve for group A can be represented as OBS_2 in Figure 4, which represents Eq. 1 (A). The supply curve for group B [Eq. 2 (A)] has the shape OAS_1 (the slope is not statistically significant). The different supply curves do not arise out of differences in tastes or leisure preferences but can be shown to arise as a result of the income effect.

Our two groups differ, then, on two grounds. Given identical production functions, the positions of the demand curve for labour are different as a result of the differences in levels of complementary inputs such as implements, and of the differences in the intensity of cultivation. Given identical leisure preferences, the positions of the supply curves differ because of the income effect. We observe, however, in Tables 3 and 4 that the input of family labour per family member does not differ significantly for the two groups. This has direct implications for the position of the demand curve for labour for group B. The family labour supplied by group A cannot exceed OC in Figure 5 because hired labour is available at the wage rate OW. Since the supply of days of work by a family member in group B is also the same (OC), the demand curve (MRP curve) for group B must pass through C. The MRP curve for group A is to the right of C.

It may be objected that we have neglected the seasonal pattern of the labour input. By adding together peak and slack seasons, we may have obtained an estimate of labour productivity which is biased downward. A more dis-aggregated specification of the inputs and outputs admittedly would enhance the accuracy of our results; but we can also examine the possibility of bias in the estimates.

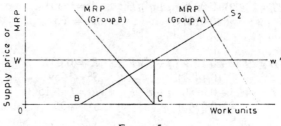

FIGURE 5.

According to the seasonality argument, we should compare the marginal product of labour in the two groups of farms in the peak season when labour input is at its peak. The zero marginal product hypothesis is properly tested, the argument goes, only if there is no net addition to output with the addition of a marginal unit of labour in the peak period.

It can be said in answer to this objection that the seasonal pattern of labour input is not likely to be different as between the two groups of farms. It cannot be shown, therefore, that on this ground the estimate of marginal product for group B is more biased than is the estimate for the other group.

Second, if it were true that the marginal product of labour is positive in the peak season and zero in the slack season, farmers with an abundant supply of labour would tend to increase labour input in the peak period. The observed inter-farm variance of the labour input to a large extent would be variance of labour input at the peak period. If this were so, the use of the annual aggregated labour input would be the same as the use of the peak labour input. Thus if labour input is measured accurately, there is no reason why bias should occur. The only reason for the existence of bias would be that in the slack season productive and unproductive labour cannot be distinguished, that the observed variance in the total input of labour would not be the variance of the input of productive labour and that this would impart a downward bias. It still remains to be shown that this source of bias affects the two groups differently before our results can be invalidated.

III

The existence in Indian agriculture of surplus labour or disguised unemployment or zero marginal product of labour has been disputed. The statistical investigations of Professors Schultz[1] and Paglin[2] are among the studies for which their authors concluded that there is no

[1] T. W. Schultz, *Transforming Traditional Agriculture*, New Haven, 1964; see, however, A. K. Sen, "Surplus Labour in India: A Critique of Schultz's Statistical Test", *Economic Journal*, vol. LXXVII (1967).
[2] M. Paglin, "'Surplus' Agricultural Labor and Development", *American Economic Review*, vol. LV (1965).

surplus labour in Indian agriculture. These investigations, however, use highly aggregated data. Schultz's data are at state level, and Paglin's are derived from group averages for different farm sizes in several states. We have approached the problem at the level of the individual farm, and thus the issues are not obscured by aggregation or by statistical problems such as heteroscedasticity in Paglin's case.[1] We have specified the production function in detail and varied its form to get some measure of the sensitivity of our results. We have shown that there do exist farms which have a zero or statistically non-significant co-efficient of labour input in the production function, and that these results make sense in the light of the observed supply curves.

One aspect of our results needs to be mentioned in some detail here. The farms with a zero marginal product of labour co-exist within a district with farms with non-zero marginal products. From evidence of the extensive use of hired labour, economists have been tempted to conclude that the marginal product of labour in the agricultural economy as a whole would be near the going positive wage rate since farmers would not be foolish enough to hire labour which is non-productive.[2] Our disaggregation has shown that the widespread exist-ence of hired labour docs not mean that every farm uses hired labour. Besides, the very notion of the marginal product of labour at the level of a state or country has dubious conceptual validity.

Data in Table 1 suggest one possible reason for the co-existence of the two types of farms. We note that farms using family labour only are concentrated in certain villages. Thus 27 of the 34 farms in group B are in three villages. This suggests that there are surplus-labour villages; they co-exist with group A farms which are in different, though not distant, geographical locations.

An important theoretical question arises here: why is it that the family workers with zero marginal product do not offer themselves in the hired labour market and force down the wage level? The persistence of the gap in marginal productivities may be due to the fact that markets for hired labour are localized markets confined to the particular village, so that "surplus" labour from other villages cannot compete in the labour market in villages where hired labour is used.

Two additional reasons for this "gap" have been given in an earlier article in *Economica* by one of us, cited above.[3] First, the probability that a family-farm worker will obtain a day's work on the market for casual labour is less than unity where the number of available jobs is less than the number of job-seekers on any particular day. Second, under the normal system of crop-sharing, the rent from leasing out the

[1] The observations used by Paglin are averages of groups of unequal size, thus violating the assumption of homoscedasticity.
[2] See, for instance, S. Wellisz, "Dual Economies, Disguised Unemployment and the Unlimited Supply of Labour", *Economica* (1968), p. 49, where he says: "With such widespread use of hired labour and leasing of land it is inconceivable that the average rural product should form a floor under rural wages."
[3] Mazumdar, "Size of Farm and Productivity . . .", *op. cit.*

4

50 TEST OF THE HYPOTHESIS OF DISGUISED UNEMPLOYMENT [FEBRUARY

land is likely to be less than the economic rent, and accordingly the supply price of labour for a worker on the family farm will be less than the market wage.

The question of surplus labour has been controversial. By attacking the problem at a disaggregated micro-level we believe we have come closer to estimating the marginal product of labour on farms. This, however, is only an isolated attempt. More work is needed on data for other districts or for other years for the same district. There is also a need to disaggregate in data according to crop, and possibly also in respect of a crop cycle. We hope to be able to report further results along these lines.

The London School of Economics.

APPENDIX

TABLE 1

The Distribution of Farms in the Sample

Village	Number of Group B Farms	Number of Farms growing Jute	Number of Farms Double Cropping
Arisingiri	0/10	7/10	9/10
Hudarait	8/10	3/10	6/10
Kadambagacchi	1/9	9/9	9/9
Khari	1/10	0/10	0/10
Akeberia	9/10	0/10	0/10
Durgapur	1/10	3/10	3/10
Krishnanagar	4/9	2/9	5/9
Krishnapara	0/10	8/10	6/10
Satberia	10/10	0/10	0/10
Srinagar	0/10	9/10	9/10
All villages	34/98	41/98	47/98

TABLE 2

Coefficients of the Labour Variable in Alternate Specifications of the Production Function

Specification	Group B (No Hired Labour)	Group A (Hired Labour)
(1) $\log$; q/A; (l,I,b)	$-0\cdot10888$ $(0\cdot13281)$	$0\cdot38417$ $(0\cdot14460)$
(2) $\log$; q/A; (l,I,b,A)	$-0\cdot07506$ $(0\cdot13574)$	$0\cdot38655$ $(0\cdot14883)$
(3) $\log$; q/A; (l,I,G)	$-0\cdot25072$ $(0\cdot10057)$	$0\cdot54789$ $(0\cdot18439)$
(4) $\log$; q/A; (l,I,G,A)	$-0\cdot23002$ $(0\cdot10114)$	$0\cdot54656$ $(0\cdot18547)$
(5) $\log$; q/A; (l,I,b)	$0\cdot20719$ $(0\cdot18239)$	$0\cdot70078$ $(0\cdot12783)$
(6) $\log$; q/A; (l,I,b,A)	$-0\cdot07280$ $(0\cdot14212)$	$0\cdot39461$ $(0\cdot15107)$
(7) q (l,I,b)	$0\cdot29736$ $(1\cdot10369)$	$3\cdot99614$ $(0\cdot34000)$
(8) q (l,I,b,G)	$-1\cdot24984$ $(0\cdot48719)$	$3\cdot47955$ $(0\cdot68410)$
(9) q (l,I,b,A)	$-0\cdot36760$ $(0\cdot50915)$	$3\cdot71568$ $(0\cdot68410)$
(10) q/A; (l,I,b)	$-0\cdot50203$ $(0\cdot53604)$	$0\cdot91473$ $(0\cdot57645)$
(11) q/A; (l,I,b,G)	$-1\cdot09062$ $(0\cdot50953)$	$1\cdot60786$ $(0\cdot83329)$
(12) q/A; (l,I,b,A)	$-0\cdot47541$ $(0\cdot54226)$	$0\cdot88776$ $(0\cdot59712)$

TABLE 3—ECONOMIC CHARACTERISTICS OF THE SUB-SAMPLES

	Group A	Group B	Difference
Family size	6·52 (3·09)	6·44 (3·32)	NS
Family size per acre	3·3019 (2·4619)	3·7714 (1·9167)	NS
Farm size	3·26750 (3·0739)	2·66088 (2·22386)	NS
Family Labour Input (in Man-days)	90·52 (79·309)	92·16706 (79·37494)	NS
Family Labour Input per Acre (in Man-days)	33·79 (22·36)	35·26792 (21·98619)	NS
Family Labour Input per member of family (in Man-days)	14·8987 (12·450)	14·1532 (10·392)	NS
Total Labour Input per Acre (in Man-days)	51·51821 (16·69750)	35·26792 (21·98619)	S
Value of Major and Minor Implements (in Rupees)	53·77938 (137·13125)	20·88382 (29·77457)	S
Value of Major and Minor Implements per Acre (in Rupees)	16·16305 (18·80921)	9·25213 (11·50527)	S S
Intensity of Cultivation	1·16254 (0·24589)	0·96613 (0·14046)	S

Notes: The figures are means, with standard deviations in parentheses.
s and NS denote significant and non-significant differences between the means at the 5 per cent. level.

TABLE 4—ECONOMIC CHARACTERISTICS OF THE SUB-SAMPLES
(Data in Logarithms)

	Group A	Group B	Difference
Family Size	1·75787 (0·50619)	1·71340 (0·57881)	NS
Family Size per Acre	0·90939 (0·71686)	1·09117 (0·70513)	NS
Farm Size	0·84858 (0·82227)	0·62230 (0·91531)	NS
Family Labour Input (in Man-days)	3·96329 (1·34814)	4·04651 (1·14069)	NS
Family Labour Input per Acre (in Man-days)	3·90264 (0·32885)	3·42428 (0·60390)	S
Family Labour Input per Member of Family (in Man-days)	2·61515 (1·79667)	2·33311 (1·21966)	NS
Total Labour Input per Acre	3·11472 (1·27915)	3·42428 (0·60390)	S
Value of Major and Minor Implements (in Rupees)	2·99548 (1·47958)	2·26588 (1·36365)	S
Value of Major and Minor Implements per Acre (in Rupees)	2·14690 (1·28473)	1·64364 (1·18262)	S
Intensity of Cultivation	0·13094 (0·19487)	0·04658 (0·16596)	S

Notes: See Notes to Table 3.

TABLE 5A—REGRESSION RESULTS: FARMS EMPLOYING HIRED LABOUR (GROUP A)

Dependent Variable	$h+f$	I	b	A	G	$R^2/\bar{s}$
log q/A	+0·38417 (0·14460)	+0·09266 (0·11686)	+0·00999 (0·03509)			0·205 0·35551
log q/A	+0·38655 (0·14883)	+0·09286 (0·03548)	+0·00942 (0·11806)	+0·00448 (0·05619)		0·205 0·35849
log q/a	+0·54789 (0·18439)	+0·09787 (0·03464)			−0·37923 (0·31464)	0·224 0·35071
log q/a	+0·54656 (0·18547)	+0·09774 (0·03464)		−0·00387 (0·05720)	−0·38120 (0·31780)	0·224 0·35491
log q	+0·70078 (0·12783)	+0·11180 (0·03771)	+0·16429 (0·11640)			0·813 0·38617
log q	+0·39461 (0·15107)	+0·09297 (0·03546)	+0·00945 (0·11791)	+0·51232 (0·15660)		0·846 0·35828
q	+3·99614 (0·34000)	+1·54412 (0·28465)	−0·19791 (0·44580)			0·852 274·13920
q	+3·46955 (0·87311)	+1·45444 (0·31706)	−0·24120 (90·45278)		+26·30726 (40·14066)	0·853 275·45183
q	+3·71568 (0·68410)	+1·47452 (0·32202)	−0·25123 (0·46263)	−15·49497 (32·72585)		0·853 275·92892
q/A	+0·91473 (0·57645)	+0·72367 (0·51026)	−0·13320 (0·72730)			0·066* 75·87456
q/A	+1·60786 (0·83329)	+0·73975 (0·50910)	−0·10105 (0·72590)		−64·88400 (56·46472)	0·086* 75·67289
q/A	+0·88776 (0·59712)	+0·72368 (0·51440)	−0·12964 (0·73342)	0·63299 (3·22180)		0·067* 76·48978

TABLE 5B—REGRESSION RESULTS: FARMS NOT EMPLOYING HIRED LABOUR (GROUP B)

Dependent Variable	$h+f$	I	b	A	G	$R^2/\bar{s}$
log q/A	−0·10888 (0·13281)	−0·01277 (0·15314)	+0·11515 (0·06350)			0·104* 0·41108
log q/A	−0·07506 (0·13574)	−0·02775 (0·15215)	+0·09834 (0·06503)	+0·09019 (0·8116)		0·141* 0·40948
log q/A	−0·25072 (0·10057)	0·17686 (0·05070)			+1·63144 (0·35183)	0·475 0·31466
log q/A	−0·23002 (0·10114)	+0·16273 (0·05157)		−0·07503 (0·06112)	+1·60488 (0·34957)	0·501 0·31204
log q	+0·20719 (0·18239)	+0·11576 (0·09005)	+0·38431 (0·18358)			0·640 0·56618
log q	−0·07280 (0·14212)	+0·09779 (0·06526)	−0·02969 (0·15400)	+0·91131 (0·17140)		0·818 0·40978
q	+0·29736 (1·10369)	+1·78931 (2·09258)	+6·05673 (2·48228)			0·430 288·67742
q	−1·24984 (0·48719)	+2·76179 (0·89297)	−0·76732 (1·20491)		+195·99889 (16·73430)	0·901 122·65445
q	−0·36760 (0·50915)	+2·73614 (0·96219)	−2·54918 (1·39310)	+175·02857 (16·38518)		0·885 132·17271
q/A	−0·50203 (0·53604)	+1·95846 (0·87298)	−0·29795 (1·27617)			0·146* 47·19076
q/A	−1·09062 (0·50953)	+2·35303 (0·78031)	−0·01606 (0·12906)		+175·45459 (56·36827)	0·358 41·61455
q/A	−0·47541 (0·54226)	+1·87173 (0·88990)	−0·33828 (1·28899)	−2·58620 (3·77986)		0·159* 47·61473

Notes to Tables 5A and 5B

1. Figures in parentheses are standard errors.
2. $\bar{s}$ standard error of residuals.
3. Asterisks denote R^2 not significantly different from zero.
4. The first column indicates specification, e.g. log q/A means that all independent variables (except acreage) as well as the dependent variable are in the form of logarithms after having been divided by acreage.
5. q indicates that the specification is linear and the dependent variable as well as the independent variables are in level form.

Oxford Economic Papers 40 (1988), 505–522

AN ECONOMETRIC APPROACH TO THE MEASUREMENT OF POVERTY

By MEGHNAD DESAI *and* ANUP SHAH

Abstract

This paper presents a method for specifying and measuring poverty defined as relative deprivation. We base our measure of an individual's poverty on the distance between his/her consumption experience relative to the norm. Consumption experience is defined in terms of events and the modal frequency of an event in the community defines the norm. Aggregation over events is made to capture the objective as well as subjective nature of deprivation. Our measure is related to that proposed by Townsend and econometric estimation is carried out using the Townsend data. Income is found to be neither the sole nor the most important indicator of deprivation.

ANY attempt to measure poverty runs into some familiar questions. First is the problem of definition. Do we mean by poverty some absolute state of existence at or below subsistence, visible to the naked eye or do we mean a state where some members of a community are relatively worse off? If the former, what determines the shopping list of minimum subsistence needs that must be met which will give us the cut-off point—the poverty line? If the latter, is there any way to avoid sinking into a morass of relativity and end up by defining poor in terms of subjective/ideological/policital criteria?

These questions are in some sense perennial and worse, difficult even to pose clearly. Notions of subsistence get revised in light of changing circumstances and "historical and moral elements" are brought to bear in such upward revision. A range of interpersonal variation in subsistence norms is easy to demonstrate even in such a basic need as nutrition [Sukhatme (1978), Srinivasan (1982)]. For relative deprivation, it is even more difficult to be precise once we disassociate the notion of poverty from that of subsistence or need. It is necessary however, to the extent possible, to reduce the element of personal bias and judgement involved and make the conceptual basis of the definition of poverty clear and its measurement adequate. In this paper we seek to do that with respect to the notion of *poverty as relative deprivation.*

Our reasons for choosing the relative definition should be made clear at the outset. For developed economies at least, poverty as relative deprivation is a notion that has gained increasing currency though its universal applicability across all countries, rich or poor, remains debatable [see Townsend (1962) (1979) for a defence of this notion. See Sen (1983) for a championing of the absolute poverty definition and Sen (1985a), Townsend (1985) for a subsequent debate]. As instances of absolute starvation become rare enough in developed economies to be really shocking, the appeal of any redistributive policy which aims to reduce poverty has to rely on a relative notion. But it is necessary to clarify the norm relative to which a household is deprived. Such a norm is often specified a priori but a better way to define it may be observing and choosing measures of normative behaviour or asking the community to define the norm. After all any redistributive policy based upon a notion of relative poverty has to be tolerated by the community which has to bear the tax burden the policy entails.

Peter Townsend in a series of papers over many years culminating in a book [Townsend (1979) and the papers by him cited therein] has attempted to make a community based notion of relative deprivation precise and to measure it for the UK (among other countries).[1] His attempt has been criticised on some grounds which invoke some of the perennial questions of poverty studies [Piachaud (1981), Townsend (1981), Hagenaars (1986)].[1] In this paper we reexamine Townsend's measure by putting it in a more formal context than he has done. In the course of this re-examination, we arrive at a measure more general than his and one that is econometrically viable. This measure is econometric in two senses. It is based, of necessity, on an empirical measurement of the consumption practice, and is thus data based. This measure cannot be defined independently of, or prior to, an empirical account of daily life in the community. It is also econometric in the sense that to meet a crucial objection to the measurement of poverty, the question of consumer tastes, an econometric specification is absolutely necessary. Since however our measure is more general than that proposed by Townsend, the available data are not fully satisfactory. We use Townsend's data as the best available for a reasonable approximation to our measure. Only a future attempt to gather data along the lines proposed in the earlier parts of the paper could fully substantiate our proposed measure.

In Section I, we outline our theory which is based on examining consumption practice in a community, defining individual experience relative to the community practice. This leads to a measure of the disparity between the individual and the community for each 'event' which is a facet of the community's consumption practice. There follows a discussion on aggregation of this disparity over different events. Here again an econometric formulation of the aggregation operation is adopted. Although we focus on consumption practices, our approach can be extended to deprivation in terms of the living environment, work environment, etc.

Section II takes up a basic objection to measures of poverty such as the one we have proposed. Recall that having obtained his measure of

---

[1] Townsend has actually proposed a variety of measures. Most of the attention and criticism have concentrated on a summary index of deprivation he proposed from which he derived a threshold level of income as a poverty line. It is this particular index we are concerned with in all the discussion that follows. We are grateful to an anonymous referee for making this distinction clear.

deprivation, Townsend proceeded to translate it with a threshold level of income as a poverty line. It may however be objected that if income is directly observable why do we need another measure of poverty which then is translated into income? This leads us to compare the conditions under which our measure generates information which is *not* contained in income. While income and our measure of poverty overlap in terms of the variable they relate to, neither can substitute for the other. Poverty is *measured* (though not *explained*) by relative deprivation. It is a function of income but it is also explained by other variables whose impact on poverty is not captured by income. Poverty is thus a multidimensional phenomenon, income being only one of these dimensions. A consequence of this multidimensionality is that policies to eradicate poverty cannot act on income alone but have to pay attention to other observable variables that explain poverty. Section II is devoted to this issue. Our measure is continuous and can be estimated for each household, also it is suitable for constructing poverty indices (such as the one proposed by Sen) where previously income has been the sole variable [Sen (1976), (1981, Appendix 2].

Having thus established the non-redundancy of our measure, in Section III, we adapt our measure of deprivation to Townsend's data. These are readily available and in as much as our interest is in improving upon Townsend's measure, it is not inappropriate that we use this data. We conclude with a brief discussion of the relevance of our results to the issues aired in earlier debates.

I

A measure of poverty has to do two things. It should be possible to classify an individual/household[2] in the category poor or not poor on the basis of such a measure. To answer this question, we have to take into account the socio-economic characteristics of the household and allow for inter-household variation. Secondly, one may also wish to obtain a measure of poverty in the community as a whole either for inter-temporal or for inter-community comparison. Our concern is primarily with the first question although our answer can tackle the second one as well.

The best way to proceed would be to start with Townsend's definition of relative derpivation:

> "Individuals, families and groups in the population can be said to be in poverty
> when they lack the resources to obtain the type of diets, participate in the

[2] The appropriate unit may be an individual, an adult equivalent ('income unit' of SB programme) or a household. To some extent, this will be largely dictated by the available data. It has been customary to think of the household as a single unit but recently there has been some interest in intra-household distribution of resources. We shall have nothing to say on this important area. In what follows we use the words individual and household interchangeably. See however Sen (1985b), chapter 15, Brannen and Wilson (1987).

activities, and have the living conditions and amenities which are customary, or at least widely encouraged and approved, in the societies to which they belong. Their resources are so seriously below those commanded by the average individual or family that they are, in effect, excluded from ordinary living patterns, customs and activities." [Townsend (1979), p15]

This definition has several features:
(a) there is a community (society) to which individuals belong, both the individuals who are deprived and those who are not;
(b) the non deprived—'the average individual or family'—set the living pattern, customs and activities which, if practiced, constitute "belonging to the community";
(c) thus individuals are deprived by not having sufficient resources to enjoy "the living conditions and amenities which are customary, or at least widely encouraged in the societies to which they belong".

The implication of (a) is to confine one's investigation to a specific social/cultural community. Then (b) requires us to measure the average, the customary or the typical style of living in the community. Having got the style of living of the typical member defined and its resource cost noted we look at the style of living of those who do not conform. We ask whether these people who do not enjoy the typical style do so because of lack of resources, or because merely of a difference in tastes from those of the typical member.

Let us begin by considering consumption occurrences which happen to the people of a community. These are best thought of as a combination of goods (and services) and individuals in a specific time space context; supper, for example. The same consumption occurrence may recur with different specific goods being consumed; indeed it may be desirable not to have identical set of goods for each occurrence. Thus one would vary the dishes for supper from day to day; not to do so may often (but not always) indicate poverty of resources. Consumption occurrences may also involve more than one person. If the unit of study is a household, then consumption events will be typically multiperson activities e.g. the household going on holiday. Other activities for an individual member of a household may require other peoples' participation, going to the pub, for example.

We can use the statistical notion of events here. Consumption experience of an individual in a particular community over a period of time could be said to comprise of a set of events. There are of course many such events. It is sufficient for our purposes to concentrate on a subset of basic or crucial events. An event will be basic in two senses. For any particular individual, there is a very high probability that the event will occur to him during the period. By the same token, every basic event will be experienced by a majority of the community. These events differ from each other according to their frequency but together they 'span' the consumption experience of the community. As an illustration consider daily events. Then, over a week, we would include in our measure an event whose frequency is high, and, on any one day, we should expect a high proportion of individuals to experience this event. Breakfast is an event of such a type. In the UK, 'have you had breakfast today' is a meaningful question to ask since a majority of people do have breakfast. It is also a high frequency event since in a week an individual is likely have breakfast almost every day.

The list of events will depend on the culture of the society and it may, over time, change for a given society. More specifically, however, the question is whether such a set of events, that is, events which happen to every one in a community sooner or later within a certain time interval, is an empty one. Thus, if, as Hagenaars points out, different households may engage in different activities, it may not be possible to define such a set across all households [Hagenaars (1986)]. There may also be the probability that consumption events are specific to class/race characteristics. Thus afternoon tea was a frequent event for the Victorian middle class but among the working class tea is a substantial early evening event. A community should therefore be defined as a group of households which has the practice of sharing a common set of events.

It should be emphasized that having a common set of events does not rule out an extreme diversity as to specific goods consumed as part of the event. There may be, of course, cultural constraints as to what is and what is not partaken in an event. Thus brandy at breakfast is unusual. Birthday parties usually involve consuming cakes etc. The inter-personal nature of events should also be kept in mind. Indeed, most events will involve other people and will not 'be the same' without other people.

It is tempting, at this stage, to define a utility function in terms of events which are themselves defined over goods and other poeple. Such a utility function would of course be different from the textbook one in involving other people as arguments. But then given the frequency dimension of events as well as their inter-personal character, a formal treatment of such a function becomes extremely complicated since we have to aggregate over time and over other people's utility functions.

This complication is avoided by presenting an empirical measure based on a hypothetical, but implementable, questionnaire. Events are indexed $i = 1,..., I$, individuals are $j = 1,..., J$ and a good knowledge of the culture of the community is presumed. Having decided upon the set of events which are typical of the community's consumption practice, an individual's experience of any given event over a specified time interval is obtained. Attached to an event i, for a given time span, there will be a maximum frequency of occurrences—seven days a week for a daily event etc. Let the frequency with which an event has been experienced be denoted by θ. Then the questionnaire method yields θ_{ij}, the number of times individual j has experienced event i. From such data a measure of deprivation can be constructed as follows.

Let $\bar{\theta}_i$ be the modal value of the ith event in the community. The definition of events and community implies that θ_{ij} will have a *unimodal* distribution. A multimodal distribution is an immediate signal that the event may be untypical or that the sample consists of heterogeneous communities. Given a unimodal distribution of θ_{ij}, deprivation for an individual relative to the community can be defined.

For the ith event and the jth person, define δ_{ij} as the disparity between the individual and the community. The function capturing this is

$$\delta_{ij} = \delta(\theta_{ij}, \bar{\theta}_i), \qquad \delta(\theta_{ij}, \bar{\theta}_i) < \delta(\theta_{ik}, \bar{\theta}_i) \quad \text{if} \quad \theta_{ik} < \theta_{ij} \tag{1}$$

where δ is a monotonic function. It can be defined linearly as $(\bar{\theta}_i - \theta_{ij})$ or a ratio $\bar{\theta}_i / \theta_{ij}$ or any general non-linear function. It can take positive or negative values if linear, or be above or below one. In measuring relative deprivation, we automatically obtain measures of relative affluence, of being above the norm.[3]

The task then is to locate individuals who may have lower than modal frequency due to lack of resources rather than due to taste differences. This was the criticism levelled by Piachaud against Townsend's measure [Piachaud (1981)]. This is done by assuming that in the questionnaire concerning events, information concerning socio-economic characteristics of the individual—income, wealth, sex, age, household size, region of residence etc.—has also been gathered. Given a sufficiently large sample, θ_{ij} can be modelled in such a way so as to separate the systematic variation in θ_{ij} from the random variation due to tastes. Thus taking tastes to be randomly distributed across the population, we posit

$$\theta_{ij} = E(\theta_{ij} \mid Z_j) + \eta_{ij} \tag{2a}$$

$$= \hat{\theta}_{ij} + \eta_{ij} \tag{2b}$$

Here Z_j is the vector of socio-economic characteristics and η_{ij} is a random error. E denotes the expectations operator. It is further required that

$$E_j(\eta_{ij}) = E_j(\eta_{ij} \mid Z_j) = 0 \tag{2c}$$

Given (2a)–(2c), (1) can be refined as

$$\delta_{ij} = (\hat{\theta}_{ij}, \bar{\theta}_i) \tag{3}$$

since the modal value should not change if $\hat{\theta}_{ij}$ is used instead of θ_{ij}.

Equations (2a)–(2c) and (3) state that if an individual does not have breakfast due to tastes but the typical person in the community with the same characteristics Z_k does, then the individual has a negative random

---

[3] An alternative is to ask the community what it thinks of the minimum tolerable frequency θ_i^+ is below which a member of that community should feel deprived. This will then be an alternative to (1) above. We have

$$\Delta_{ij} = f(\theta_{ij}, \theta_i^+)$$

We do not pursue this alternative here. See however Mack and Lansley (1985) for data which allow one to implement such a measure.

error. Another individual may have low θ_{ij} due to differences in Z_j and that will persist in $\hat{\theta}_{ij}$.

Thus the problem of tastes is in principle soluble. A deprivation measure based on the notion of distance of actual frequency from modal frequency of an event which has unimodal distribution is the first step. The second step is to be able to get Z_j such that condition (2c) will be satisfied. Given these two conditions, $\hat{\delta}_{ij}$ is the appropriate distance measure. It is the specification of the error structure for θ_{ij} that allows us to tackle the problem of tastes and it is in this sense that our measure is econometric.

Aggregation

A simple approach would be to sum the θ_{ij} i.e. give them equal weights. This was Townsend's procedure. In our terms, Townsend's procedure is to pre-assign a frequency θ_i^* for each event and then define

$$t_{ij} = 1 \quad \text{if} \quad \theta_{ij} < \theta_i^*$$
$$= 0 \quad\quad \theta_{ij} \geq \theta_i^* \tag{4a}$$

Then the Townsend index (T_j) for deprivation is

$$T_j = \sum_i t_{ij} \tag{4b}$$

There is however no clear justification for equal weighting. Events have unequal expenditure implications even for a particular household. Households may also have different priority over events and they may economize on some but not on others. We have to therefore seek other weighting schemes which are less restrictive, but which will do justice to the inter-personal variation without losing the social dimension of deprivation.

One way of weighting events unequally is to ask about the *subjective feeling* of deprivation in addition to the *objective incidence* of deprivation. Thus, while $\hat{\delta}_{ij}$ is the objective incidence of deprivation, we might weight each $\hat{\delta}_{ij}$ in relation to the proportion of total community *not* deprived to capture the subjective feeling of being deprived. Thus a deprived person may feel more deprived if s/he was in a minority than if half the community was similarly deprived. Of course this would require that the event in question was relevant to the majority of the community i.e. that the mode should be above the median value for each θ_i. But even if that were not the case, the implication is that our weighting scheme should be robust whether the median is above the mode or below it. A simple scheme would be to weight θ_{ij} by the proportion of the community above the mode in the total community. Thus

$$\hat{D}_j = \sum \lambda_i \hat{\delta}_{ij} \tag{5a}$$

$$\lambda_i = J_i'/J_i \qquad J_i' = (\#j \mid \theta_{ij} \geq \bar{\theta}_i) \qquad j \in J \tag{5b}$$

Thus λ_i is the proportion of the non deprived (i.e. those above the norm) in the total population for the ith event. The advantage of λ_i is that it is robust against the range of the question being relevant for only a small minority of the population e.g. Have you had caviar for breakfast today? Such an 'event' will have a small λ_i and therefore will get a small weight in the overall index. The weights λ_i could be thought of as *objective* measures of *subjective* feelings of deprivation i.e. people *feel* more deprived if they see many more haves than have nots for any event, when they are among the have nots themselves.

II. Income and the proposed measure of poverty

In what sense does such a measure which involves gathering much information improve upon a straightforward use of income as an alternative and much simpler measure? Poverty measures have been based in the past on income as the basic variable treating income in its own right or as a surrogate for utility to indicate economic status. Is it worth abandoning this simple approach in search of a more elaborate, more information intensive measure such as $\hat{D}_j$?

There are two responses to this, one is a minor point and the other the major crucial distinction. Most poverty measures need to specify a minimum income level $\bar{y}$ arbitrarily and one could defend our data intensive procedure as a way of getting a more explicit and endogenous motivation for $\bar{y}$.

But the more crucial response is that a measure such as $\hat{D}_j$ should capture certain elements of living style which income does not capture. As we said above, events represent multiperson activities and an element of reciprocity is basic to being able to enjoy them. The aggregation of separate disparity measures based on particular events also attempts to capture social as against personal aspects of deprivation.

The best way to pose this issue is in terms of the information content of a measure (such as $\hat{D}_j$) which is a linear combination of individual event disparities and compare it to that of income, not measured income but permanent income for the adult equivalent household size taking account of other dimensions of household characteristics.

The framework we use is that of canonical correlation [Hooper (1959)]. On the one hand we have a linear combination of the variables $\mathring{\delta}_{ij}$. We can represent this as

$$\delta\alpha = \zeta_1 : \zeta_1'\zeta_1 = 1 \tag{6}$$

where α is the vector of linear coefficients (weights) of individual δ_i. The canonical variate ζ_1 has the property that its inner product with itself is unity. [It is not argued that $\hat{D}_j$ necessarily satisfies this orthogonality property.]

The vector of socio-economic variables Z_j introduced in (2a) can be thought of as including measured income y as its first component. Then

$Z_{2j},..., Z_{kj}$ are other relevant socio-economic characteristics. Now define another canonical variate ζ_2 as combination of Z_{kj}

$$Z\beta = \zeta_2 : \zeta_2'\zeta_2 = 1 \tag{7}$$

The extent to which the deprivation measures δ have the same information as the income and household characteristic variables Z can be answered then in a straighforward way. The canonical correlation between the two sets of variables is defined as

$$|\mu| = \zeta_2'\zeta_1 \tag{8}$$

If $|\mu| = 1$ then the deprivation measures are redundant since we get no more information from them than from the Z variables. The composite income measure ζ_2 will contain information different from the deprivation aggregate ζ_1 as long as $|\mu| < 1$. If the correlation were zero, then deprivation would be random in the sense that it will be independent of the usual sort of variables thought to influence it. In this case, one could claim with Piachaud that it is a matter of taste. Thus the question of whether the deprivation measure is redundant can be answered in principle by computing the canonical correlation. We do not however propose to compute μ for our data set.

But while our measure of deprivation may have different information than income does, one may still wish to translate deprivation into income to determine a threshold level of poverty income. It is this attempt to locate a level of income which can be called a poverty line which has proved controversial. In terms of our discussion in the Introduction, income may not be sufficient as a sole variable to capture the complex phenomenon of poverty. Leaving that issue aside, can one locate a value of income y^* below which we could say that people are poor. Townsend's procedure was to fit one linear segment of high values of T_j to the corresponding Y_j (relative to the supplementary benefit entitlement of j) and another segment to lower values of j. These turned out to have statistically significantly different slopes. [For the test Desai (1986)]. But there is still arbitrariness about classifying some T_j as 'high' and other as 'low' and also about choosing two linear segments rather than a smooth nonlinear curve to represent the relationship of T_j to Y_j.

In our case this arbitrariness is removed. This is because implicit in the measure itself we have $\delta_{ij} = 0$ as the cut-off point. This leads to the appropriately aggregated $D_j = 0$, as the deprivation level corresponding to which we can locate the threshold income level.

To continue in the framework of canonical correlation mentioned above, we will seek to find out the value of ζ_2 which corresponds to $0 = \delta\hat{\alpha}$. Call this ζ_2^*. ζ_2^* is then the synthetic income measure below which deprivation will increase and above which it will decrease (since μ will be negative). Now measured income is only one of the components of $Z\beta = \zeta_2^*$ but it would be a straightforward matter to extract the value of measured income implied by ζ_2^*. Note that in view of the criticisms of Piachaud and Hagenaars mentioned above we can calculate such a threshold from a single continuous function. The difficulty in Townsend's case arises from the fact that since he prespecifies θ_i^*, $\tau_{ij} = 0$ does not have the same interpretation as our measure $\delta_{ij} = 0$ has. Thus in his case the location of a critical value of T_j involves an additional problem and this is why it requires an ad hoc specification of two segments to identify the threshold.

We have thus established that it is possible to provide a firm conceptual basis for a non-utilitarian, socially oriented view of poverty as relative deprivation.[4] This was the aim with which Townsend advanced his measure. We have shown that a more general approach can avoid many of the criticisms levelled against his measure. By relating Townsend's questions to an underlying concept of events, we can define deprivation as distance relative to the community norm. It provides a way of tackling the thorny problem of tastes. Aggregating event specific deprivation disparity into aggregate index we obtain a continuous measure of deprivation for the household. They could be viewed as alternative to income which has been used in many poverty indices as the relevant microeconomic measure. Thus from our D_j measures we could generate Sen's measure of poverty or Atkinson's measure of inequality [Sen (1976), Atkinson (1970)]. We have argued that our measure provides information other than that conveyed by the income measure. It is possible also to obtain a measure of the threshold level of income below which deprivation is a serious matter.

We do not however have the data to construct our $\hat{D}_j$ measure. In the next section, we implement many of our ideas with the data obtained by Townsend.

III. A Measure of poverty: empirical implementation

The task now is to implement our measure empirically. The largest data set currently available is that due to Townsend (op cit). The data set consists of 2,052 households interviewed in 1968–69. Each household was asked a list of sixty questions on 'style of living'. From these, Townsend chose twelve questions intended to represent the sixty and also apply equally to the different sexes and age groups in the sample. They covered 'major aspects of dietary, household, familial, recreational and social deprivation' in order to prepare a deprivation index. (See Appendix Table A1 for a list of these questions). As is readily apparent, all the questions with the exception of 9 and 10 captured what we call events. But note also that these questions are framed in a restrictive way.

Thus, instead of asking households 'how often have you had cooked meals in the last week?', they were asked 'have you had cooked meals more often than four times in the last week?'. In terms of the model in the

---

[4] Since we wrote our paper, Lewis and Ulph (1987) have advanced an argument based on utility maximization for the phenomenon of a threshold income which defines a poverty line.

previous section, this means that θ_i^* was set before the questions were asked. Households who had a frequency below this norm were scored 1 (deprived) and those at or above the stated frequency scored 0 (not deprived). Thus, we have a problem of censored data here; we observe a discrete rather than a continuous variable.

Balanced against this, we have the advantage that along with the questions, a lot of information was gathered on the socio-economic characteristics of house-holds—income, wealth, family type, health, education achievement of the head of the household etc. We can thus implement our equation (2) and separate the effects of tastes from those of systematic factors.

Given the data, we only observe households with $\theta_{ij} \geqslant \bar{\theta}_i$ and $\theta_{ij} < \bar{\theta}_i$ where $\bar{\theta}_i$ is now to be interpreted as the preassigned norm θ_i^*. We wish to transform this zero/one classification into the probability of being deprived or not being deprived. Let p_{ij} be the probability attached to the (random) event that the jth household is *not* deprived with respect to the ith (consumption) event. Then obviously those households recorded with $\theta_{ij} \geqslant \bar{\theta}_i$ are most likely to have $p_{ij} \geqslant \frac{1}{2}$, and those with $\theta_{ij} < \bar{\theta}_i$ have $p_{ij} < \frac{1}{2}$.

This transformation of the observed discrete variable into a probability enables us to obtain a deprivation index similar to $\hat{D}_j$ (5a) above. Since it is based on T_{ij} rather than δ_{ij}, but the weights are as in (5b) we label it TD_j

$$TD_j = 1/I \sum \lambda_i \delta(\hat{\theta}_{ij}, \bar{\theta}_i) = 1/I \sum \lambda_i (1 - \hat{p}_{ij}). \tag{10}$$

In (10) $\hat{p}_{ij}$ is the probability of not being deprived as calculated from $\hat{\theta}_{ij}$ rather than θ_{ij}. Whereas the measure in (6) is defined over the entire real line, the measure in (10) is confined to being positive. There is clearly some loss of information involved due to the nature of the underlying data. But the advantage of interpreting $\hat{\delta}(\hat{\theta}_{ij}, \bar{\theta}_i)$ as the probability is that (10) can be seen as analogous to an entropy measure. Thus if we take $\lambda_i = p_i$ i.e. the proportion in the population *not* deprived then we can interpret this observed frequency as a probability. Thus

$$TD_j = 1/I \sum \lambda_i (1 - \hat{p}_{ij}) = 1/I \sum \hat{p}_i (1 - \hat{p}_{ij})$$

$$= -1/I \sum \hat{p}_i \log \hat{p}_{ij}. \tag{11}$$

In (11) we approximate $(1 - \hat{p}_{ij})$ by $-\log \hat{p}_{ij}$. Of course (11) is only an approximation and is presented here for its suggestiveness. The usefulness of the deprivation index in (6) and in (10) does not depend on the closeness of its approximation to the entropy measure.

Returning to our empirical implementation, it seems appropriate given the one/zero nature of the data to posit a logistic specification for $\hat{p}_{ij}$

$$\hat{p}_{ij} = [1 + \exp(-Z_j \hat{\beta}_i)]^{-1} \tag{12}$$

TABLE 1[a]

Logit estimates of events

Event i / Variable	$i=1$	$i=2$	$i=3$	$i=4$	$i=5$	$i=6$	$i=7$	$i=8$
Intercept	−0.316	−0.544*	0.284	−0.482*	−0.568*	−0.438	0.089	−0.104
FAM 2	−1.036*	−0.251	0.051	−0.433*	−0.126	0.376	−0.048	0.224
3	0.160	0.547*	−0.124	−0.226	−0.208	0.424*	−0.064	−0.513*
4	0.060	0.102	−0.030	−0.582*	−0.028	0.056	−0.302	−0.475*
5	−0.170	−0.048	−0.631*	−0.670*	−1.147*	0.160	0.160	−0.308*
6	−0.490*	−0.059	−1.086*	−0.809*	−1.181*	0.069	0.051	−0.350*
7	−0.361*	0.038	−1.167*	−1.095*	−1.662*	−0.024	0.092	−0.485*
8	−0.353*	−0.018	−1.134*	−0.801*	−1.201*	0.177	0.296	−0.010
9	−0.300	0.071	−1.570*	−0.200	−1.061*	0.369	0.578	0.083
10	−0.026	−0.003	−1.054*	−0.828*	−1.343*	0.162	0.470*	−0.084
11	−0.385*	0.153	−1.253*	−1.153*	−1.510*	0.063	0.547*	−0.109
12	−0.103	−0.181	−0.557*	−1.056*	−1.867*	0.234	0.380*	−0.111
13	0.122	0.092	−0.617*	−0.681*	−0.859*	0.261	0.773	0.322
14	−0.267	−0.073	−0.763*	−0.970*	−1.193*	0.426*	0.370*	−0.212
ED 2	−0.152*	−0.058	0.092	−0.252*	−0.053*	−0.147*	−0.090	0.012*
3	−0.286*	−0.223*	−0.249	−0.463*	−0.212*	−0.274*	−0.447*	−0.339*
4	−0.420*	0.051	−0.355	−0.290	0.236	−0.372*	−0.532*	−0.622*
5	−0.367*	−0.287*	−0.087	−0.206	0.112	−0.467*	−0.274*	−0.219
6	−0.504*	−0.281*	−0.482*	−0.302*	0.320*	−0.471*	−0.835*	−0.239*
INC 2	−0.004	−0.103	−0.054	−0.018	−0.023	−0.066	−0.029	0.160
3	0.010	−0.128	−0.176	−0.350*	−0.251*	−0.295*	−0.020	−0.147
4	−0.094	0.056	−0.193	−0.198	−0.250*	−0.388*	−0.097	−0.129
5	−0.300*	−0.079	−0.459*	−0.638*	−0.375*	−0.633*	−0.113	−0.101
WLTH 2	−0.063	−0.093	0.121	−0.248*	−0.021	−0.170*	−0.175*	−0.194*
3	0.087	−0.175*	−0.137	−0.191	−0.126	−0.322*	−0.323*	−0.483*
4	0.144	−0.254*	0.175	−0.271	0.021	−0.533*	−0.051	−0.049
5	0.205*	−0.278*	0.107	−0.242*	−0.329*	−0.512*	−0.180*	−0.298*
−2 Log Likelihood[b]	2278.8 (223.79)	2257.9 (89.25)	998.05 (168.81)	1683.5 (334.53)	1600.0 (490.43)	2268.2 (289.64)	2342.4 (212.48)	2201.7 (151.13)

[a] The regressions also include REG 2–REG 9, HEALTH AND ORIGIN (see Table A2). The sample size is 1850.

[b] The figure in the brackets is the difference between −2 log likelihood value for the estimated equation and the constrained equation in which all the coefficients except the constant term are set equal to zero and thus provide a likelihood ratio test for the null hypothesis that $\beta = 0$.

* The coefficient value is at least twice the standard error.

where $\hat{\beta}_i$ are the maximum likelihood estimates of the coefficients of Z_j. The vector Z_j comprises many socio-economic variables. These are listed in Appendix Table 2. The $\hat{\beta}_i$ estimates are listed in Table 1.

Looking at Table 1, it is obvious from the last row which gives the likelihood ratio statistic that the variables do contribute to the explanation of the observed data.

TABLE 2
Log likelihood values for alternative specifications

	All variables present	Income omitted	Wealth omitted	Family type omitted	Education omitted
DF	36	32	32	23	31
Event 1	223.79	201.64(R)	217.64(A)	168.21(R)	198.90(R)
Event 2	89.25	86.19(A)	79.22(R)	57.29(R)	78.25(A)
Event 3	168.81	155.34(R)	166.69(A)	95.78(R)	162.13(A)
Event 4	334.53	276.42(R)	325.54(A)	260.44(R)	317.33(R)
Event 5	490.43	474.57(R)	484.85(A)	268.79(R)	480.72(A)
Event 6	289.64	224.25(R)	254.38(R)	268.71(A)	265.12(R)
Event 7	212.48	210.31(R)	199.01(R)	141.23(R)	157.92(R)
Event 8	151.13	141.69(A)	127.07(R)	95.39(R)	127.47(R)

A—Accept the null hypothesis that the variable subset has a zero parameter subvector
R—Reject the null hypothesis

In arriving at the coefficient estimates given in Table 1, only a small number of alternative specifications was tried. The main experiment was introducing the actual amount of income and wealth and the number of years of education. Since there was hardly any change in the explanatory power of the independent variables, this was dropped in favour of the chosen specification where these variables are converted into step dummies. This allows for any nonlinearity in the influence of these variables on the probability of deprivation. The second major experiment was to drop subsets of variables and Table 2 lists the likelihood values for the unrestricted specification and for each set of restrictions that was imposed. The null hypothesis is that this restriction, i.e. omission of a subset of variables, does not lead to a significant loss of likelihood. Using twice the difference in the log likelihood values and comparing it to the χ^2 values for 95% and the appropriate degrees of freedom, the accept/reject decision can be made. As the table indicates, the omission of the family type variables set is a restriction which is rejected by the data in seven out of eight cases and in the eighth case it is rejected at the 90% level. Broadly speaking, the omission of income is also a restriction that is rejected by the data for it is only in two cases that the null hypothesis is acceptable at 90% level. On the other hand, omission of wealth is acceptable in more cases. Education falls in between income and wealth.

The deprivation index

From the coefficient estimates in Table 1, the $\hat{p}_{ij}$ can be calculated and the deprivation index constructed. Given the large number of variables, it is possible to construct as many as 75,600 separate $\hat{p}_{ij}$ but this would be an

TABLE 3
The effect of selected variables on measured deprivation

	TD_j^*		TD_j^*
INC 1	1.057	FAM 1	1.274
INC 2	1.033	FAM 2	1.197
INC 3	1.000	FAM 3	1.247
INC 4	0.993	FAM 4	1.160
INC 5	0.862	FAM 5	1.142
WLTH 1	1.000	FAM 6	1.053
WLTH 2	0.937	FAM 7	1.000
WLTH 3	0.888	FAM 8	1.102
WLTH 4	0.952	FAM 9	1.193
WLTH 5	0.900	FAM 10	1.145
ED 1	1.000	FAM 11	1.208
ED 2	0.960	FAM 12	1.169
ED 3	0.832	FAM 13	1.274
ED 4	0.822	FAM 14	1.206
ED 5	0.851	HEALTH	1.261
ED 6	0.753		

Base Value $TD_j^* = 1$ for a couple with 2 children, $120 \leqslant$ income < 140), WEALTH $<$ 2500, ED $\leqslant 9$ years, good health, born in the UK and living in Greater London.

absurd task to undertake. We therefore proceed as follows. For the sample a base value for TD_j is calculated. This is done by setting all the dummy variables equal to zero except that for FAM 7 (a couple with two children) and INC 3 ($120 \leqslant INC < 140$). This family is also assumed to be living in Greater London, born in the UK and in good health. It appears that such a base is the most representative of the average but, of course, if warranted different bases can easily be computed. The specific value for Base TD_j happens to be 0.176. Now let $TD_j^* = \dfrac{TD_j}{\text{Base } TD_j}$. For the base case chosen obviously $TD_j^* = 1$. Table 3 then lists TD_j^* for someone with all the characteristics of the base case except the one indicated. Obviously the lower the value of TD_j^* the less deprived a person is.

As expected, the first five entries in Table 3 show that deprivation falls with income. The noteworthy feature is that the index falls sharply as income increases from INC 4 ($140 \leqslant INC < 160$) to INC 5 ($INC \geqslant 160$). The implication is that income has a sizeable influence on deprivation only at the highest levels. Whereas deprivation is inversely and monotonically related to income its relationship with wealth is non-monotonic. Increasing wealth from WLTH 1 (WLTH < 2500) to WLTH 3($5000 \leqslant$ WLTH $\leqslant 7500$) produces a sizeable drop in the index but thereafter there appears to be a limit below which deprivation cannot decrease with increases in wealth. The relationship between the index and education is also non-monotonic. The most interesting feature of this relationship is that as ED increases from EC 2 (10 years) to ED 3 (11 years) there is a sharp fall in deprivation. Therefore staying at school for two extra years beyond the minimum school leaving age has a major impact on reducing deprivation but this may also represent a vintage effect since the older generations have fewer years of education. An almost equally powerful impact accompanies an increase in education from ED 5 (13 years) to ED 6 (14 years or more). This roughly coincides with a degree course at an institution of higher education. Finally, turning to family type, the influence is not regular as there is not a natural way of ordering the different types. Nevertheless, a few features can be noted. The lowest level of deprivation is for family type 7—couple with two children and the highest is for family type 13—All others without children. For adults only, deprivation appears to have a distinct relationship with number and age. Thus single person households are as greatly deprived as families with four adults. Among single person households, pensioners are highly deprived.

Several lessons emerge from this econometric exercise. Debates about poverty have frequently conflated various issues. In the debates surrounding Townsend's attempt to locate the poverty line as being at a certain multiple of the British Supplementary Benefit (SB) level, questions of measurement, behaviour and causation have been mixed up. What we have done amounts to saying that the *measurement* of poverty defined as relative deprivation can be based rigorously on the underlying consumption practices of the community and an individual's experience relative to the community. Then we have the issue as to whether a single 'objective' indicator of poverty, a marker to separate the poor from the not so poor, can be found and whether income is such an indicator. Our answer to that is no. Income is one of the variables besides wealth, education, health, ethnic origin etc. which defines the position of a household in the deprivation space. For some events, income has no influence; for others wealth does not. It would be a mistake therefore to look for just a single variable. A satisfactory indicator for poverty has to be vector valued rather than a scalar. After all, given such a complex phenomenon as poverty, it would be surprising if such a crude variable as income could capture it.

Conclusion

We have in this paper provided a firmer conceptual basis for measuring deprivation than has hitherto been advanced in the literature. By defining relative deprivation as relative to the community norm and making the norm the modal behaviour, we make the sociological view of poverty empirically measurable. The key here is to define consumption in terms of certain crucial events which are highly frequent and highly probable. We then proceed to define the modal value of frequency of consumption events and the difference between an actual value and modal value as a simple measure of deprivation for any particular event. By making a suitable econometric specification, we finess the problem of tastes. In aggregating the differences between the actual and the modal value over the different events, we propose a procedure that weights events unequally but in a way that is robust against the inclusion of 'minority events'. This done, we explore the question as to whether our aggregate measure had any different information content from the income variable. We propose that one way to check this might to be use the canonical correlation approach. We we implement a modified measure with Townsend's data.

Our empirical results show that it is possible to use Townsend's data in a sophisticated way to extract from them information that can locate who the deprived are. In terms of family size there are at either end of the distribution—single person households and large adult dominated households. The state of health matters as well. As far as income is concerned, there is a sharp decline in the deprivation index beyond the 160% of SB level. But income is far from being the only or even the most important variable.

Thus we hope to have shown that while Townsend's measure has been criticised, it is possible by a suitable formalisation to meet most of the limitations. The notion of relative deprivation is more general than Townsend's particular measure of it and this notion is obviously worth formalising and measuring econometrically. Our approach produces a measure for each household and it captures the social, interpersonal aspects that are basic to the concept of relative deprivation.

Much further work remains to be done. The robustness of our measure could be tested by extending to more questions within the Townsend sample than the set used here. It could also be tried out on other samples. Ideally, of course, it should be tested by linking it to a questionnaire which allows the event specific distance to be measured. This however remains for the future.

London School of Economics
University of Newcastle Upon Tyne

M. DESAI AND A. SHAH   521

APPENDIX

TABLE A1
List of events

Event	% of Sample
1. Has not had an afternoon or evening out for entertainment in the last two weeks.	40.9
2. Has not had a cooked breakfast most days of the week.	67.0
3. Has gone through one or more days in the past fortnight without a cooked meal.	9.7
4. Does not have fresh meat (including meals out) as many as four days a week.	23.5
5. Household does not usually have a Sunday joint (3 in 4 times).	25.2
6. Has not had a week's holiday away from home in last 12 months.	53.0
7. Has not been out in the last 4 weeks to a relative or friend for a meal or snack.	46.4
8. Has not had a relative or friend to the home for a meal or snack in the last 4 weeks.	33.2
9. Household does not have a refrigerator.	43.8
10. Household does not have sole use of four amenities indoors (flush WC; sink or washbasin and cold-water tap; fixed bath or shower; and gas or electric cooker).	19.8

* The following two events apply only to children:

11. Has not had a friend to play or to tea in the last 4 weeks.
12. Did not have party on last birthday.

TABLE A2
Definitions of variables

FAM 1–FAM 14:	Fourteen family types. (1) Single man ≥ 60 years, (2) Single man <60, (3) Single woman ≥ 60, (4) Single woman <60, (5) Couple, (6) Couple with a child, (7) Couple with 2 children, (8) Couple with 3 children, (9) Couple with 4 or more children, (10) 3 adults, (11) 3 adults with children, (12) 4 adults, (13) All others without children, (14) All others with children.
ED 1–ED 6:	Six education categories. (1) Years of education ≤ 9, (2) 10 years of education, (3) 11, (4) 12, (5) 13, (6) ≥ 14.
INC 1–INC 5:	Five income categories. (1) Income $<100\%$ of supplementary benefits scale rates, (2) $100\%–120\%$, (3) $120\%–140\%$, (4) $140\%–160\%$, (5) $>160\%$.
WLTH 1–WLTH 5:	Five wealth categories. (1) Wealth $<2,500$, (2) $2,500–5,000$, (3) $5,000–7,500$, (4) $7,500–10,000$, (5) $\geq 10,000$.
REG 1–REG 9:	Nine regions. (1) Greater London, (2) South East, (3) Anglia and East Midlands, (4) South West and Wales, (5) West Midlands, (6) North West, (7) North East, (8) Northern Ireland, (9) Scotland.
HEALTH:	1 = Poor health, 0 Otherwise.
ORIGIN:	1 = Born outside U.K., 0 Otherwise.

BIBLIOGRAPHY

ATKINSON, A. B. (1979). "On the Measurement of Inequality", *Journal of Economic Theory*, Vol 2, 244–263.

BRANNEN, J. and WILSON, G. (1987). *Give and Take in Families: Studies in Resource Distribution* (London: Allen and Uwin).

CLARK, S. and HEMMING, R. (1981). "Aspects of Household Poverty in Britain", *Social Policy and Administration*, Vol. 15.

CLARK, S., HEMMING, R. and ULPH, D. (1981). "On Indices for the Measurement of Poverty", *Economic Journal*, 91, 515–530.

DESAI, M. (1981). "Is Poverty a Matter of Taste? An Econometric Comment on the Townsend–Piachaud Debate", (LSE, Unpublished).

DESAI, M. (1986). "Drawing the Line: On Defining the Poverty Threshold", in Golding (1986).

GOLDING, P. (1986). *Excluding the Poor* (London: CPAG).

HAGENAARS, A. J. M. (1986). *The Perception of Poverty: Contributions to Economic Analysis* (Amsterdam: North Holland).

HAGENAARS, A. J. M. and VAN PRAAG, B. M. S. (1985). "A Synthesis of Poverty Line Definitions", *Review of Income and Wealth*, Vol 31, 139–153.

HOOPER, J. (1959). "Simultaenous Equations and Canonical Correlation Theory", *Econometrica*, April, 245–256.

LEWIS, G. W. and ULPH, D. T. (1987). "Poverty Inequality and Welfare" (Paper presented at AUTE meeting Aberystwyth, forthcoming in Conference Papers).

MACK, J. and LANSLEY, S. (1985). *Poor Britain* (London, Allen and Unwin).

PIACHAUD, D. (1981). "Peter Townsend and the Holy Grail", *New Society*, 10 September.

SEN, A. K. (1976). "Poverty: An Ordinal Approach to Measurement", *Econometrica*, 44.

SEN, A. K. (1981). *Poverty and Famine: An Essay on Entitlement and Deprivation* (Oxford: Claredon Press).

SEN, A. K. (1983). "Poor, Relatively Speaking", *Oxford Economic Papers*, 35, 153–169, reprinted in Sen (1985b) as Chapter 14.

SEN, A. K. (1985b). *Resources, Values and Development* (Oxford, Basil Blackwell).

SRINIVASAN, T. N. (1982). "Malnutrition in Developing Countries: The State of Knowledge of the Extent of Its Prevalence, Its Causes and Its Consequences", Yale University, Mimeo.

SUKHATME, P. V. (1978). "Assessment of Adequacy of Diets at Different Economic Levels", *Economic and Political Weekly*, Special Number, August.

TOWNSEND, P. (1962). "The Meaning of Poverty", *British Journal of Sociology*, 8.

TOWNSEND, P. (1979). *Poverty in the United Kingdom* (London: Allen Lane and Penguin).

TOWNSEND, P. (1981). "Reply to Piachaud", *New Society*, September 17.

TOWNSEND, P. (1985). "A Sociological Approach to the Measurement of Poverty—A Rejoinder to Professor Amartya Sen", *Oxford Economic Papers*, 37, 659–668.

[3]

The Role of Exchange and Market Relationships in the Economics of the Transition Period: Lenin on the Tax in Kind*

MEGHNAD DESAI

London School of Economics, England

1

The question of the role of markets in a Socialist economy has been discussed by economists and socialists for many years. On the level of economic theory, most issues regarding the old questions of rationality of 'collectivist' planning or the new ones regarding centralization versus decentralization in computing planning prices, etc., are now non-controversial, though many technical refinements need to be made. While there is consensus within the economics paradigm, no such agreement exists among socialists. Recently we have witnessed a debate between Bettelheim and Sweezy[1] on the question of market in a socialist economy in the context of the Czechoslovak economy and the Russian intervention. As on many other questions in Marxian political economy, intense sectarian debate has continued on this issue. It is interesting in this context to examine Lenin's discussion of the importance of trade in an economy in transition to socialism. As we shall see later, Lenin argues both on the basis of theoretical considerations and policy problems, the contribution trade has to make. His contribution is of interest also because his theoretical paradigm is different from that assumed in economic theoretic discussion. Since not much is known about Lenin's economic writings, we start with a brief description of his work and then proceed to his pamphlet *The Tax in Kind*[2] which contains a discussion of the role of markets.

Lenin's economic writings are a small proportion of his total output. There is

*This paper was originally written for a Lenin Centenary Conference at Delhi University during my stay as Visiting Fellow at the Delhi School of Economics during 1970–71. Though the Conference never took place, my interest in the topic was further encouraged by discussions with Professor Sukhamoy Chakravarty and Professor Khaleeq Naqvi. The many suggestions they made have improved the paper, though this does not in any sense implicate them for the views or the errors expressed herein.
  1. P. Sweezy and C. Bettelheim, *On the Transition to Socialism*, Monthly Review Press. (New York and London, 1971).
  2. Lenin, 'The Tax in Kind' in Lenin, *Selected Works in Three Volumes*, Vol. 3, pp. 589–619. (Progress Publishers, Moscow, 1971).

a difficulty, of course, of classification here. By 'economic writings' we mean those works in which the major issue under discussion pertains to economics. Needless to say in all his writings, the economic aspect is discussed along with political implications mixed with observations and frequently the call to battle. But, one is still justified for example in classifying *The Tax in Kind* as primarily economic while *State and Revolution* or *Two Tactics of Social Democracy* as primarily philosophical and political.

Following this classification, one can divide Lenin's economic writings into those written before the October Revolution and those after it. The pre-Revolution writings are concerned mainly with analysing the development of capitalism in Russia and the international economic forces of Imperialism. In the early period, one of the major themes is Lenin's controversy with Narodniks about the question of the shrinkage of home market under capitalism. In *A Characterisation of Economic Romanticism*[3] and in the first chapter of *The Development of Capitalism in Russia*[4], Lenin discusses this problem. The problem is whether the emergence of large scale industry and the displacement of handicrafts lead to a shrinkage of the home market—to impoverishment of the general population. Lenin shows by using Marx's analysis of generation of surplus value that such a view is romantic and antiscientific. Other themes in the pre-Revolution economic writings are the analysis of agrarian class structure and growth of capitalist relations in Russian agriculture and the growth of monopoly capitalism–Imperialism internationally.

In the post-Revolution period, Lenin is concerned much more with issues of economic policy. The main themes in this period are state capitalism, cooperatives, importance of exchange between agriculture and industry during the phase of New Economic Policy (NEP), the role of national accounting, control and supervision. All these themes are inter-related to form a comprehensive statement of the problem of policy in the period of transition from capitalism to socialism in a predominantly small-peasant economy. In as much as there are only a few hints in Marx's writings on the problems of transition, Lenin's writings constitute the first Marxist treatment of these policy problems.

All the major themes of the post-Revolution period are discussed by Lenin in *The Tax in Kind*[5]. The pamphlet was written in April 1921 and published in May 1921. Following the decision of the Tenth Party Congress to launch NEP, Lenin wrote the pamphlet to explain the role of exchange between agriculture and industry in the period of transition, especially in light of the serious economic dislocation prevailing at that time. In the pamphlet, Lenin takes up the problem of trade in

---

3. Lenin, 'A Characterisation of Economic Romanticism : Sismondi and Our Native Sismondists.'
4. Lenin, 'The Development of Capitalism in Russia', *Collected Works of Lenin*, Vol. 3.
5. *op. cit.*

conjunction with the issue of state capitalism and his analysis of both is embedded
in a description of the Russian economy. The most important aspect of his description of the Russian economy is his demonstration that several overlapping
modes of production, from partriarchal peasant agriculture to socialism, existed
simultaneously in the economy, and trade-free or capitalist trade had therefore
a progressive role to play in that situation. In what follows, we shall outline Lenin's
arguments and put them in a general perspective of Marxist economic theory.

2

Through the years of Civil War and War Communism, a compulsory appro-
priation of surplus grain was in force. This was to feed the Army as well as cities.
In many cases, not only was the surplus appropriated but even a part of subsistence supplies were taken. The policy of War Communism was partly forced
by the circumstances of war and devastation but it was also thought of as an
experiment of running an economy without market relationships or money.
The transition from War Communism to NEP was seen by many as a retreat or
a going back to capitalist forms.

The tax in kind was a scheme whereby a part of the urban requirements of grain
was collected as a tax in kind or output while leaving the peasant free to sell the
balance of his surplus grain in the free market in exchange for manufactured
goods. It was thought desirable to confine such free trade only to local exchange.
Since large scale industry's output was low, the farmer could buy only the products
of small scale, local industry. Local exchange was therefore both necessary and
desirable. The desirability of local exchange rose from the need to check growth
of capitalist relations in the economy. Lenin's pamphlet is mainly concerned with
the question of allowing free trade in the industry–agricultural exchange.

Before discussing *The Tax in Kind* any further, let us look at the following quotation from the conclusion of *The Tax in Kind* in which the argument is summarised
by Lenin.

"To sum up.
"The tax in kind is a transition from War Communism to the proper Socialist exchange of
products.
"The extreme ruin rendered more acute by the failure of the harvest in 1920 made this transition urgently necessary owing to the fact that it was impossible to restore large-scale industry
rapidly.
"Hence, the first thing to do is to improve the conditions of the peasants. The means to this
are the tax in kind, the development of exchange between agriculture and industry, the development of small industry.
"Exchange is free trade, it is capitalism. It is useful to us in as much as it will help us to overcome the scatteredness of the small producer, and to a certain degree to combat bureaucracy;
to what extent will be determined by practical experience. The proletarian regime is in no danger

as long as the proletariat firmly holds power in its hands, as long as it firmly holds transport and large scale industry in its hands.

"The fight against profiteering must be transformed into a fight against larceny and against evasion of state supervision, accounting and control. By means of this control, we shall direct capitalism, which is inevitable and to a certain extent necessary for us, into the channels of state capitalism.

"The fullest scope must be given for the development of local initiative and independent action in encouraging exchange between agriculture and industry. This must be done to the utmost extent and at all costs. The experience gained in this must be studied, and this experience must be made as varied as possible."[6]

The only step in the argument which is not included in the quotation above but is in the pamphlet relates to the desirability of channelling local exchange through peasant cooperatives. Lenin held that this would help check the growth of private capitalist tendencies since cooperatives being collectivist private enterprises were a form of state capitalism in the Soviet economy and hence subject to accounting, supervision and control by the proletariat.

3

Lenin begins his analysis of the tax in kind with a long quotation from his 1918 pamphlet—*Left-Wing Childishness and Petty-Bourgeois Mentality*[7]. In that pamphlet, discussing State Capitalism, he lists the various socio-economic formations or modes of production which existed in Russia then.
These are :

(1) "patriarchal, i.e., largely natural peasant economy;
(2) small commodity production (this includes the majority of those peasants who sell grain);
(3) private capitalism;
(4) state capitalism; and
(5) Socialism".[8]

It is the intermingling of these forms—the simultaneous existence of overlapping modes of production which determines according to Lenin, the existence of an economy in transition. Also being a predominantly small-peasant economy, the small-peasant or the petty-bourgeois element predominated. The main struggle was between small commodity production and private capitalism on the one hand and state capitalism and socialism on the other.

6. *op. cit.* pp. 618–619.
7. *Selected Works*, Vol. 2, pp. 685–709.
8. *op . cit.* p. 590

It was the predominantly small-peasant/petty-bourgeois character of Russia as well as the state of extreme devastation and ruin which made trade necessary and inevitable. Trade was also politically necessary in the short run to alleviate the discontent that led to peasant riots and as part of a long term strategy of alliance between peasants and workers. 'The correct policy of the proletariat, which is exercising its dictatorship in a small-peasant country is to obtain grain in exchange for the manufactured goods the peasant requires. Only such a food policy corresponds to the tasks of the proletariat; only such a policy can strengthen the foundations of socialism and lead to its complete victory.'[9]

Trade is also seen by Lenin as an antidote to bureaucracy. Bureaucracy is rampant mainly because the peasants are scattered and trade is absent, and hence trade combats bureaucratic tendencies. After discussing the roots of bureaucracy in capitalist countries, Lenin analyses Soviet bureaucracy as follows, "Bureaucracy in this country has a different economic root, viz., the atomized and dispersed character of small production, its poverty, lack of culture, absence of roads, illiteracy, absence of *exchange* between agriculture and industry, the absence of connection and interaction between them."[10] Trade is thus a better, more efficient way of mobilising surplus in a small peasant economy than bureaucracy. This is because "the atomized and dispersed character of small production" implies that surplus occurs in small amounts or each of many small scattered units of production—the small peasant farms. The technology being backward surplus only occurs in small amounts (low productivity) and the property relations being precapitalist (numerous small peasants) surplus is scattered and can only be mobilized by exaction or trade. Trade, however, is economically more efficient and as already seen above, was politically the better policy.

What is more, trade is not only more efficient but may prove to be the instrument for overcoming the atomised character of small peasantry. This is because trade may encourage higher forms of association among the peasantry. Six months after the publication of *The Tax in Kind*, Lenin returned to the question of trade in October 1921. "The proletarian state must become a cautious, assiduous and shrewd 'businessman', a punctilious *wholesale merchant*—otherwise it will never succeed in putting this small-peasant country economically on its feet. Under existing conditions, living as we are side by side with the capitalist (for the time being capitalist) West, there is no other way of passing on to Communism. A wholesale merchant is an economic type as remote from Communism as heaven is from earth. But this is one of the contradictions which, in the actual conditions of life lead from a small-peasant economy via state capitalism to socialism. Personal incentive will develop production: and our primary task is to increase production at all costs. Wholesale trade economically unites the millions

9. *op cit.*, pp, 600–601.
10. *op cit.*, p. 607.

of small-peasants; it gives them personal incentive, links them up and leads them to the next step, namely, to various forms of association and union in the process of production itself."[11]

One such form of association, though not in the process of production, but in the process of trade and exchange, already existed; namely, the producers' co-operatives. The small commodity-producers' cooperatives were the predominant and typical form in the economy but they strengthened petty-bourgeois capitalist relations and facilitated their development. But despite this drawback, if free trade, which would inevitably lead to fostering capitalist tendencies, was to be allowed, then it was preferable that such trade be carried on through Cooperatives. This was because given the class-character of the State—the dictatorship of the proletariat—cooperative capitalism was a form of State capitalism. "Cooperative capitalism resembles State capitalism in that it facilitates accounting, control and supervision and the establishment of contractual relations between the State (in this case, the Soviet State) and the capitalist'.[12]

Trade is thus seen as a way of overcoming the isolation of the small-peasantry, and trade through cooperatives ensures the regulation and control of capitalist tendencies. The cooperative form of organisation of peasantry was cited again and again by Lenin in the NEP years as a way of binding together the atomised and scattered small-peasantry and also an appropriate private but collectivist form suitable for the transition to socialism. "As a matter of fact, all that we need under the NEP is to organise the population of Russia in co-operative societies as a sufficiently wide scale, for now we have found that degree of the combination of private interest, trading interest, with state supervision and control of this interest, that degree of its subordination to the common interests that was formerly the stumbling block for very many Societies."[13] As an instrument of economic policy in the period of transition, trade, especially trade by cooperatives, was linked through accounting, supervision and control as a form of state capitalism: state capitalism in its turn was a higher form of economic organization than private capitalism and facilitated the transition to socialism.

4

In as much as the question of market relationships in Socialist countries has again recently risen into prominence, it may be helpful to bring out the relevance of Lenin's remarks on the general question of trade and market relationships in Marxist economic theory and problems of economic policy in Socialist countries.

11. The Fourth Anniversary of the October Revolution, in *Selected Works*, Vol. 3, pp. 647–648.
12. The Tax in Kind, *op. cit.*, p. 604.
13. On cooperation, in *Selected Works*, Vol. 3, p. 760.

Let us first take Lenin's argument about trade in small-peasant countries. Small-peasant production is not entirely for the market because a part of the output is consumed by the producer. What remains has the character of surplus. It is misleading however to draw an analogy with capitalist production and attempt to separate output into constant and variable capital and surplus value. If surplus grain is exchanged for manufactured goods for consumption by the peasant family, then grain retained for consumption on the farm and surplus grain both have the character of variable capital. If the peasant also hires agricultural labour then the more conventional categories may come into play. But even then, if part of the product is consumed by the peasant as well as given as wages in kind, the peasant cannot be said to be producing for the market and value categories which are appropriate for the commodity mode of production may not apply. The existence of trade and exchange in a small-peasant economy either in the specific form of barter or in the generalised form of money sales and purchase is thus not the same as capitalist production for the market. If other modes of production coexist with small-peasant production, market relationships also share both pre-capitalist and capitalist features.

Lenin's argument is more concerned with the problem of mobilising grain surplus and the usefulness of trade as an efficient instrument for doing that. As already mentioned above, the crucial facts here are the scatteredness of producers and the small size of surplus on each farm due to backward technology. The form in which the surplus occurs dictates the forms in which it can efficiently be mobilised. Bureaucracy and trade are the two choices and trade tends to be more efficient. Under War Communism surplus was mobilised physically by bureaucratic methods; after the civil war, surplus had to be 'realized' by exchange with manufactured goods.

The important question is whether market relationships are inseparable from the capitalist mode of production or can they survive in post-capitalist period? Lenin, relying mainly on the political capacity of the Soviet state to control and supervise the growth of market relations, takes the view that in the period of transition market relationships are useful. The usual tendency however has been to rely more on direct (bureaucratic) methods of allocation in socialist countries rather than on controlled and supervised trade. This, I believe, rests on a misunderstanding of the nature of market relations.

Exchange either in the specific form of barter or in the generalised form of buying and selling for money is historically a precapitalist phenomenon. Production for the market i.e. specialisation necessitating realisation of the total value of output by sale on the market is a capitalist form. This also extends to the sale of labour-power by the labourer. The exchange that the labourer undertakes of labour-power for wages is mutually beneficial although for the labourer it is the only way he can survive. Exploitation in the sense of creation of surplus value is not due to exchange. It is not as if the system of trading due to monopoly or market imperfections leads to exploitation in the Joan Robinson sense (i.e., gap between wage and marginal product as in her *The Economics of Imperfect Competition*). It is because the act of exchange *alone* cannot explain the existence of surplus value that one has to look at the *relations of production*—the class monopoly ownership of means of production, the category of 'free' labour, etc. Since capitalism cannot function without the market and also since it leads to exploitation (in the Marxian sense), market relationships have been identified as the exploitation mechanism.

If the relations of production are different, i.e., if there is total public ownership of means of production, the problem of market takes on a different context. It becomes a 'technical' relationship like the method of double entry book-keeping and its efficiency considerations become paramount. This is the familiar Lange-Lerner type of socialism. Our argument regarding *The Tax in Kind* however adds one additional dimension to it.

The question of market in matters of exchange between productive units—purchase of raw materials can be taken separately from exchange between producing units and consumers—the question of retail distribution. If several modes of production are co-existing, Lenin's argument about the need for exchange extends to the purchase of raw materials, etc., by productive units. If all productive units are large scale and publicly owned, market purchases of raw materials can be simulated by book transfer or an efficient planning mechanism which can arrange the 'trade' at shadow prices. In this case, the problem of the market is trivial in the sense that we need it only in the absence of efficient planning techniques.

The question of the market for exchange between producing units and consumers is different. Retail trade has many of the characteristics of small-commodity production. It is atomised and scattered since consumers are scattered. The alternative way of affecting exchange is to rely on a bureaucratic network and allocate consumption goods by some form of rationing. The choice is similar to that posed by Lenin in *The Tax in Kind*. A cooperative retail trade mechanism is a preferable alternative to private retain trade but trade is preferable to bureaucracy.

The problem of market relationships in socialist countries also extends to the purchase of labour power by the productive units and the role of profit calculus as a decision rule. These matters are not discussed here since they go beyond the scope of this paper and also since they deserve detailed treatment. The important consideration in all these discussions of possible revival of capitalism is to determine the class character of the state. If political power is in the hands of the proletariat and the state owns all means of production, then reliance on market is not likely to lead to the revival of capitalism. It may successfully combat bureaucracy.

4

Economic Alternatives for Labour, 1984–9

Meghnad Desai

A Labour Government that comes to power in 1984 (or before) will face the biggest challenge that a new Government has faced for years – a challenge comparable to that of 1945.[1] The economy will be in a critical condition after five years of dry monetarism; unemployment is likely to be between 4 and 5 million; the decline in output in 1980–2 is unlikely to have been substantially reversed. Barring upheavals in the Conservative Party leadership, the most likely estimate is that an election-winning budget from the present Government will take the form of tax cuts – for the middle- and upper-income groups, for the private corporations and for the wealthy. There will probably have been little substantial economic recovery, and it is unlikely that the economy will be back to its postwar trend level of output below which it has operated since 1974.

Unemployment, bankruptcies and loss of production capacity are not the only problems. The potential for future growth has been harmed by a persistent decline in output and the senseless cutting of expenditure on education, research and development. But the most serious matter for an incoming Labour Government to consider will be that the welfare state launched by the policies of the Coalition Government and the Labour Government of 1945 will have been severely damaged. The Keynes–Beveridge design for welfare capitalism fell short of a socialist alternative; even so, inadequate as it was, its implementation was niggardly, and its full potential was never realised.[2] Despite this, it is only now, when it has been rejected as official policy, that we have begun to appreciate how much we took it for granted. In abandoning full employment as an objective, in jettisoning even a nominal commitment towards a guaranteed minimum standard of living, in running down the health and social facilities provided under the state's aegis and, above all, in attacking the ideology that sustained the arrangement, the present Tory Government has precipitated a radical departure from the postwar policy consensus. In many ways, policies since 1979 (if not those before that year, as we shall see below) have been a replay of the deflationary episode of 1921 which inaugurated the long interwar period of high unemployment and conflict that lasted until 1939. Only the outbreak of the war made it imperative that mass support be secured for a successful war effort; full employment and a substantial welfare state were the almost inevitable consequences of the nation's total involvement in the war — as if there had been a social contract between the Government and the people.[3] That a reversal of such a long-standing policy could come about raises questions about the sources of political as well as economic power and about the best way of guaranteeing that such reversals do not recur.

Thus a new Labour Government will not only face the immediate short-term tasks of restoring and rehabilitating the economy after five years and more of devastation. It will also have to regain the ground that has been lost in the public provision of health, education and social services. But it cannot be desirable — nor is it feasible — to see the task as one of restoring the *status quo ante*: there will have to be a restructuring of the economy.

Diagnosing the British disease

In diagnosing the British disease, it is tempting to rake over recent failures of economic policy. The backsliding by the Wilson and Callaghan Governments from their avowed promises, a panic boom inaugurated by the Heath Government, the mistiming of the devaluation decision by the Wilson Government — all these can be rehearsed. The postwar period saw both an unprecedented quarter-century of full employment, with real income growth, and the realisation that such could not be the permanent condition of the British economy. 'You Never

Had it so Good' was true in 1959 but could not be repeated a decade later. The realisation that full employment and growth were difficult to achieve simultaneously crystallised during Maudling's years as Chancellor of the Exchequer. At first the problem seemed to be the balance of payments and the overvalued pound, then high wages which were causing inflation, then the expanding share of public sector or the unrestrained growth of money supply. These were not unrelated, but each surfaced at various times as the fashionable explanation of the British disease.

What they hid, however, was the deeper structural reasons for the predicament, which go back to the 1870s. Indeed, what needs to be explained is the miraculously easy period of 1948–63. Various conjunctures – the growth of world trade that resulted from the simultaneous adoption of full employment policies in all developed capitalist countries, the preoccupation of Britain's potential trade rivals with the immediate task of postwar construction, the sluggish growth of the US economy in the 1950s, etc. – helped to ease the British problem. The structural causes of British economic stagnation were thus hidden for a while, but it is on these that we must focus.

By the 1870s it was clear that the British economy was no longer the most dynamic capitalist economy. Its growth rate, its rate of innovative activity, its international competitiveness had all suffered, and it was facing competition from the USA and Germany in all the markets to which it exported. The response of the political and economic community in Britain in the years 1870–1900 determined the course of the long-run stagnation.

The first Industrial Revolution took place in the second half of the eighteenth century, preceded by an Agricultural Revolution, and between 1790 and 1840 the British economy witnessed tremendous expansion and structural transformation. The dominant pattern of industrial organisation was the privately owned firm managed by the owner. While there were many competing firms in each industry, internationally Britain was in a monopolistic position. She did not face any serious competition from domestic or foreign rivals in the various countries where she sold goods. Captive markets were also created by the policy of imperial expansion – the loss of the American colonies was quickly recouped by the gain of the Indian Empire – and these markets were immediately penetrated by British textile and engineering firms. This was the period during which Britain exported new manufactured goods as well as new technology.

But the second Industrial Revolution, which occurred in the 1870s and 1880s with the introduction of electrical-mechanical technology, passed Britain by. The favoured form of industrial organisation in Britain was unsuitable for exploiting the economies of mechanised production, and it hindered the adoption of new managerial practices. The American economy, by contrast, underwent this technological-managerial revolution, which encouraged the growth of large, vertically integrated firms managed by personnel who could use new methods of cost accounting and production control. The British firms in many ways revealed their crafts origins and remained small-scale. From the 1870s onwards the British economy began to lose its competitive edge in third markets to the USA and Germany.[4]

This loss was noticed by contemporaries, and many attempts were made to identify the ingredients of the foreigners' success. But the responses of the Establishment were exactly the opposite of what was needed. Instead of responding to this new challenge by changing the structure of industry, the economy increasingly took the character of a *rentier* economy. The domination of finance capital over industrial capital dates from this period, when banking became concentrated in and around London, at the expense of country banks. The educational system, far from changing over to technical and scientific subjects, inculcated the anti-industrial values of the landed aristocracy. There was no democratic spread of education as there was in the USA. Workers learned their craft skills on the job and not at polytechnics. There was no managerial education, and even if there had been, there would have been no opportunities for the employment of the graduates of such education, since firms continued to be owner-managed.

The *rentier* economy flourished by specialising in the export of capital. There was a shift from direct investment abroad to passive equity or fixed-interest debenture participation. The City of London could raise money from British savers for almost any project anywhere in the world, and much of this was in debenture form. The gentleman who drew his income from interest on past investment was ranked above the industrialist. The heirs of industrialists preferred to become gentlemen if they could buy their way into the gentry by education and marriage.

Faced with international competition, one political response was to rely on imperial expansion to assure markets. The idea was to keep the imperial territory as a protected area from which competition could be shut out, as Joseph Chamberlain urged. While the protectionists did not win the argument, there were many ways of excluding rivals from imperial markets, not least important of which was to instruct the natives of India and the African colonies that British was best.

The Empire provided an area of effectively (though not formally) protected markets, and in the functioning of the Gold Standard India was pivotal. Her trade surplus was transferred by means of a complex web of financial arrangements to finance the British balance of payments deficit, which arose from the large volume of capital exports that exceeded the commodity trade surplus. Freedom to export capital was vital to the *rentier* economy and to its nerve centre – the City of London.

The *rentier* economy experienced high and cyclical unemployment in the 1860–1914 period, but in the absence of political pressure *laissez-faire* policies could be maintained. The trade union movement had won over skilled craft workers but was spreading to general industrial workers only slowly. Nevertheless, all workers, skilled or otherwise, benefited from the Victorian arrangements, since Britain could import cheap consumables and raw materials from the Colonies and could export finished manufactures at prices which were favourable to herself.

It was precisely this delicate compromise that fell apart in the 1914–40 period. The inadequacy of the compromise in dealing with poverty and distress had already been apparent in the discussions following the Boer War. The increased electoral pressure after the 1884 extension of the franchise, the growth of union activities evidenced by the Taff Vale retaliation and the débâcle of the Boer War had led to a pressure for a welfare state. The Liberals conceded this in the Lloyd George budgets, but the advent of the First World War changed the entire political context in Britain.

The year 1915 was perhaps the first since recorded unemployment statistics began to be kept that unemployment fell under 1 per cent. The war effort required mass co-operation, and this meant giving the trade unions official recognition in tripartite committees. The full employment prevalent in the 1914–20 period boosted Labour's share in total income from a 60 per cent average between 1860 and 1913 to 65 per cent. Another extension of the franchise had taken place, so that all adult males were now entitled to vote.

The war prompted a tremendous structural change in the *rentier* economy. During the war many of the Empire countries and other markets in which Britain used to have dominance (e.g. Argentina) began to industrialise. The USA emerged as a creditor nation and New York as a rival financial centre to London. The response of the British Establishment was to renege on the wartime compromise with workers. A severe deflation designed to restore the pound sterling to its old parity of $4.86 was inaugurated without any consultation with trade unions in 1921. This was followed by various wage-cutting exercises and an end to tripartite co-operation. The interwar period saw a higher level of unemployment on average than in the prewar period. The British economy was squeezed through a long deflation from 1921 until 1939 in order to restore the City of London to its former prominence. The period from 1921 to 1932 was perhaps the worst because much of the unemployment was concentrated in the traditional export industries which were adversely affected by the high exchange rate. Despite the squeeze, however, no fundamental restructuring of the economy took place in terms of managerial or industrial organisational change.

The Second World War forced the Establishment to revive the contract of the First World War, but this time firm guarantees had to be given that there would be no backtracking. Also since 1928 full adult franchise had been established and now the obsolete economic and political machine had to cope with mass democracy. The war not only prompted much egalitarian sentiment; it also encouraged modernising tendencies. The economic orthodoxies were shown to be those not of a dynamic competitive economy but of protective, inefficient cartel arrangements behind which reactionary owners hid. The needs of war – manpower planning and the application of new techniques – showed what could be done if this moribund capitalism were modernised. But the war had also shown that the regulation of production and of labour allocation increased rather than reduced production efficiency, just as the rationing of consumer goods improved nutrition and health. War conditions enlisted egalitarianism and change in the service of a spirit of community, playing down conflict.

Postwar reconstruction thus consisted of the guarantee of full employment and the carrying out of a package of reforms in welfare provision – health, social security, pensions, unemployment benefit. The rationalisation of industry took the form of the nationalisation of the most obsolete and reactionary of the old industries, especially coal-mining. But the financial structure was unchanged, and the City was left in private hands except for the nationalisation of the Bank of England. Instead of the abolition of the privileged private educational system, or even its reform, a binary system was adopted whereby state education grew up side by side with public schools. But the much more drastic plans of industrial reconstruction proposed in the war years were never realised. The tripartite equilibrium between Government, employers and unions was re-established and cemented by the employers' willingness to concede some public ownership and the closed shop; the state's guarantee of full employment and the adoption of an orthodox scheme for financing the welfare state; and the unions' display of interest not in the control of production but only in free collective bargaining.[5]

Even so, some fundamental change in the industrial structure on the managerial and on the union side was inevitable. With the loss of India, it was obvious that colonial markets were no longer secure. But there was a temporary reprieve. Although the financial burdens of the war weighed more heavily on Britain than on the defeated countries, for a while there was not much competition from Germany and Japan. Much of Europe was recovering from war damage. There was also a sustained growth in world trade because of the full employment policies that were being followed in the developed capitalist countries. Britain's *rentier* economy faced no immediate crisis; it faced instead easy conditions in the world markets. After the immediate problems of physical shortages in the period 1946–9, the economy began to enjoy growth of exports and income, with full employment, through much of the 1950s.

The pivotal position of India in the financing of British capital exports has been mentioned above. Once India had gained independence, this benefit disappeared. There were also large wartime credits due to India as well as to other Empire countries. To stave off immediate repayments, it was essential to preserve the sterling area. This and the creation of the Commonwealth gave a breathing space to the *rentier* economy and the City of London.

With the re-establishment of free convertibility of European currencies, the revival of the Western European economies and the establishment of the Common Market, the breathing space came to an end. From the beginning of the 1960s the economy faced severe challenges, which took the form of an inadequate growth rate, incipient inflation and growing concern about the burden of sterling as a key currency.

Rapid economic growth became the universal solution to the problems of the *rentier* economy. It was needed to preserve the wartime social contract. In fact, as Crosland clearly saw, it also obviated the need for any drastic redistribution of income. But even if it had been achieved, more was asked of rapid growth than could be delivered. Indeed, it became the only way to avoid hard choices.

But the breathing space of the 1950s had revived the City of London, which adjusted remarkably well to the decline of sterling as a key currency and regained its status as the major banking and financial centre of the developed capitalist world. It was assisted by the fact that the now prospering Western Europe economies had weak banking sectors and that despite the growth of New York as a financial rival, proximity to Europe helped London to hold its own. The City had thus an abiding interest in strengthening its links with Europe and in resisting any drastic change required for, and contingent upon, rapid growth.

The real problem in the 1960s, however, was international competition. While world trade was still growing, the British economy faced many industrial rivals. The development of new products which could cut costs, investment in research and innovation, the rapid retraining of the work force as demands for new skills emerged – all these were important. But nothing had been done in the 1950s (or indeed during the previous years of the twentieth century) to instil a culture of industrial capitalism in this *rentier* economy. The relative position of the British economy in the growth league began to slip badly from the early 1960s onwards. All those postponed decisions of the previous hundred years had now to be taken. But as the pressure on sterling, the subsequent abandonment of the National Plan and the resort to short-term fiscal and monetary manipulations since 1966 show, the decisions have still not been made.

Future policy and prospects

What lessons can be drawn from this conspectus of long-run problems? Much discussion today, on the left especially, about the problems of the British economy holds international economic forces responsible for the British decline. Thus multinational corporations, the EEC, the ideology of free trade which leaves British markets open to competitive imports, the free flow of international capital in and out of the country, competition from the newly industrialising countries of the Third World are all blamed for de-industrialisation and the loss of economic and political sovereignty. The openness of the economy is seen as the major structural weakness by many writers on the left. Those who argue along these lines would not much dispute the main lines of my narrative above, but precisely because of that I wish to make explicit my departures from their interpretation (see Cripps *et al.*, 1981; Singh, 1980).

The growing internationalisation of the world economy (and not merely of the capitalist First World) has been evident since

46   Socialism in a Cold Climate

1945. In this respect the world economy has resumed the course on which it embarked after the Napoleonic Wars, which was interrupted by the First World War and its aftermath. In the nineteenth century national sovereignty in economic affairs could be afforded by very few countries. Britain's economic and political sovereignty was sustained by her Empire abroad and her lack of democracy at home. But in the recent period every country, including the USA, has increasingly felt that its economic autonomy is being compromised. Multinational corporations and the other international forces mentioned above are not peculiar to Britain. If their impact on the British economy is more severe than on (say) that of West Germany, the reasons lie precisely in the structural weaknesses outlined above. To blame Britain's economic decline on foreign economic forces is once again to evade the question of the responsibility of deep-seated historical and institutional forces for the present malaise.

It is also to demonstrate a signal failure to learn from history. The imperial props of Britain's much vaunted sovereignty are now gone. Indeed, it was the presence of the Imperial Alternative that lured Britain down the path of compromise which created the *rentier* economy. The various devices used to preserve British prosperity at home and imperial hegemony abroad reflected the wrong choices. Instead of revolutionising educational institutions and industrial practices, restructuring the pattern of trade to meet competition from abroad, defensive attitudes were adopted which postponed change. The culture of industrial capitalism was never inculcated, either on the factory floor (indeed, the expression 'shop floor' betrays its pre-industrial origins) or in the educational institutions. The costs were borne by the natives of the imperial colonies or by the poor at home who were beyond the Pale of industrial employment.

Whatever the outcome then, it would be a mistake now to use again the same devices, even with a radical rather than an imperial-chauvinist rhetoric. The decline in living standards, the erosion of social capital and the rapid obsolescence of industrial capital all point to the limited room left for manoeuvre in the urgent task of restructuring the economy. It would be a mistake to cocoon the economy against change once more. The cost of any new attempts to resist change and innovation, no matter how radical the language in which they are clothed, will have to be borne entirely by the domestic population, and societies have many ways of shifting such costs inevitably on to the poorest. If one is to fashion a socialist economic programme, such evasions must be made explicit and avoided. The achievement of a socialist economy must remain the ultimate goal, and in devising short-run and medium-run policies we must be on our guard against foreclosing socialist options. The need for a modernising, innovative economic strategy is profound, however. In what follows I shall concentrate on policies that would enhance the chances of successful restructuring while at the same time ensuring that short-term economic policies generate as much employment and income as possible.

Whatever reservations one may have about specific details, the Alternative Economic Strategy (AES) has been discussed very widely in Labour and left-wing groups.[6] Although its beginnings go back to the discussions preceeding the 1974 Labour Government, since 1979 there has been a veritable explosion of debates, articles and books on the AES. Seldom before have so many different groups taken part in an economic debate, but even now there is need to involve more people.

There seems to be general consensus that AES involves five ingredients:

- reflation through increased public expenditure or devaluation
- the expansion of public ownership and the extension of control over the industrial sector via planning agreements
- import controls and restrictions on capital exports
- policies for job creation, worksharing, early retirement and a 35-hour week
- price control.

In what follows I wish to assess the adequacy and the feasibility of the AES as it now stands, to make explicit some of the implicit assumptions about the nature of the economy that a Labour Government will wish to achieve by means of the AES and to fill out a skeletal statement of general principles with some illustrative macro-economic projections.

The full-employment aspect of the AES strategy is in the Maudling–National Plan tradition. Thus the notion is that of expanding aggregate demand by higher government expenditure, or by devaluation, or by tax cuts. While higher government expenditure, especially on the capital side, will be absolutely essential, if only to replace what has been depreciated, what is not clear is that reflation would lead to more jobs rather than to higher imports or, if import control is imposed, to higher prices and profits. Such doubts persist in the absence of any detailed plan for correcting the structural weaknesses of the British economy.

Although no detailed projections have been made in any of the AES publications, work is now available which clarifies the structural constraints on any reflation plan. In recent years a number of studies has been carried out with econometric models which have some common features. These exercises were undertaken on the Treasury Model by the Fabian Society group coordinated by David Blake and Paul Ormerod in 1980 (Blake and Ormerod, 1980); again in 1981 in a series of articles in *The Times* by David Blake (Blake, 1981); by Terence Barker using the Cambridge Multisectoral Dynamic Model (Barker, 1982); and, in early 1982, Peter Shore launched a five-year alternative plan for full employment.

David Blake's 1981 calculations are of the most immediate interest to us. Barker's analysis with a more detailed interindustrial model does not in any way contradict Blake's conclusions, so let me summarise Blake's conclusions first. Blake's calculations are given as alternatives to the current strategy over the 1981–4 period. Barker also concentrates on alternative policies for generating extra employment, but he looks at the short run (1982–5) as well as at projections to 1990.

David Blake tried three separate policy packages, all consistent with the AES. These were:

- a reflation package of £4 billion, comprising (i) an investment programme costing £1 billion; (ii) an income tax cut of £1.25 billion, obtained by indexing threshold levels; (iii) a cut in the National Insurance Surcharge by 1.75 percentage points

- 20 per cent devaluation, bringing the pound down from the June 1981 level of $2.07 to a level of $1.60
- protection plus public spending: a £6 billion increase in demand, plus a 30 per cent tariff on all imports of manufactured goods as well as of semi-manufactured goods.

The effects of these policies on output growth, unemployment, inflation and consumption growth are shown in Table 1.

One can only say that the results make terribly depressing reading. None of the three packages cuts unemployment by even 0.5 million by early 1984. Taking into account the increased participation in the labour force that such job creation entails, the net reduction in unemployment is at most 400,000 compared with present policy in Option III. Given that all these estimates are surrounded by a penumbra of error, the difference between II and III can hardly be significant. The major difference, then, between a purely reflationary policy without import controls/devaluation (I) and a mixed policy with import controls (II/III) seems to be of the order of between 250,000 and 450,000 jobs, with unemployment above 3 million in all cases.

The import control/devaluation strategy, however, involves a reduction in the standard of living of between 4 and 4.5 per cent more than the purely reflationary strategy. On the other hand, the purely reflationary strategy generates a lower output growth rate than the mixed reflationary strategy. Indeed, the output level is between 1.5 and 2 per cent higher by 1984 under II/III than under I. As against this, the inflation rate is between 3.5 and 4.5 per cent higher in II/III as compared with I.

What this calculation reveals is that a mixed strategy such as II or III succeeds in achieving growth and high employment but also redistributes income in favour of profits. Thus the real wage decline is much more pronounced in the case of such policies than in that of the purely reflationary strategy, as can be seen by comparing the figures for the standard of living. Thus import control or devaluation is a way of generating growth by increasing the share of profits (i.e. it is a method of cutting real wages).

This is said not to detract in any way from the merits of the

Table 1 *Likely impact of alternative economic strategies*

	Present Policy	I	II	III
Output (percentage growth of GDP)	−1% by summer 1982 0% 1982–3 +1.5% 1983–4	0% 1981–3 1.5% 1983–4 (on average 1% above present policy)	0% until end 1982 2% 1983–4 (on average 3% higher than present policy)	1.5% growth by early 1982, followed by stagnation (2.4% above present policy by 1984)
Inflation	Falls slowly to 9.6% by early 1984	Falls faster over mid-1981 to end 1982 but is 10.3% in early 1984	Up to 14% by end 1981. 19% by end 1982 but falls to 13.8% by early 1984	17% in winter 1981/2 19½% by summer 1982, then down to 14.7% by early 1984
Living standards	Stagnant to end 1983, then rises to early 1981 level	On average 1% higher than present policy	Falls by 3.5% by late summer 1982, then rises by 2% by autumn 1983 and by 3% by summer 1984 (on average 3% below present policy by 1984)	Falls by 3.5% in summer 1982, rises by 1% by summer 1982 then at rate of 2% per annum until early 1984 (on average 3.5% below present policy by 1984)
Unemployment, including school-leavers	More than 3 million in winter 1981/2, then rising gently to 3.5 million by 1984	Just over 3 million in winter 1981/2, rising to 3.38 million by early 1984	Over 3 million in winter 1981/2, rising to 3.265 million by late 1982, then falling to 3.185 million by early 1984	Rises very gently to above 3 million in late 1982, then falls during rest of the year but rises to 3.05 million in early 1984
Extra jobs created		175,000	420,000	600,000

Source: Blake (1981).

import control strategy but to make explicit the effects of the policy. Since profitability is a problem in British industry (and this is so for the private sector as well as for nationalised industries), one way in which to examine the political aspects of any policy is to see how it deals with that problem. An import control policy allows domestic firms to increase their prices in relation to import prices net of tariffs. This depresses real wages (in terms both of product and of wage goods) and increases profits. These profits are presumably invested in output expansion, and this gives the extra output.

The best alternative with which one should compare such a policy is a reflationary package with an incomes policy. Incomes policies have been used as short-term devices for cutting real wages. Unfortunately, this was not simulated by David Blake, but it is clearly another way of altering the relative share of wages and profits. It would be interesting to examine whether it would have milder effects on standards of living or equally severe ones. Incomes policy is one issue on which AES has been coy, since unions take a stand on free collective bargaining and other radical analysts have castigated it as merely a wage-cutting device. We are aware that an import control policy is also a wage-cutting strategy: the choice between them should be made on the grounds of their contribution to the other objectives of the overall economic plan.

Terence Barker, using the Cambridge Multisectoral Model, arrives at similar conclusions. After considering a variety of policies such as import controls, National Insurance and tax cuts, investment projects and employment subsidies, he writes: 'The conclusion is that the changes required to reduce unemployment appreciably are probably too large to be feasible within the life of the present Government and represent a daunting task for the next one' (Barker, 1982, p. 19). Barker tried ten different policies separately in a simulation exercise. The aim was to find the change in the policy instrument that would generate 100,000 jobs by 1984 (starting in 1982) and then to project the result to 1990.

In Table 2 I have provided information on the ten policies with regard to their effect on employment, inflation, income and consumption growth as well as on PSBR as a proportion of

Table 2 *Effectiveness of alternative employment-creation policies*

Measure	To generate 100,000 jobs by 1984	Increase in employment (000)		Inflation (%)		GDP Growth (%)		Consumers' expenditure (%)		PSBR as % of GDP		
		1982–4	1990	1982	1984	1982	1984	1982	1984	1982	1984	1990
Tariff on manufactured imports	22.2%	355	−73	14.1	12.4	2.1	1.8	−2.3	0.1	1.3	0.7	−2.3
Permanent incomes policy	3%	156	621	9.1	9.2	1.1	1.9	−1.3	0.7	3.3	3.3	−0.8
Temporary incomes policy	3.3%	162	178	8.9	9.6	1.1	1.9	−1.3	0.9	3.3	3.4	2.4
Devaluation	3.5%	224	128	9.9	11.5	1.4	1.9	−1.2	1.0	3.4	3.7	3.4
Import quotas on engineering and motor vehicles	12.4%	160	250	10.9	11.1	1.1	1.8	−0.8	1.2	3.4	3.7	2.7
Employment subsidies	76,000 jobs	294	109	10.8	11.0	1.0	1.6	−0.7	1.2	3.5	4.1	4.4
Current government expenditure	1.9%	242	112	10.9	11.1	1.1	1.7	−0.8	1.2	3.4	4.1	4.4
National insurance surcharge	−2.8%	231	171	9.8	10.7	1.5	1.9	1.4	1.6	4.0	4.6	5.0
Investment projects	extra £1.37 billion	226	197	10.9	11.1	1.4	1.9	−0.7	1.2	3.8	4.8	5.2
Income tax: standard rate	−3.8%	264	113	10.7	11.1	1.7	1.9	1.3	2.2	4.7	5.6	7.4
Present policy				10.9	11.1	1.0	1.6	−0.8	1.0	3.4	4.0	4.2

Source: Barker (1982).

GDP. Each policy was tried separately, but their effects are not additive. It is clear that for short-run employment creation tariffs are the best policy by far. Incomes policies and import quotas generate about 160,000 jobs over three years, whereas tariffs generate 355,000 jobs. In terms of long-run job creation, tariffs do worst and incomes policies do best. Import quotas also show a high job-creation rate in the long run.

Tariffs achieve the best GDP growth rate, though the effect declines over the next two years, whereas with all other policies the 1984 growth rate exceeds the 1982 one. Tariffs also require a large drop in consumption growth and again the long-run effects are better with all other policies. In terms of inflation, incomes policies do best and tariffs worst.

The investment project policy steps up government expenditure each year from 1982 to 1984 to inject an extra £1,370 million into the economy by 1984. This creates 226,000 jobs over three years or about £6,000 per job. This is considerably less than the cost implicit in David Blake's calculations, which is about £20,000 per job. Barker directed the extra investment to public construction projects, which have higher employment multipliers than manufacturing industries. It is a typical result of many of these calculations that the generation of extra jobs in manufacturing is much more costly than in non-manufacturing industries, especially services.

If one is to plan a full-employment strategy, then, it would seem that on present information employment effects are likely to be higher if the final demand is such that the non-manufacturing sector will have a greater share. Similarly, public goods have a lower import content than private goods. Since construction, public utilities, transport and communications are all non-manufacturing, initially demand will have to be directed at these sectors. Indeed, expenditure directed mainly at capital investments in the public sector – schools, hospitals, sewers, roads – will seem to be a good way in which to achieve low import content and high employment-generating growth.

This means, however, that initially it will not be possible to promise increases in the consumption of private goods and that industrial revival will have to come from directions other than a reflationary package. These are both quite drastic implications of a capital construction programme, and we need to look at them.

The emphasis on import control in AES is justified by the need to afford British industry breathing space while it reverses its decline of the last fifteen years. This is to be supplemented by an industrial strategy which relies on planning agreements to force the private sector to direct investments into channels laid down by the Government. As David Blake's calculations show, import control will increase profits. One question remains, however: should they be allowed to be ploughed back in the old declining industries? To some extent, the strategy of affording protection to existing industry from competing imports conflicts with the need to restructure the economy. The industries which have lost their competitive edge have done so, to some extent, because of their inability to provide products at low cost. By channelling resources into them, other activities would have to be starved.

It is best at this stage to confront the issue of profitability openly. Should a Labour Government be following a policy designed to restore profitability, or should it be launching a socialist policy designed to abolish the capitalist system? Should a Labour Government be managing capitalism or smashing capitalism and building socialism? It must be strongly contended that such a dilemma is a false one. There is no immediate prospect that an incoming Labour Government will have the electoral strength, the mass support or the objective conditions that would be conducive to launching a fully socialist economy. Indeed, any incoming Government will be taking over when the economy is in a dire condition (but not propitious for a socialist revolution) and, as any left-wing Government would, it will face immense international pressures. It will have to manage capitalism in order to put through even a reformist or transitional programme. (The analogy with the Mitterrand Government's actions in its first year, especially as regards the speculative pressure on the franc, is very instructive.) The real test will be the extent to which such immediate pressures do not detract from the transitional/reformist tasks which such a Government should be engaged in.

The test of any AES is, then, not the narrow question of

whether profit share is restored but how it looks upon the role of profit in a long-run perspective and how different elements of the policy add up to a left-wing policy. Since the British economy will be a mixed one, even after a Labour victory, profits will continue to constitute a crucial determinant of investment and output growth. Consequently, low profitability will mean low growth of output and employment. The crucial issue is not whether profits will be raised but the extent to which the Government can ensure that profits are channelled into investment and not into consumption, exports or speculation. It will also matter whether the Government can channel them into areas which, in its long-term view, have priority. The only justification for profits in a modern economy is as a source of investment funds. But since market forces can be myopic in channelling investment, the Government will have to take over the task of controlling the direction of investment. Profitability (in terms of size and rate of profits) will continue to signal, in a majority of cases, the desirability of continuing to pursue a certain activity. If the economy pursues a loss-making activity continuously, it will only be taxing other sectors of the economy. Such a decision may still be the correct one according to some criteria (social need, long-run viability), but it should be made explicit that losses are a tax on the economy, and such losses are frequently visited on the least well-off sections of society.

The merit of an AES, then, is to be judged by the extent to which it alters the shape of the economy by using the profitability generated by sacrifice on the part of the mass of workers. It should also make explicit how much sacrifice will be made by other groups (i.e. what concomitant tax policies are followed). Thus if profits are to be channelled into investment, businessmen's consumption privileges afforded by the tax system must be taken away and corporation tax must be at a level which will enable the Government to channel these resources either into priority investment (e.g. a hospital building programme) or into increasing the social wage.

The need for import control should be therefore argued as a part of an overall macro-economic plan – a medium-term strategy. Such a strategy would need to generate surpluses for investment into a whole range of new industries which could afford growing employment, competitive advantage and, eventually, a rising real wage. Thus import control has to be seen as *a strategy for regulating the growth of private consumption*. The profits generated in the protected industries should be diverted, via taxation or other arrangements, into new growth industries such as micro-electronics, biotechnology or other R & D-intensive industries. The UK has a work force with high literacy and an educational establishment which has a good record in basic research. It would be part and parcel of any policy for restructuring the economy to reshape the educational system to take more advantage of the opportunities in these R & D-intensive industries. Hence what is needed is a phased withdrawal from the products with which the UK has lost her competitive edge and the establishment of new industries. This will require massive investment in the retraining of workers as well as in the training of new entrants into the work force (school-leavers, for example) into new skills. To freeze the present employment pattern will not lead to the creation of new jobs or to any rise in real wages.

I acknowledge that any proposal that there be phased withdrawal from existing, uncompetitive industries is bound to raise much resistance on the part of the unions as well as the management of these industries. Extensive experience of high unemployment, except for brief boom periods between 1870 and 1940, has ingrained certain defensive practices concerning job preservation in union bargaining. Even the long period of high employment in the postwar period did not alter these practices, perhaps because this period, though quite long by previous standards, was still short in relation to any cohort's working life. Thus if we consider man's working life as stretching from 15 to 65 years of age, the longest period of full employment in recent decades has been thirty years (1940 to 1970) or, more usually, about twenty years (1946 to 1966). Thus it is probable that every working man (to say nothing of working women, whose experience is much worse) born in any year since 1900 has experienced one or more spells of unemployment in his life. It is not surprising, therefore, that unions who represent workers' interests are conscious of job losses and resistant to the introduction of new technology that may threaten jobs.

But these defensive practices are an endogenous response to the long-run stagnation of a *rentier* economy. Workers have long been fobbed off with a high level of real income but have suffered from a low growth rate of income (relative, say, to the USA), and in terms of lifetime income – i.e. weighted by spells of low-income unemployment and high-income employment – they have lost out by comparison with workers in other countries. British wage-bargaining practice is to settle for a regular overtime component in the pay packet, though with a low regular real wage and job protection. The final effect on lifetime income is still adverse; the working week continues to be long; and the investible surplus generated by such activities remains small. Management practices are equally influenced by the *rentier* economy psychology – snobbish aloofness from the shop floor, lack of technical or professional knowledge of industrial practices, the appointment of managers by reference to old school tie considerations, the failure of top management to work as hard as their counterparts elsewhere and so on.

To understand these practices is not to assign blame, nor to seek to perpetuate them. There is much that is undesirable about them, and it is no defence to say that they are justified by the nature of capitalist social relations. We have frequently noticed in the past that socialists have condoned workers' resistance to new technology when capitalist relations have prevailed, only to turn around after the 'revolution' and insist on these very practices as progressive (Lenin on Taylorism is a good example of this). If we are to inaugurate the long period of transition to socialism, we have to affirm that many of these pre-industrial labour practices are obstacles to the restructuring of the economy. We have to welcome new technology and to speed up its invention and introduction. The fear of new technology is related to the threat of job loss. But we can generate jobs which afford high real income with a shorter working week only if we adopt new technology and restructure the economy. The need to generate investible surpluses and to invest them in new technology would be paramount even if the entire economy were collectively owned; otherwise the stagnations of real incomes and the precarious nature of employment will never be cured.

It is precisely for these reasons that arguments for thinking again about work and income are the strongest. It is quite likely that micro-electronics will make small production units viable and will allow both for work to be decentralised and for firms to be smaller. Working from a home base or from a small industrial unit will have obvious advantages in terms of work satisfaction. In addition, the possibility of the work stoppages and industrial conflicts to which large multiplant units are prone will be reduced (Prais, 1977). Small units of this type will also afford the possibility of new patterns of ownership – they might be co-operatives or enterprises that are owned by the Government, by a private individual, by the workers or jointly by workers and management.

Arguments for reducing the length of working week and for early retirement have been made mainly along the negative lines of work-sharing. But if such work-sharing is to mean not the reorganisation of the work process but only a lower real income, then there is bound to be resistance. One radical proposal in this area, from the women's movement, has been to rethink the nature of income from work. It has been argued by Anna Coote, for instance (Coote, 1981), that AES has been pursuing a male-oriented strategy of full employment with high real wages without having explored more radical arrangements of the work process.

The need to organise the working week or even the working year around the social needs of child-rearing, work satisfaction and some autonomy over the work process means that once again the arguments for new small-scale industrial units with high potential productivity and decentralised locations are very strong. Thus flexitime, the abolition or blurring of the distinction between full-time and part-time work (say, by reducing the working week to thirty hours), the provision of sabbatical leave for everyone in the active labour force, arrangements for day-release or short-term leave for taking up educational opportunities – all these must be important ingredients of any AES. They are not idealistic, but neither can they be implemented except through a planned medium-run strategy over perhaps ten or fifteen years. They are of great importance because they raise fundamental questions about the purpose of jobs and wages and economic activity in general.

A concomitant of these arrangements would be some down-grading of the role of private consumption and a boost for the role of publicly provided consumption goods. Such a rearrangement in favour of public consumption makes sense on several grounds. First, the need to restrict the growth of private consumption is imperative if funds are to be available for investment and if growth is not to lead to heavy imports. The strategy of increasing public investments in non-manufacturing industries and concentrating on new growth products dovetails with this. Second, the need to channel profits from existing protected industries to new growth industries will require a planned incomes policy which regulates wages, salaries, perks and prices. This will mean not only regulating the overall rate of growth of wages but also implementing a policy whereby wages in the protected industries do not grow more rapidly than in other sectors. A planned incomes policy should also tax managerial consumption privileges and surplus profits, and it should fashion a plan for wage income which will regulate its growth over the period of ten or fifteen years that will be needed to work through a restructuring of the economy. Thus the fiscal policy needed to redirect resources from consumption to investment and from old to new industries will require a downgrading of private consumption and the regulation of the growth of personal incomes.

The growth of public consumption, on the other hand, is necessary both to achieve traditional egalitarian aims and to facilitate the emergence of new work practices which treat women and men on an equal footing. Publicly provided meals, crèches, medical facilities available at places of work, access to educational opportunities at work or away from it, the financing of sabbaticals and short holidays as well as the adequate provision for the many income assistance schemes – all these will be necessary. Any medium-term plan will also need to stipulate a growth in leisure facilities – libraries, theatres, art galleries, museums, etc.

Thus a plan for restructuring the economy would require the growth of both public and private investment and public consumption over a period of five to ten years, if not longer. This would entail a planned incomes policy, an industrial restructuring policy, and an import-control policy (though with the proviso described above concerning the ploughback of profits). It would also require a fiscal package for raising resources through taxation and borrowing. It is best, therefore, to provide some detailed calculations for such a five-year plan.

A five-year plan for full employment

If we accept the multiplier pessimism illustrated by some of the projections discussed above, a plan which could create 500,000 jobs per year for five years would require a public investment programme of £10 billion per annum, growing cumulatively to £50 billion by the end of the fifth year. Public investment will be 6.5 per cent of GDP by 1989. Along with private investment, this would take up 20 per cent of GDP. Such a high rate of investment would be necessary if each extra job cost anything up to £20,000. The economy would have to grow at a rate of 6.5 per cent per annum over this period to allow room for productivity growth as well as extra employment. This is an extraordinarily high growth rate and would put a strain on wages and prices if these were not made part of a plan. But the regulation of take-home income is also necessary because the needs of investment – public and private – and of public consumption mean that *there would be virtually no room for the growth of real take-home pay in the five years required to achieve full employment.*

This contention is based on the very crude illustrative macro-economic calculation which is given in Table 3. It is based on the figure of £20,000 per job as a necessary investment. The numbers involved assume a steady rate of inflation, 10 per cent per annum. The share of capital formation in government expenditure rises from its 1979 level of 6.5 per cent to its 1966 level of 13 per cent by 1989. Allowing for 20 per cent of GDP as investment's share, 25 per cent for exports and imports and government consumption at 25 per cent, there is only 55 per cent left for private consumption. If we translate this into the share of disposable income in GDP, it comes to 62 per cent by 1989. It is currently in the region of 80 per cent. So all the income growth has to be taken out of personal incomes

Table 3   *Hypothetical projections for a maximal growth plan*

	Actual GDP	Potential GDP	Actual GDP (current prices)	Price level (1975 = 100; 1980 actual, other years projected)	Government expenditure (current prices)	Government consumption and investment (current prices)	Government consumption plus investment (1975 prices)
	1975 prices						
1980	101		193	200	105	64	
1981	98		215	220	118	69	
1982	96		230	242	128	76	
1983	98		260	266			
1984	101(102)	104.7 120	280	293	140	95	33
1985		108.6		322		110	
1986		112.6		354		128	
1987		116.8		389		150	
1988		121.1 136.7	570 640	470	315	205	44
1989							

Note: All absolute figures are in £ billions.

and put into investment and public consumption. There is just no room for a real wage explosion if full employment is to be achieved and the economy is to be restructured. The growth of public consumption (social wage), however, will be about 3.5 per cent per annum over the five years under this plan. Private income can grow by no more than 10 or 11 per cent – barely up to the assumed rate of inflation.

This is obviously a drastic proposal, but there is no reason to believe that it exaggerates the difficult situation that Labour will face when it comes to power. As the French resort to price freeze and devaluation in June 1982 showed, an employment-creation plan can rapidly run into trouble if such difficulties are not foreseen. These difficulties have to be made explicit and subjected to the widest public discussion if they are to be visited on the people. The promise of full employment, a restructured economy, the room that it will afford us for a drastic rethinking of income, work and leisure are the benefits. They will have to be delivered, of course, and this means no short-run blowing off course. The political task of the Labour Party is to discuss these questions openly and honestly with its supporters and to arrive at broad, democratic agreement that the sacrifices are worth the benefits. It can then begin to define the next step in the reshaping of the economy which will mark its progress towards a socialist society.

Notes

1 Comments by Jane Lewis, Julian Le Grand and Henry Neuberger as well as members of the 'Labour Seminar' are gratefully acknowledged. Christine Wills was patience itself in the production of each of the four drafts through which the paper went. To her my thanks.
2 Upon reading Beveridge and Keynes again, one realises how much tougher they were on the kinds of reform that private capitalism had to undergo to become welfare capitalism. Thus Keynes' views are even today far ahead of the policies pursued in his name by postwar Governments: 'The state will have to exercise a guiding influence in the propensity to consume partly through its scheme of taxation, partly by fixing the rate of interest, and partly, perhaps, in other ways. Furthermore it seems unlikely that the influence of banking policy on the rate of interest will be sufficient by itself to determine an optimum rate of investment. I conceive, therefore, that a *somewhat comprehensive socialisation of investment* will prove the only means of securing an approximation to full employment. . . . If the state is able to determine the aggregate amount of resources devoted to augmenting the instruments and

the basic rate of reward to those who own them, it will have accomplished all that is necessary' ('Concluding Notes on the Social Philosophy Towards Which the General Theory Might Lead', *The General Theory*, ch. 24, p. 378; emphasis added). Beveridge had envisaged that, with full employment, the central direction of the labour force along the lines of wartime manpower budgeting would be required. He also clearly saw the case for state regulation of the wage bargain. See 'The war time triangle, 1941–5', ch. 10 in Middlemass (1979).

3 'There existed, so to speak, an implied contract between Government and people; the people refused none of the sacrifices that the Government demanded from them for the winning of the War; in return, they expected that the Government should show imagination and seriousness in preparing for the restoration and improvement of the nation's well-being when the War had been won. The plans for reconstruction were, therefore, a real part of the war effort' (Hancock and Gowing, 1953, p. 541).

4 For the US experience of the second Industrial Revolution, see Chandler (1977, 1978). For British experience in this period, see Payne (1978). The transformation in British attitudes towards industry has been charted in Weiner (1981) and also Hutchison (1951).

5 Middlemass (1979).

6 Publications on AES are appearing at a steadily accelerating rate. The main references are: CSE London Working Group, *The Alternative Economic Strategy*, and articles by Adam Sharples, Terry Ward, Sam Aaranovitch and Pat Devine in Currie and Smith (1981). Among these the Sharples paper is a very good overall survey and critique of AES, and it also contains a full bibliography. See also Glyn and Harrison (1981) and Aaranovitch (1981). There have been articles in *New Socialist* by Sapper (1981) and Coote (1981).

References

Aaranovitch, S. (1981) *The Road to Thatcherism* (London: Lawrence & Wishart)

Barker, T. (1982) 'Long term recovery: a return to full employment?', *Lloyds Bank Review*, Jan., pp. 19–35

Blake, D. (1981) 'Is there an alternative to the Government's economic strategy?', *The Times*, 1–3 June

Blake, D., and Ormerod, P. (1980) *The Economics of Prosperity: Social Priorities in the Eighties* (London: Grant McIntyre)

Chandler, A. (1977) *The Visible Hand: the Managerial Revolution in American Business* (Cambridge, Mass.: MIT Press)

Chandler, A. (1978) 'The United States: evolution of enterprise', in Mathias and Postan (1978), Part 2, pp. 70–133

CSE London Working (1979) *The Alternative Economic Strategy* (London: Conference of Socialist Economists)

Coote, A. (1981) 'The AES: a new starting point', *New Socialist*, Nov./Dec., pp. 4–7

Cripps, *et al.* (1981) *Manifesto: A Radical Strategy for Britain's Future* (London: Pan)

Currie, D., and Smith, R. (1981) *Socialist Economic Review* (London: Merlin Press)

64 *Socialism in a Cold Climate*

Glyn, A., and Harrison, J. (1981) *The British Economic Disaster* (London: Pluto Press)

Hancock, K., and Gowing, M. (1953) *The British War Economy* (London: HMSO)

Hutchinson, K. (1951) *The Decline and Fall of British Capitalism* (London: Cape)

Keynes, J. M. (1936) *The General Theory of Employment, Interest and Money* (London: Macmillan)

Mathias, P., and Postan, M. (eds.) (1978) *The Cambridge Economic History of Europe*, vol. 7 (Cambridge: CUP)

Middlemass, K. (1979) *Politics in Industrial Society: The Experience of the British System since 1911* (London: Deutsch)

Payne, P. (1978) 'Industrial entrepreneurs and management in Great Britain', in Mathias and Postan (1978), Part 1, pp. 180–230

Prais, S. (1977) *The Strike Proneness of Large Plants in Britain*, Discussion Paper No. 5 (London: National Institute of Economic and Social Research)

Sapper, A. (1981) 'The Alternative Economic Strategy', *New Socialist*, Sept./Oct., pp. 19–24

Singh, A. (1980) 'UK industry and the less developed countries: a long-term structural analysis of trade and its impact (Department of Applied Economics, University of Cambridge)

Weiner, M. (1981) *The Decline of the Industrial Spirit in Britain* (Cambridge: Cambridge University Press)

[5]

3

THE ECONOMICS OF FAMINE

Meghnad Desai

INTRODUCTION

Famines were thought to have disappeared from the scene so much that there was no discussion of them in economics in the twentieth century until recently. The Malthusian threat lost its credibility in the developed Western world and famines were thought unlikely. They were not unknown; in the aftermath of World War I, the revolution and civil war in Russia saw a severe famine leading to a detailed but little-cited study of the influence of hunger on human affairs by the sociologist Pitrim Sorokin (Sorokin 1975). Famines, in view of the West, happened elsewhere. In the period during and after World War II, mass hunger was seen in many occupied countries especially the Netherlands. Again this could be dismissed as an extraordinary event. It was the emergence of the newly independent countries in Asia and Africa that brought issues of development and poverty on the economics agenda.

Even in this area the first two decades of discussion and theorizing were marked by a Panglossian optimism; calculations were made for target growth of per capita income, the required investment and a search was made for resources domestic and foreign. Given enough aid, it was thought the problems of underdevelopment could be overcome. At the onset of the 1970s this optimism broke down. Harvests had already failed in India in two successive years 1965–6 and 1966–7, though no famine deaths were admitted to. (A famine also occurred in China in 1960–1 but this did not become widely known till much later.) The newly-independent Bangladesh was seen quite widely as needing special help – 'basket case' in US State Department jargon but also inviting a concert by former Beatle George Harrison prefiguring the Live Aid of recent years. The year 1972 also saw low harvest in the US and the spectre of raw material shortage caused by too much growth was mooted.

The bad harvests of 1972 were followed by the oil shock of 1973. Suddenly resource shortages were not only a problem for the second and the third world but came home as it were to the first world. The Keynesian optimism was lost and a general search ensued for ways of tackling the age-old problems of scarcity. Unsurprisingly many of the nineteenth-century arguments were revived and refurbished to tackle the recurring problem. Malthusianism became fashionable especially as directed towards the less-developed countries. Hunger was said to be caused by a lack of food and too many mouths to feed. The global perspective that had been quite rightly advanced, by Barbara Ward, for example, was now distorted into the paradigm of a life raft from which some had to be ejected to save the rest. Little imagination is needed to gauge how the third world ranked in those stakes. In macro-economic affairs the revival of *laissez-faire* policy was in tune with these trends.

Against this background, it was Amartya Sen's study of the Great Bengal Famine that offered an alternative but general theory of famines (Sen 1977). This was followed by Sen with further 'applications' of the theory to the famines of the 1970s – Bangladesh, the Sahel, and Ethiopia. This work has been followed up by a number of studies of various regions and historical episodes (for a bibliography, Sen and Dreze 1987). The theory has also been criticized as being either nothing that was not well known or as no more than a minor curiosum in neo-classical economics (Mitra 1982; Srinivasan 1983). Others have sought to extend and generalize Sen's argument (Desai 1984, 1986a; Rangasami 1985).

In this chapter I shall argue that the economic theory offered by Sen has a great potential for extension and development. While the theory could be generalized beyond the case of famines, I concentrate here on the ways in which it needs to be supplemented for a study of famines. A major problem is that the theory lacks a dynamic framework. It needs to be articulated in a system of blocks which bring out the dynamic and simultaneous interdependence of the physical and the economic aspects of famines. Sen's theory will be outlined first and then I look at the criticisms. The following section extends the theory in various ways to meet the critics' objections. In the last section a systems representation will be given in which the dynamic extensions will be made. All along I shall have occasions to mention other studies and examples of the basic approach.

THE THEORY OF EXCHANGE ENTITLEMENTS

The theory of exchange entitlements was advanced by Amartya Sen specifically in an attempt to explain the paradox of one of the most tragic famines of this century – the Great Bengal Famine of 1943. After a careful calculation of the available food supplies, he concluded that the total amount of food available had not declined since the previous years, but despite this there were widespread deaths. Looking further into this, he found that the pattern of mortality was systematically different in rural areas as between people connected in some way with the rice-farming activity and those groups who were in the non-rice and non-agricultural activities. With a further look at how people moved from their usual occupations to new ones as a way of averting the worst consequences of famine, it became clear that the drift was towards agricultural labour or any other activity that would bring them closer to the rice-growing activity. In one sense what happened was that the price of rice had risen relative to that of other goods and services. While this is obvious, it was also true that those not growing rice had less to sell and also that they could purchase less rice with each unit of goods they could sell, i.e. they suffered a loss of quantity as well as adverse terms of trade. But even within the rice-growing sector, those who could appropriate rice directly – as sharecroppers or as labourers paid in terms of rice – suffered less than those who had to 'translate' what they had – money or goods and services – into rice by exchange.

Sen built up his theory further by examining some more recent famines – Bangladesh in 1974, the Sahel famines of the early 1970s, and the Ethiopian famines of 1973 and 1974. In economics the usual practice is to build up a theory *a priori* on axiomatic or other sparse foundations and then subject it to test. Sen's theory was built up with an empirical (not empiricist) approach (see Thompson (1978) for the distinction). The extension of his investigation to African famines enabled Sen to examine a wider class of food and non-food activities. Thus if the main non-food activity in Bengal was fishing, in Africa the pastoral activity was the alternative. In stating his thesis in the book four years after his article, the argument is couched in terms of an attack on the 'Food Availability Decline' (FAD) hypothesis. FAD argues that it is decline in the overall per capita availability of food as a result of the twin pincers of population growth and agricultural stagnation that famines occur. Shifting attention away from this aggregative approach, Sen argues that FAD is neither necessary nor sufficient for famines to occur. In one sense Sen's theory can be seen as a series of arguments demolishing one after another of the monocausal arguments about famines. Thus, for example, droughts and such other extreme natural events are also neither necessary nor sufficient. Famines have occurred with and without FAD, with and without the food grain price rising, and with and without natural disasters occurring.

To understand famines, it is important to place the various economic groups in relation to the food-growing economy. Given their abilities and their endowments as well as the existing set of property rights, etc. one can define the exchange entitlements of each person in terms of the food he can obtain in the 'normal' course of events. If this entitlement is less than the amount required to subsist then the person will starve. One could think of poverty as endemic low entitlements. This happens because the poor have low-ownership entitlements; whatever the configuration of relative prices, they can obtain inadequate amounts of food (or in a more general context a basket of goods) with what they have to offer. But for those who may have normally adequate entitlements in terms of what they own, famines are situations in which their exchange entitlements to food can suddenly shrink below starvation levels. It is necessary, therefore, to examine the nature of entitlements both as they relate to individuals and as compared between different groups of individuals. (In what follows I rely on Desai (1984).)

Each person, no matter how poor, has some endowments. They may consist of personal attributes – age, sex, race, height, weight, and more elusive personal qualities such as charm, beauty, etc. In terms of economic measures every person has at least his capacity for work – his labour power – unless too young or too old or infirm or severely handicapped. Others may have additional endowments – land, money, durable goods, financial assets, etc. There are certain legal rules which define what can and what cannot be owned. Thus a slave does not have any endowments which he can call his own except the personal attributes which may have made him more marketable. Serfs were not free to dispose of their labour power as they chose. Modern societies do not permit slaves as part of one's endowment.

Given the endowments, there are various ways of converting them into goods and services which constitute consumption baskets. Some endowments can be directly traded into goods, e.g. money is such a universal solvent. Others have to be put into a production process – seeds or ploughs – so they can yield output – things – which can be converted into other goods. Labour power has a dual status in this scheme. It can be directly sold for wages which can be converted into consumption goods. It can also be engaged into a production process along with other inputs which will yield output which again can be sold. All these exchanges whether of labour directly or of labour and inputs via output presume a market and they are all mediated via money in almost all modern economies no matter how 'less developed'. There also has to be sufficient demand for these 'vendible commodities' (to use Adam Smith's expression) for one to be able to obtain other goods for it.

Now, given one's endowments there are various ways of converting them into goods. If I have land, I could sell it outright and live off the sum of money with or without additional interest earned by investing the capital sum. I could alternatively rent the land out and live off the rent. Or I could give it to a sharecropper for half the output though I may also have to provide some of the inputs. I may, lastly, cultivate the land myself with or without hired labour.

Thus, from the ownership of one asset – land, here are various possibilities each of which will convert into a basket of consumption goods. Selling the land or renting it at a money rent will yield me sums of money which I could trade for consumption goods at the prevailing retail prices. If, however, I have let it for a rent in terms of a portion of the output, the situation is similar to sharecropping and to own cultivation. I have to *sell* the output and then buy consumption goods with the money revenue earned from the sale. Here again it is crucial for the probability of my experiencing starvation whether I grow edible or non-edible crops. For the former at least some portion of the output can be directly consumed and the price does not enter into the question. For non-edible crops there has to be a sale before there can be a purchase.

Now all the various combinations of consumption bundles I can obtain for my land traversing these routes is what Amartya Sen calls my 'exchange entitlements'. If I owned only my labour power, then I have the choice of working for a wage as an agricultural (landless) labourer, or as a non-agricultural labourer, or perhaps a sharecropper. The labourer and the sharecropper are similar because they own nothing but their labour power. They may turn out to have different exchange entitlements, however.

In 'normal' times, the wage of the worker will be enough to provide subsistence, if not more. Thus the subsistence bundle is within his exchange entitlement. The same, let us assume, is true for the sharecropper, the tenant, and the landlord. Now, if for some reason – drought, war, black-market hoarding – the price of grain were to go up, some of the participants will find their entitlement shrinking. This may be so drastic that they may not even get a subsistence bundle. They may starve.

But even within this context of shortage, caused either by demand shock (war, hoarding) or supply shocks (drought, floods, locusts), we must examine the mode of income receipt to appreciate the uneven incidence of famine on different people. Take as an extreme case two landless labourers – one paid money wages, and one paid in kind. Let us assume that the wage is fixed before the harvest *ex ante* at Rs1000 for the season, or 100 kg of grain. If the rains fail, or due to some other reason harvests are very low, the output will be below expectations. If this is a widespread phenomenon, grain prices may rise. If 50 kg is a subsistence bundle, a price rise of grain of more than 100 per cent would push the worker paid in money wages below the subsistence line. Thus his exchange entitlements shrink due to *relative price changes*. The worker paid in grain will then be that much safer (assuming the employer does not arbitrarily renege on the contract to pay him 100 kg).

Take now a sharecropper and a worker paid in money wages. Let us say the sharecropper may normally expect 150 kg of grain – one half of normal output of 300 kg. Again if output were to be anywhere lower than 100 kg due to, say, drought, then the sharecropper would be pushed below subsistence. So he will suffer not so much from relative price change as from a pure quantity change.

Take lastly a cattleman. The nomadic herdsmen of the Sahel raise livestock and take it from one place to another for grazing. They sell cattle or dairy products to buy grain. A drought would mean decline in cattle output (in terms of weight) and/or in dairy output. If, in addition, grain prices have also risen, then a cattleman would suffer relative price loss (grain is more expensive in terms of dairy products or meat) and from output loss (leaner cattle/less milk). His entitlement of grain would thus shrink due to both these reasons and he will be doubly vulnerable, as it were, to starvation.

Thus, whatever the macro-economic dimensions of food shortage, the micro-economic incidence of starvation would depend on how individual households are placed in terms of their endowments, and through these endowments, in their exchange entitlements. To some extent these endowments relate to ownership of the means of production as in the case of sharecropper/labourer but they also depend on *access* to the means of production. But here again – ownership or access to the means of production are not sufficient to define the likelihood of entitlement loss though they may serve to determine the class to which an individual belongs. If you have two modes of production coexisting, say a nomadic one with livestock as the principal means of production and an agricultural one, the class position of a rich cattle owner does not render him immune from entitlement loss if the cattle/grain price ratio changes. Thus entitlement leads to a more complex classification than a Marxian-class analysis.

CRITIQUES

The entitlement approach to famines has not gone without criticism. A major criticism has been that in some sense what the approach says is obvious and well known. Thus in an early review of the book, Ashok Mitra was dismissive of Sen's contribution saying that after all this is what our grandmothers always knew about famines (Mitra 1982). Srinivasan in another review has taken the view that the only thing Sen says is that the real wage, in terms of grain, falls when the price of grain goes up. The purchasing power having shrunk, people buy less than required for survival. Hence they starve. 'The "entitlement approach" is a fancy name for elementary ideas fairly well understood by economists, though not necessarily by policy makers' (Srinivasan 1983, p. 200). Srinivasan also points out that the shifts in purchasing power have to be drastic and sudden for the analysis to have any bite; 'A less drastic and gradual shift (in real purchasing power) would have given enough time for authorities to take appropriate action and individuals to adjust on their own' (Srinivasan 1983, p. 201). Once we take such dynamic considerations into account 'the role of price expectations and speculative changes in food stock have to be analysed for the dynamics of price–wage movements to be understood' (Srinivasan 1983, p. 201).

A criticism of a different sort has been made by Amrita Rangasami (1985). Her point is that famine and starvation are not results of sudden and drastic collapses in purchasing power or food supply. There is a process which starts much before which has already rendered some groups more vulnerable than others. Rangasami's points about the dynamic process that ends in starvation can be summarized as follows (all quotes from Rangasami 1985, p. 1748):

(a) ... that starvation is a process and that it is long drawn, hardly sudden;
(b) ... that the biological process has a socio-economic dimension: that such a process has clearly marked phases. The phases correspond with biological changes and deterioration in the health of the affected community and socio-economically by transfer of assets from victim to beneficiary. The socio-economic process is completed with the loss of all the victim's assets including his ability to labour;
(c) ... that the state does not appear to intervene until the third and irreversible phase;
(d) ... that the perceptions of famine we have today only relate to the terminal phase and not the entire process. Consequently, they have a limited validity. I will, therefore, conclude that the definitions in use insofar as they hinge on the elevation of mortality may be set aside. Consequently, Sen's work which is based on such a definition is inadequate.

Rangasami's focus is wider than the narrowly economic theoretic criticisms of Srinivasan. She is concerned both with the biological process whereby there is a dynamic interplay between inadequate food intake and undernourishment which may eventually lead to starvation. Citing various nutritional and clinical studies on starvation, she says, 'Together these studies demonstrate that the individual passes from a well nourished stage through successive stages of starvation. Far more significant that the body can adapt itself at a low equilibrium – a plateauing effect that can endure for weeks to several months ... ' (Rangasami 1985).

Rangasami's consequent concern is that famines are defined too partially. Even in normal times some poor individuals may die of starvation: 'Famine is a condition that affects large numbers of people within a recognisable, spatial unit such as a village, a country or an entire geographical region.' Citing studies of the famine in the Netherlands during Nazi occupation, she lists the three stages of famine as dearth, famishment, and morbidity. Within this dynamic process there is a steady loss of the assets of the victim and a deterioration in the terms at which he trades with the beneficiary. The movement from dearth to morbidity is via famishment. Famishment indicates movement from a state of dearth where there is still some hope of returning to the original stage before morbidity when such hope is abandoned. It is at this stage that 'strategies to prevent death ... become imperative. These can include acceptance of slavery, conversion to other religions, permanent migration as indentured labour. What is significant is that a large number of families resort to one identical stratagem' (Rangasami 1985, p. 1750).

Rangasami also points out that an examination of Indian Famine Codes and actual practice relief confirms that Sen's entitlement approach was understood by the administrators. That does not mean that they knew of its formal structure but the logic of looking at the variety of factors determining the exchange entitlements of individuals. Thus they looked not only at food shortages, but also unemployment and real wages. They devised work programmes to generate purchasing power for those most likely to suffer from high food prices, 'The relationship between drought and famine was not so much a reduction in total food output as a decline in the level of employment' (Rangasami 1985, p. 1798).

I have described Rangasami's critique at length because it introduces crucial non-economic factors while broadening the economic factors to include dynamic considerations. In spirit, it is not hostile to the entitlement approach but wishes it to move beyond the static, one-period consideration. In this sense one can say that while Sen's theoretical framework is static as well as partial equilibrium, in his concrete studies of the four famines many of the other considerations do play a role. It is important, however, for our purposes, to supplement and extend Sen's framework to take account of some of the criticisms.

EXTENSIONS OF THE ENTITLEMENT APPROACH

THE ENTITLEMENT APPROACH: SOME SIMPLE ANALYTICS

There are two strategies which I shall pursue in extending the entitlement approach. In a narrow economic theoretic framework I shall explore ways of clarifying and extending the model. Taking Sen's theoretical framework in his book and his QJE article (Sen 1981*b*), I shall extend it to a general equilibrium argument demonstrating the asymmetry between food markets and other markets. Somewhere in the course of a famine, food becomes a pivotal commodity, displacing all other commodities to a peripheral status. How is one to account for this in a formal model? Having done that in the context of a two person–two good economy, I shall next ask how we can incorporate the dynamic considerations emphasized by Rangasami.

   To begin with let us look at the diagram used by Sen in his book and in his article in the *Quarterly Journal Economics*. This is given here as Fig. 3.1. An individual requires OA amount of food to avoid starvation. The area DAE is thus outside the starvation set. He has an initial endowment of *x*** representing a combination of food and non-food commodities. Initially the rate at which he can exchange his endowments for food is given by the price slope *p* and the line AB (the slope is tan of angle BAO). It is clear that if he is at *x***, he can, by converting all his non-food endowments into food, get beyond OA and be outside the starvation set. Now if the endowment set were to drop (quantity shock) from *x*** to *x***, the individual would get food less than OA. But even without this quantity shock, if the price of food were to rise from *p* to *p** (tan of angle CAO), then even with *x***, the individual will get less than OA. Famines can thus happen either with or without a food rise or with or without a quantity shock. Of course in actual famines, individuals often suffer from both quantity and price shocks.

   It will be helpful to begin by considering a modification of Fig. 3.1. A

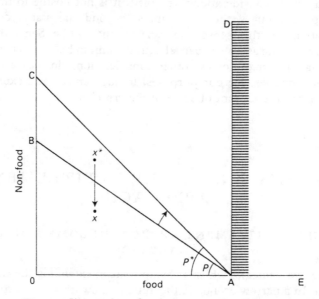

Fig. 3.1. Illustration of endowment and entitlement.

person may either offer labour services as non-food endowment or another
commodity. In either case the initial endowment will be a point on the non-
food axis rather than in the interior, i.e. a combination of food and non-
food. For someone who supplies labour services, a point such as L_1
represents the number of hours he can work, the price slope then
representing the real wage in terms of food. Let this food commodity be
rice. Fig. 3.2a is an adaptation of Fig. 3.1. For a labourer supplying labour
power above OB at price (i.e. real wage) p, there is no fear of starvation. If

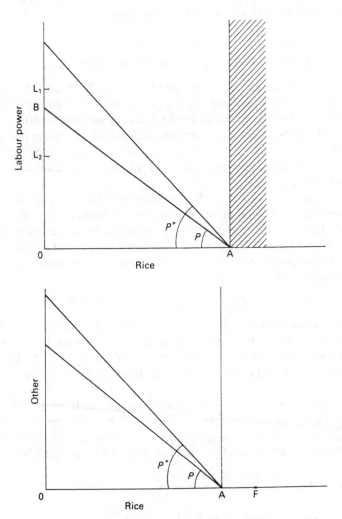

Fig. 3.2(a). Labourer's entitlements. **(b).** Farmer's entitlements. Note: farmer's
endowment is independent of price variation.

prices move to $p\star$ (real wage falls) or if he is debilitated and cannot work more than OB hours, then he will begin to face the process which will eventually culminate in starvation.

By contrast, a rice farmer will have his endowment as the output of rice. As long as this is beyond OA he will not starve (Fig. 3.2b). Typically, he may wish to be much beyond this if he is hiring a labourer. But notice that if the rice farmer's output is at some point beond OA, he may not wish to purchase any non-food commodity, i.e. not hire labour. A shortage of food endowment will not only impoverish the farmer but also shrink the demand for other products and services by the farmer.

A GENERAL EQUILIBRIUM EXTENSION

It is obvious, therefore, that we should examine food demand and food supply together with demand and supply of other commodities that non-food producers have to exchange for food. Let us suppose that there are two such commodities, rice and fish, and two individuals, the fisherman (A) and the farmer (B). Let us look at the possibility of a famine-type entitlement failure in this static but general equilibrium framework. (I am drawing here on Desai 1986*a*.)

I assume, not unreasonably, that both the individuals regard rice as their basic food and fish as something extra worth having but not crucial to survival. Indicate the amount of rice required as a minimum by each individual as $X_{1A}^\star$ and $X_{1B}^\star$. No such minimum amount is necessary for fish but fish yields utility to the consumer. The formal representation of such a utility function is:

$$U_i = \alpha_1 \log(X_{1i} - X_{1i}^\star) + (1 - \alpha_1)\log X_{2i}, \quad i = A, B \tag{1}$$

Each individual derives utility from rice consumption if he gets more than $X_{1i}^\star$ not otherwise. The weights α_1 and $(1 - \alpha_1)$ attach to rice and fish consumption. Now the rice farmer's income will be $p_1 \cdot X_1$, X_1 being total output and p_1 the unit price, and the fisherman's income will be $p_2 \cdot X_2$, X_2 being fish output.

Given the form of the utility function in (*1*), it is easy to derive the demand functions of the farmer and the fisherman for rice and fish. (Formally this is done by maximizing U_i subject to the constraint that total expenditure of each individual does not exceed his income.) We have:

$$X_{1A} = X_{1A}^\star + \frac{\alpha_1(p_2 \times X_2 - p_1 X_{1A}^\star)}{p_1} \tag{2a}$$

$$X_{2A} = (1 - \alpha_1)\frac{(p_2 X_2 - p_1 X_{1A}^\star)}{p_2} \tag{2b}$$

$$X_{1B} = X_{1B}^{\star} + \alpha_1 (X_1 - X_{1B}^{\star}) \tag{2c}$$

$$X_{2B} = (1 - \alpha_1) \frac{p_1 (X_1 - X_{1B}^{\star})}{p_2} \tag{2d}$$

Each equation gives us the demand of an individual for a commodity given his income and prices except in the case of the farmer's demand for rice (X_{1B}). Here note that prices play no role whatsoever. The farmer decides his consumption of the pivotal commodity at the outset. He consumes above his subsistence requirement a proportion of his total output above his subsistence requirement, i.e. trivially rewrite $(2c)$ as:

$$(X_{1B} - X_{1B}^{\star}) = \alpha_1 (X_1 - X_{1B}^{\star}) \tag{2c'}$$

This, however, means that the fisherman only gets the excess above X_{1B} i.e. $(X_1 - X_{1B})$ as a possible quantity he can purchase. There is no guarantee at all that this quantity will suffice for him i.e. that $X_{1A}^{\star} < (X_1 - X_{1B})$. Being away from the production of the foodstuff, he cannot guarantee that he will be able to obtain his subsistence requirement in exchange. Another way to put this is that in equation $(2a)$ there is nothing to guarantee that $X_{1A} > X_{1A}^{\star}$ i.e. that $(p_2 X_2 - p_1 X_{1A}^{\star}) > 0$. It will depend on the amount of marketed surplus $(X_1 - X_{1B}^{\star})$ that the farmer will release and the resulting terms of trade.

As far as the terms of trade are concerned, we can explicitly solve them out given the output quantities X_1 and X_2. We have

$$\frac{p_1}{p_2} = \frac{\alpha_1 X_2}{(1 - \alpha_1)(X_1 - (X_{1A}^{\star} + X_{1B}^{\star}))} \tag{3}$$

If for some reason enough is not produced to cover the subsistence requirement for *both* the individuals $X_1 < (X_{1A}^{\star} + X_{1B}^{\star})$, the price ratio turns negative, i.e. trade breaks down. Of course, in case output of rice is actually below the subsistence requirements of the two individuals, what will happen is that the farmer will grab X_{1B} and leave the fisherman $X_1 - X_{1B}$.

This is a simple and stylized example to show how if we require minimum food for subsistence and let one person (or group) specialize in food production, then that person (or group) occupies an asymmetric position in exchange. Their food entitlements are always guaranteed and the other groups, not in food production, become marginalized. The price ratio p_1/p_2 will be steeper as food output above subsistence needs falls. Let us look at some examples.

We consider three examples. The first example sets up a 'normal' situation to set the scene and the following ones are variants with differential drops in output of the two commodities.

Example 1: assume that $\alpha_1 = 0\cdot6$, $X_{1A}^* = X_{2B}^* = 500$ kg. Outputs are $X_1 = 3000$ kg, $X_2 = 1000$ kg. Put $p_2 = 1$ by assumption. Then we get:

$$p_1/p_2 = 0\cdot75, \qquad X_{1A} = 1000 \text{ kg}, \qquad X_{1B} = 2000 \text{ kg}$$

Example 2: let the output of rice be halved, $X_1 = 1500$ kg. Everything else as above:

$$p_1/p_2 = 3\cdot0, \qquad X_{1A} = 400 \text{ kg}, \qquad X_{1B} = 1100 \text{ kg}$$

Thus the price ratio quadruples because though output declines by 50 per cent, marketed output in the new situation is a quarter of what it was before. The farmer gets 55 per cent of his former consumption but the fisherman only 40 per cent.

Example 3: let both outputs be halved, $X_1 = 1500$ kg, $X_2 = 500$ kg:

$$p_1/p_2 = 1\cdot5, \qquad X_{1A} = 400 \text{ kg}, \qquad X_{1B} = 1100 \text{ kg}$$

This is a strong 'invariance' result whereby the rice farmer's rice consumption is unaffected by the fall in the output of fish and the consequent fall in the relative price of rice. The relation between the two individuals is not symmetric but asymmetric and 'recursive'. The rice economy determines the rice allocation independently of the fish economy.

BOOM FAMINES AND SLUMP FAMINES

But, of course, famines can arise without the output of the pivotal commodity going down. Amartya Sen has distinguished between boom famines and slump famines. The Great Bengal Famine of 1943 was caused by the demand shift due to the wartime needs of the military and the consequent upturn in the activity it caused in urban areas. Thus without the fish/rice output balance changing in any way, prices could still go up due to a demand shock.

To demonstrate this, we should ideally have a more elaborate model with several income groups all interacting. One such model is presented in Appendix B of Poverty and Famine (Sen 1981a). This has five different classes and is designed to show the uneven incidence of a rise in the minimum ration on the different economic groups. We can do the same in a slightly amended version of the model above. Thus assume that apart from the two individuals A and B there is an outside 'urban' economy. From this economy, two types of shocks can be felt. One is that a sudden influx of purchasing power denoted m can be injected to buy rice. This is a demand shock. (Technically, one could think of m as an unexpected deviation from normal demand which is already accommodated in the economy.) On the supply side, a shock can come from forced requisition of rice. Such things happen during civil wars. Call this shock $\hat{X}_1$.

Without much ado, we can write down the modified equation (3) as a result of these two shocks

$$\frac{p_1}{p_2} = \frac{\alpha_1 X_2 + m}{(1 - \alpha_1)(X_1 - \hat{X}_1 - \Sigma X_1^*)} \qquad (3a)$$

Thus the effect of m and of $\hat{X}_1$ is to raise the price ratio p_1/p_2. But notice again that the incidence of the two shocks is very different on the farmer as against the fisherman. Let us take the two shocks in turn

(a) Demand Shock: $m > 0$, $\hat{X}_1 = 0$

It is quite clear from our earlier analysis that the farmer's rice consumption stays as it was in equation $(2c')$. The burden of the extra demand falls on the fisherman. Take again Example 1 but say that $m = 1000$ (money units). Then the resulting equilibrium is:

Example 1m:

$X_1 = 3000$, $\quad X_2 = 1000$, $\quad p_1 = 0.6$, $\quad p_2 = 1$, $\quad m = 1000$

$p_1/p_2 = 2.0$, $\quad X_{1A} = 500$, $\quad X_{1B} = 2000$, $\quad X_{1m}(= m/p_1) = 500$

Example 2m: as Example 2 above but with $m = 1000$

$p_1/p_2 = 8.0$, $\quad X_{1A} = 275$, $\quad X_{1B} = 1100$, $\quad X_{1m} = 125$

Example 3m: as in Example 3 above but with $m = 1000$

$p_1/p_2 = 6.5$, $\quad X_{1A} = 247$, $\quad X_{1B} = 1100$, $\quad X_{1m} = 153$

The demand shock examples illustrate several things. First, if examples 1 and 1m were two successive years where everything else was unchanged except an injection of extra demand we see how the fisherman's consumption of rice is cut to the bare bones and he suffers the entire incidence of the extra demand. This occurs without any decline in rice output. The next interesting contrast is between examples 2m and 3m as compared to examples 2 and 3. In the case of 2 and 3, there was invariance in the rice allocation as between the farmer and the fisherman, although fish output halved. Now when fish output halves, in the presence of outside demand of the nominal magnitude, the fisherman is worse off. He has now suffered quantity shock and price shock.

While it is not strictly legitimate to think of these examples as occurring successively through time, one can imagine that a transition from the world of example 1 to that of example 3m, sees the fisherman going from 1000 to 247 in his rice entitlement due to (i) drop in rice output, (ii) drop in fish output, (iii) presence of outside demand.

(b) Supply Shock $\hat{X}_1 > 0$, $m = 0$

The supply shock story is straightforward in as much as it acts in a similar way to a drop in output. There may be some difference if the grain is collected at the farm gate and the farmer is left with only $X_1 - \hat{X}_1$, from which to meet his own requirement $X_{1B}^{\star}$ as well as sell some output. On the other hand if $\hat{X}_1$ is collected from the marketed output, i.e. from $(X_1 - X_{1B})$ the effects would be wholly on the fisherman.

Example 1x:

Take $\hat{X}_1$ as a lump sum tax of 500. $X_1 = 3000$, $X_2 = 1000$, $\alpha_1 = 0.6$ as in Example 1 before. Then by $(2c')$ $X_{1B} = 1700$, $X_{1A} = 800$ and $\hat{X}_1 = 500$. If on the other hand it is collected from marketed output we could have $X_{1B} = 2000$, $X_{1A} = 500$, $\hat{X}_1 = 500$. The price ratio p_1/p_2 is the same in the two cases which is a consequence of the equation $(3a)$ above, i.e. $p_1/p_2 = 1$. But given the independence of the farmer's consumption of relative price, the two different methods of procurement have different effects.

Example 2x:

Again with $\hat{X}_1 = 500$ and the values of Example 2, we get

Direct requisition $X_{1B} = 500$, $X_{1A} = 500$, $\hat{X}_1 = 500$

Indirect requisition $X_{1B} = 1100$ with not enough left over to even collect $X_1 = 500$ let alone have $X_{1A} > 0$.

Examples of such direct requisition are not totally unrealistic. The Soviet famine of 1920 had as one of its causal factors the policy of direct requisition of food grains. At a time when food output was only 60 per cent of its 1913 value (industrial output barely 20 per cent), the policy of direct requisitioning from farmers to feed the urban workers led to a tremendous hardship, and reportedly the death of between 2 to 3 million in 1920 (Jasny 1972, p.12; Sorokin 1975). It was on recognition of the cost of such direct requisition policy that Lenin decided to shift to market-based agricultural requisition policy (Lenin 1971; Desai 1971).

There are various directions in which we can extend such analysis further. Thus, one well-established sign of distress is when people start selling their assets in order to obtain cash to buy food. Such distress sales only result in the assets not bringing in as much as they would in normal times because those who have the cash to buy such assets have a strong bargaining position. But the presence of financial assets does modify the stark results given in examples 1, 2, and 3, especially the last two. Having established the foundations in our earlier equations, the extension to the case where the two individuals have financial assets is straightforward.

Let us see this by a simple extension of our example above. Let m_A be the value of assets of the fisherman, m_B of the farmer. Then it is easy to see that the equations $(2a)$–$(2d)$ above are modified as:

$$X_{1A} = X_{1A}^{\star} + \frac{\alpha_1(p_2 X_2 + m_A - p_1 X_{1A}^{\star})}{p_1} \tag{4a}$$

$$X_{2A} = \frac{(1 - \alpha_1)(p_2 X_2 + m_A - p_1 X_{1A}^{\star})}{p_2} \tag{4b}$$

$$X_{1B} = X_{1B}^{\star} + \alpha_1(X_1 - X_{1B}^{\star}) + \alpha_1 \frac{m_A}{p_1} \tag{4c}$$

$$X_{2B} = (1 - \alpha_1) \frac{p_1(X_1 - X_{1B}^{\star})}{p_2} + \frac{(1 - \alpha_1)m_A}{p_2} \tag{4d}$$

We see that each person's demands are augmented by the presence of assets. Also now the farmer's demand for rice (X_{1B}) is no longer insensitive to prices. The price level itself is influenced by the assets and equation (3) has to be modified to:

$$\frac{p_1}{p_2} = \frac{\alpha_1(X_2 + (m_A + m_B))}{(1 - \alpha_1)(X_1 - (X_{1A}^{\star} + X_{1B}^{\star}))} \tag{3a}$$

We can again work out three examples with financial assets added:

Example 1M: all the values of example 1 but with $m_A = m_B = £1000$. Then:

$$p_1/p_2 = 2{\cdot}25, \qquad X_{1A} = 734, \qquad X_{1B} = 2266$$

Example 2M: all the values of example 2 with $m_A = m_B = £1000$. Then:

$$p_1/p_2 = 9{\cdot}0, \qquad X_{1A} = 434, \qquad X_{1B} = 1166$$

Example 3M: all the values of example 3 with $m_A = m_B = £1000$.

$$p_1/p_2 = 7{\cdot}5, \qquad X_{1A} = 420, \qquad X_{1B} = 1180$$

Several things are noteworthy about these examples. Thus, the invariance of the farmer's rice consumption to prices is now modified but note that by assigning equal money balances to the two individuals, we have tilted the entitlement ratios even more in favour of the farmer than before. When the rice output falls, again his relative advantage improves with assets rather than without. Finally in example 3M, we see that a fall in fish output hurts the fisherman even further in terms of food entitlement than when fish output was normal. Thus example 3M is an illustration of the adverse price and quantity effects persisting even when the individuals have financial assets.

These are again stylized examples, but they serve our purpose. More realism can be added by allowing each individual to demand money balances as well as the two commodities, by linking money balances to past savings and by letting interest rates exert some effect but I will not follow that road here.

One further dimension along which we can explore the implications of the model is to ask how sensitive the outcome is to the parameters α_1 and $X_{1i}^\star$, the minimum quantities. Let us concentrate on the fisherman. From (2a) we see that if the quantity in the parenthesis $(p_2 X_2 - p_1 X_{1A}^\star)$ is negative, the fisherman will get less than his subsistence. For what ranges of the parameters is this likely? Clearly, it is sufficient that:

$$X_2/X_{1A}^\star < p_1/p_2$$

for $X_{1A} < X_{1A}^\star$. Exploring this further by substituting equation (13) for p_1/p_2, we get the condition that:

$$\frac{(1 - \alpha_1)}{\alpha_1} < \frac{X_{1A}^\star}{(X_1 - \Sigma X_{1i}^\star)} \qquad (5)$$

is sufficient for $X_{1A} < X_{1A}^\star$. Notice that (5) is independent of the value of X_2 as long as it is positive. The fisherman will starve if (5) is fulfilled. In (5), the denominator is the surplus above the farmer's and the fisherman's subsistence and the numerator is of course the fisherman's subsistence. It is clear that the higher α_1 is, the more likely, *ceteris paribus*, that the fisherman will get less than his subsistence.

AN ALTERNATIVE MODEL

The above exercises with a simple general equilibrium model have brought out various aspects of the theory of entitlement. In particular, the asymmetric position of the food producer *vis-à-vis* the person outside the pivotal commodity production is dramatically brought out. The influence of an aggregate demand shock as well as supply shock can be explored in a way that is simple and transparent. The drawback is that we rely on a rather restrictive utility function such as equation (1). While it is patently realistic to require that people need minimum quantities before they derive any utility from consumption, this may yet be found to restrict the generality of our results. We proceed therefore to explore an alternative formulation which preserves the asymmetry of the two commodities but does not require minimum quantities of rice to be consumed.

Instead of equation (1) as our utility function, let us posit the following:

$$U_i = X_{1i}^\alpha (\beta X_{1i} + X_{2i})^{1-\alpha} \qquad (5)$$

Equation (5) is a modified version of the well-known Cobb–Douglas form familiar to economists. The presence of $\beta \neq 0$ is the new element here. As long as $\beta > 0$, the commodity X_1 will be more important in the consumer's mind than X_2. Indeed U_1 has the property that the consumer can go without X_2 and have $U > 0$ but for $X_1 = 0$, $U = 0$. Thus X_2 is inessential and X_1 is essential but in a different sense than in *(1)* above where both were essential but X_1 was required to be in excess of a minimum quantity.

Like *(1)*, equation *(5)* is easy to manipulate. Corresponding to *(2a)–(2d)*, we can derive the demand conditions for the two person–two good economy:

$$X_{1A} = \alpha \frac{p_2 X_2}{(p_1 - \beta p_2)} \tag{6a}$$

$$X_{1B} = \alpha \frac{p_1 X_1}{(p_1 - \beta p_2)} \tag{6b}$$

$$X_{2A} = \frac{X_2((1-\alpha)p_1 - \beta p_2)}{(p_1 - \beta p_2)} \tag{6c}$$

$$X_{2B} = \frac{p_1 X_1((1-\alpha)p_1 - \beta p_2)}{(p_1 - \beta p_2)} \tag{6d}$$

The structure of demand equations *(6a)–(6d)* sets some limits to the movements of the relative prices. Thus for the X_1 demand equations it is easy to see that we require the denominator to be positive so that X_{ij} can be positive. Hence $p_1/p_2 > \beta$ is a necessary condition. But given that $p_1/p_2 > \beta$, for demand for X_2 to be nonnegative we require $p_1/p_2 > \beta/(1 - \alpha)$ as can be seen from *(7c)* and *(7d)*. Since $0 < \alpha < 1$, it is only the latter condition that is of interest.

Thus in the asymmetric world described to us by equation *(5)*, there is a limit above which the price of X_2 cannot rise relative to that of X_1. When the ratio p_1/p_2 falls to $\beta/(1 - \alpha)$, consumers stop buying X_2. At this stage people buy only X_1 but given that no one buys X_2, the producer of X_2 has no income to spend on buying X_1. In this sense, a decline in the output of the peripheral commodity will not benefit its producers. They will lose their entitlements to food (X_1) if the price of their product rises too high. Thus, adverse effects are not compensated by favourable price effects for the producers of the peripheral commodity. The asymmetry is reinforced but in a different way.

We can also work out the equilibrium price ratio corresponding to *(3)*, for the new model. We get:

$$p_1/p_2 = \frac{\beta}{(1 - \alpha)} + \frac{\alpha}{(1 - \alpha)} \frac{X_2}{X_1} \tag{7}$$

Thus the price ratio can fall to the limit when demands for X_2 are zero only if the output of X_2 is zero, since otherwise X_2 and X_1 should be positive.

It is instructive to work out numerical examples on the lines of examples 1 to 3 above. We label them 1, 2 and 3.

Example 1: $\alpha = 0{\cdot}6$, $\beta = (1 - \alpha)$, other values as in Example 1

$$p_1/p_2 = 1{\cdot}5, \qquad X_{1A} = 545, \qquad X_{1B} = 2455$$

Example 2: α and β as in 1 and other values as in Example 2

$$p_1/p_2 = 2{\cdot}0, \qquad X_{1A} = 375, \qquad X_{1B} = 1125$$

Example 3: α and β as in 1 and other values as in Example 3

$$p_1/p_2 = 1{\cdot}5, \qquad X_{1A} = 545, \qquad X_{1B} = 2455$$

It is clear that in this economy the relative entitlements of rice (X_1) are determined by the ratio of outputs of X_1 to X_2. From (6a) and (6b):

$$\frac{X_{1B}}{X_{1A}} = \frac{\alpha}{(1 - \alpha)} + \frac{\beta}{(1 - \alpha)}\frac{X_1}{X_2} \qquad (8)$$

Notice that in (6b) the farmer's demand for rice is no longer independent of the relative prices.

This makes a substantial difference to the farmer's supply response when the relative price changes. Thus if we compare 1 to 2, the proportion of rice marketed (X_{1A}/X_1) goes up from 12·5 to 36·3 per cent as output drops by 50 per cent and the price goes up by a third. By contrast in examples 1 and 2, the proportion marketed falls from 33·3 per cent to 26·6 per cent. The presence of $X_{1i}^{\star} > 0$ and $X_{2i}^{\star} = 0$ in equation (1) thus strongly shapes the supply response. In the second model there is still an asymmetry since there are limits to the price ratio p_1/p_2 in the downward direction but not in the upward direction. Of course, the strength of this asymmetry will depend crucially on the relation of α to β.

The purpose of these two models has been pedagogic. In as much as the entitlement approach has been criticized as either not novel or mistaken in the context of the neoclassical economy theory, I have been at some pains to point out that it can be formulated in fairly general terms and interesting conclusions can be derived from it without violating postulates of neoclass-ical economics. The case of minimum consumption requirements has been well known to cause problems of existence of equilibrium (Koopmans 1957). While this is well known it has not been sufficiently explored in the literature. What does it precisely mean to say equilibrium does not exist? We see in example 2 that a positive and finite price ratio can be worked out as long as X_1 exceeds the sum of the minimum requirements $X_{1i}^{\star}$. This however leads to a peculiar sort of equilibrium where one of the parties gets less than the minimum requirements. In one sense this violates the utility function but in another sense this represents the best that individual A can do. The fisherman derives 'infinitely negative utility' when $X_{1A} < X_{1A}^{\star}$. But then it is realistic to say that he would rather have a half a loaf than none. In Rangasami's terms he is in the process of famishment. One would need to reformulate the model with not only utility maximization but some food security motives to put some realism into the choice behaviour. Thus it is not utility of consumption but the reproduction of daily existence that may have to become the objective function. But this is clearly an area for future research.

A major omission in the entitlement approach is the dynamics of situations which start from a drought or even normal rainfall but deteriorate into famines. This is not to say that we lack descriptive studies of famines which bring these dynamic aspects out. It is the lack of a theoretical framework that is at issue. Here I have no new analytical models to propose but it is appropriate to list some considerations which may be tackled in the future. One dynamic consideration is the state of the overall economy/ecology within which a trigger event such as drought takes place. If the economy is already weakened by such previous episodes, it will have limited reserves for coping with such a crisis. It is also very likely that if there is no quick and adequate relief, one year's crisis may affect future output. This is especially true in livestock operations where, if some cattle die during a famine, restocking may take several years due to the usual gestation lags. The institutional structures of land ownership and developments in non-agricultural parts of the economy would also be important. Thus while the Great Bengal Famine of 1943 occurred in absence of a decline in food availability, the enormous damage it caused can only be understood if seen in the context of a secular decline in Bengal's economy. The highly concentrated land ownership, the multiple layers of subinfeudation, and the stagnation in the region's industrial economy in the inter-war years had already made Bengal's economy/ecology vulnerable to a shock (Greenough 1982).

Another sort of dynamic consideration is at the individual level. As Rangasami points out, there is a gap between the first shortage – dearth – made good by selling financial assets and the final stage of starvation. Nutritionists have studied the process by which the body adjusts its activity rate to lower food intake, etc. But this slowing-down of activity has consequences for future output since lack of adequate nourishment influences effort and productivity adversely. This process has been studied in general but not integrated into the economics of famine (Bliss and Stern 1978; Dasgupta and Ray 1986/7). But is is clear that low output this year would lead to low employment and low wages which in turn perpetuate such low output in the following years. Thus droughts in one year can lead to famines in subsequent years, notwithstanding that the rainfall in the subsequent year may have been normal.

A third set of dynamic considerations are in terms of the interactions between different socio-economic groups. The asset holdings of these groups, their saving propensities, and the opportunities for investment open to them in normal times would to a great extent decide how long they can last when faced with shortage. In some sense, adequate reserves of grain and assets confer social power and determine who benefits from famines. After the famine is over, the changed distribution of assets means that those who sold their assets start again in a vulnerable position and those who were prosperous to begin with have strengthened their position. *In extremis* people may move from one group, say pastoralists to another, landless labourers, or may migrate to urban areas. Thus Sen noticed that in the Great Bengal Famine many people tried to get work in rice-harvesting and other such operations though previously they were in the non-agricultural part of the rural economy. Large-scale migration of refugees has been a noticeable feature of the Sahel and the Ethiopian famines.

For those who have assets and stocks of foodgrain, famines may afford opportunities for profits. A perennial controversy about famines is whether they are caused by the hoarding of foodgrains by the farmers or by the grain merchants. Standard economic theory has been somewhat divided on the issue as to whether speculators cause instability or they help markets clear more rapidly and hence prices may be lower than otherwise. The issue concerns the profitability of stockholders' behaviour about hoarding or releasing foodgrains. This brings up the question of the expectations of the traders as to how the prices are going to move and whether such expectations reveal stabilizing influences or not. But the issue concerns not only how traders form expectations but also how consumers and producers form them as well. Only empirical work can give us a classification of markets where stockpiling is stabilizing and where it is not. Ravallion has investigated this question for Bangladesh and found some evidence of destabilizing speculative behaviour (Ravallion 1985).

MODELLING FAMINES

We now have the benefit of a number of descriptive studies of famines, most of them inspired by the entitlement approach. From them a number of common elements emerge as well as significant differences. It is possible to construct a model of the famine – a model in the sense of a set of articulated blocks or systems which interact in specified ways. These systems link with each other through time and display the usual properties of recursivity or simultaneity, exogeneity, or endogeneity. Any such general model must not only be comprehensive in the sense that it must capture the main features of the known famines but it must also leave the possibility open that at the end a famine may or may not occur. Also it must capture the basic premise of the entitlement approach, that none of the usually cited causes for famine – e.g. decline in food availability due to drought, stockpiling, population pressure – is either necessary or sufficient for the famine to occur. Famines are social rather than natural events in this sense.

The basic blocks of this model are:

- The Nature System
- The Socio-Political System
- The Economic System:
     The Food Production System
     The Non-Food Production System (Rural)
     The Non-Food Production System (Urban)
     The Food Delivery System

THE NATURE SYSTEM

Of these systems, the nature system is exogenous with respect to the rest. There is a very long-run connection between the utilization of resources by the economic system which may damage the ecology as in the creation of the US Midwestern dustbowl but for the time perspective within which famines occur, we can take the nature system as exogenous. The nature system will comprise certain stock variables, e.g. the ecology, the land quantity and quality, the other natural resources available. But more important in a temporal context are the flow variables, especially rainfall. It will be the amount, timing, and the geographical incidence of rainfall that will be a crucial exogenous variable. Too much rainfall (floods) or too little (drought) can be a trigger for the chain of events which end in famine. Whether such is the end result or not depends on the conditioning stock variables – the ecology and the structure of the other systems.

Although the nature system is exogenous, it is not necessarily unpredictable. There are regular cycles in rainfall, for example, which can be statistically modelled to gain an early forecast of the likelihood of high or low rainfall. The availability of such a forecast combined with the ability of the socio-political system to respond can avert a trigger such as drought from developing into a famine. (The pioneering work on climatic history is Lamb (1982). See also Wigley *et al.* (1981). For forecasting of droughts see Heathcote (1985).)

A related aspect of the nature system is animal behaviour. Attacks of locusts can cause a collapse of food output even after a normal rainfall, good planting, and fertilizing. The migratory behaviour of locusts is an exogenous but increasingly predictable variable. A different but equally important shock can be the outbreak of disease among the cattle. This can influence both the food and the non-food production systems.

THE SOCIO-POLITICAL SYSTEM

The working of the economic system cannot be divorced from that of the socio-political system. At the macro-level, this involves the nature of the state and of the society. A state hostile to groups within its territory either on racial, ethnic, religious, or class grounds can deliver severe shocks to the availability and distribution of food. The Soviet famine of 1932–3 was most probably a result of the collectivization campaign which led to wholesale destruction of cattle by the peasantry. Civil war is another frequent occurrence which disrupts the production and delivery of food-stuffs. Russia in 1920 and Ethiopia in recent years have witnessed civil wars which seriously disrupted the flow of food as between different regions. Civil wars also illustrate an aspect of the entitlement approach which has not been sufficiently brought out. Entitlements presume a legal framework of property rights; in civil wars there is a dispute precisely about legality. Property owned by someone belonging to one side is seized by the opposite side. Thus entitlements become precarious due to non-economic reasons in civil-war periods.

The socio-political system also tells us about the structure and incidence of taxation. The taxation of agricultural output in one form or another is a central source of revenue for most less-developed countries and even for today's developed countries in their historical period. The method of taxation – direct requisition, income tax, or indirect tax – will determine allocative effects on relative food entitlements. One example of this was given above but more work is needed here.

The socio-political system is also crucial for the administrative/political response to the threat of famine. The Famine Code devised by British civil servants in India during the late nineteenth century has been much studied recently as an example of the practical response based on an implicit entitlement approach (Rangasami 1985). In more recent famines in India the effectiveness of different provincial administrations even within a common famine-relief tradition has been contrasted as between Maharash-tra and Bihar (Dreze (1986) on Maharashtra; Brass (1985) on Bihar). It is not clear what it is that determines the competence of different socio-political systems in responding to threats of famine. Thus in the Sahel and Ethiopia, it is often international rather than domestic famine-relief that seems to be bearing the brunt whereas in Kenya in the 1984/5 famine, it was the domestic administration which was able to avert the famine.

A much deeper aspect of the socio-political system is the social struc-ture–kinship, behavioural norms, inter-group conflicts, religious taboos, etc. These will determine whether the food is shared out equitably and at what level of social aggregation. Certain groups, e.g. single, unmarried, or widowed women, may get systematically marginalized, or allocation norms may discriminate against the old and infirm and concentrate on the survival of the able-bodied who have the best chances of survival. Such micro-variables can only be captured by anthropological fieldwork and economics has little to say on such things.

The socio-political system has to be thought of as exogenous to the economic system. Again if a famine condition becomes endemic, this may have repercussions on the stability of the socio-political system, but for the purposes of understanding famines and devising measures to avert them, it is best to take them as given.

THE ECONOMIC SYSTEM

The economic system will, in general, be endogenous. Variables such as stocks of foodgrains or of capital equipment or of cattle will be given by past decisions, i.e. be lagged endogenous. So will be the given distribution of financial assets and other endowments. The vulnerability of a community to a shock such as failure of rainfall will depend to a large extent on the size and distribution of its reserve stocks of foodgrains as well as assets which can be cashed to buy food.

In normal times again the interaction between the food and the non-food systems is simultaneous. They determine the mutual demand for each other's products and the relative prices. But as we have seen in abnormal periods (in the various senses described in the section above) the food production system becomes pivotal and asymmetric with respect to the non-food system. Thus we look first at the food production system.

The Food Production System

Famines are ultimately about the insufficient access of a large part of the community to food. The food production system is the crucial block. The input-output lag, between sowing and harvesting, is a fundamental feature. The dependence of the system on rainfall as against other sources of water, the cropping pattern, and the technology of cultivation are all important variables. Thus, if the rains fail, the possibility of changing the sowings to another less water-demanding crop will allow the farmers to salvage something out of the situation. The size of crop standing in the field was used as an early indicator of size and harvest in Indian revenue assessment (the so-called annawari system). The vulnerability of the harvest to slight delays in getting the labour or equipment is another factor.

These various factors – dependence on rainfall, possibility of changing the crop, the size of the standing crop as an early indicator of final harvest, the vulnerability of the harvest to last-minute delays – are ordered in time along the input–output lag, i.e. the former occur earlier in the input–

output sequence. The earlier the signal of a possible failure in harvest, the more time there would be for the socio-political system, especially the administrative system, to respond to the signal.

The food production system in normal times determines the output of food, as well as its demand for inputs. Chief among the inputs is hired labour as far as the famine incidence is concerned. If a harvest failure is indicated at an early stage – low sowings, low rainfall – then we know that there would be little demand for hired labour. This would be a sure sign that the labourers' entitlements will shrink unless a relief works programme is immediately initiated. The labourers would otherwise face low employment and low wages. The mode of wage payment, cash or kind, will further determine the size of the price effect. (Some of these points are developed further in Desai (1986b).)

The tenurial relations in food production – sharecropping, tenancy, owner cultivation, co-operative cultivation – as well as the distribution of cultivable land will be the next set of variables to look for. They determine the income of the various agents. Depending on the size of the harvest, the wage bill (in kind) paid out, farmers' own consumption, we can calculate the size of the marketed surplus. The price at which food will be sold to those who have to purchase it as against those who can appropriate it directly will depend on the size of this harvested surplus along with the demand emanating from the non-food production system.

The Non-Food Production System (Rural)

Descriptive studies of famines have revealed a variety of non-food-growing activities which are the second major source of livelihood. Fishermen in Bengal, pastoralists in Sahel, jute growers in Bangladesh – all such activities typify this sector. The point is that the bulk of the poor in LDCs are in rural areas and they are frequently net purchasers of food rather than sellers. Thus, while much development literature talks of the terms of trade between agriculture and industry or between rural and urban areas, it is the intra-rural terms of trade between the food and non-food sectors which matter in times of shortage.

The rural non-food production system can be as much affected by a weather shock – lack of rainfall, for example – as is the food production system. The state of the ecology will matter equally to this system. Thus the nature system has an equal impact on both the rural economic systems. In addition the non-food system may be affected by cattle disease, mercury poisoning of fish, etc. which are specific shocks to this sector. Thus a famine could start because, say, the incidence of foot and mouth disease reduces the incomes of the pastoralists and hence their entitlement to food even without the food supply having suffered.

In normal times, there would be mutual dependence of the food and non-food sectors. They will demand things from each other and sell products as well. To the extent that the non-food system sells inputs to the food system, if activity rates are low in the food sector, then the repercussions will be felt everywhere. If the non-food sector sells consumption goods or services, the impact of a rise in the relative price of food will be adverse. This is because, as I showed above, the share of food expenditure will rise and money spent on other items will fall. Thus during the Great Bengal Famine many who were providers of rural services, e.g. the village barber, suffered from a collapse of the market for the things they had to sell.

The Non-Food Production System (Urban)

This block is mainly a demander of food, and to the extent that the food production system may use sophisticated inputs, e.g. fertilizers, a provider of inputs. In general, it controls credit flows into the food production system. In many famine-prone economies this sector is underdeveloped and hence unable to provide infrastructural support such as transport which would help improve the food delivery system. In famine situations, this system is a demander of food and often has limited quantity of goods to offer in exchange. Such for example was the case in Russia during the Civil War.

But although this sector is a burden on the economy in famine periods, typically there is a grain storage capacity here. Thus the people seeking food and work often migrate from rural areas to urban areas. This is where they are likely to find jobs and also where there is a better chance for food to be available. Urban deaths are also more visible and bring pressure to bear upon relief agencies, national or international.

The Food Delivery System

This system is the network of traders and transporters who store, transport, and sell grain. The merchants who hoard grain are part of this system as is any public distribution system. The ability of this system to cope with famine will depend upon the density of the network. Thus in the Sahel, it has been difficult to organize relief chiefly because the transport network has been thin, lacking roads as well as suitable transport equipment. This can happen if food markets are isolated and the transport of foodgrains is a seasonal activity. In such a case, the transport of food from the coast to the interior becomes problematic. The efficiency of the public relief system, domestic or international, presumes the existence of a dense network.

As already mentioned above, a contentious aspect of the food delivery system is the role of traders, especially their stockholding behaviour. Economics does not support the popular prejudice against the trader/ middleman (often also ethnically different from the local population). By buying at harvest time and selling at lean times, the trader makes a profit but smooths out price fluctuations. The debate then centres around whether, by delaying release of foodgrains from stock on the expectation that prices will rise even further, the trader makes excessive gain. Theoretically, the argument can be made on both sides and can only be settled by empirical investigation. Much more work is necessary on this aspect as on the influence of public distribution systems on price fluctuations.

A common misconception about the entitlement approach to famines is that somehow bringing in food from outside is irrelevant. This is not true. Famines may occur with or without food shortage but increasing food availability is an important plank of famine relief. The other plank, of course, is to initiate an income generation (relief work) programme that will enable people to buy the food.

THE MODEL AND ITS INTERRELATIONS

The interrelations between the different blocks are given in Fig. 3.3. The exogenous blocks – the nature system and the socio-political system – have arrows emanating from them but not directed at them. Beside each arrow the major influencing activity is also given but this is only as a signal for a cluster of variables. Thus 'taxation' is a summary term for a whole gamut of ways in which the state extracts resources from the economic system as well as the benefits it may give. The economic system is endogenous and there is a simultaneous interaction amongst the various blocks as is clear from the chart. Although there are no econometric models available at the present of famines, any future modelling activity will have to start with a system structure such as given in Fig. 3.3. Indeed as details are filled out we shall learn more about the dynamics of the system.

An alternative way to characterize the system would be by examining the relationship between different socio-economic groups within and across the various blocks. Thus the food production system has landlords, farmers, sharecroppers, and landless labourers. Other systems will have similarly employers, self-employed, employee groups. Their interrelations would be structured by the causal flows in the 'objective' system structure but there would also be modifications due to social and political features. Thus there may be ways of putting pressure on the socio-political system from the economic system to alter the burden of taxation on the pace of relief operations. Some of the disaggregated pattern of interrelationships

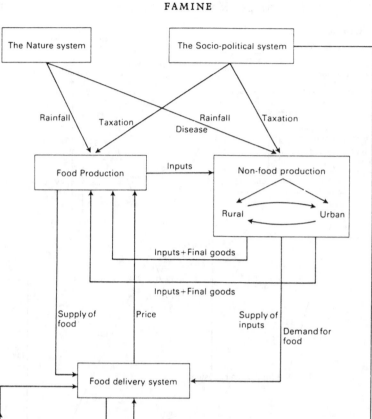

Fig. 3.3. The systems structure of famines.

have been formally covered in Appendix B of Sen's book (1981a) and the actual case studies in his book, and subsequently have filled out the details.

In Fig. 3.4 these interlinkages are described as in normal (non-famine) times. In the food production system we have landlords, tenant farmers, owner cultivator farmers, sharecroppers, and landless labourers. They exchange land for rent (landlord–tenant), labour for wage (landlord–tenant farmer–owner cultivator–labourer), inputs for grain (farmer–sharecropper). Each of the parties except the landless labourer (though unlikely for sharecropper) sells their surplus grain to the trader. The non-food system has been collapsed into three groups, employers, self-employed, and employees. They appear mainly as purchasers of foodgrains. There is no

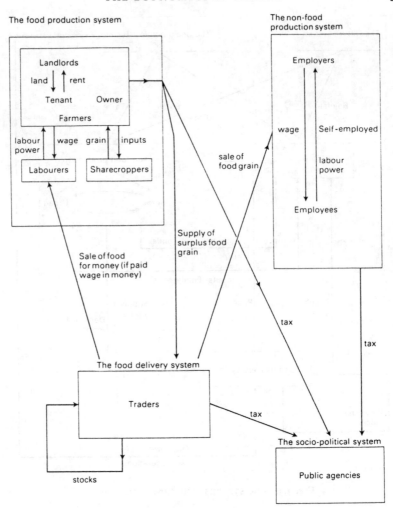

Fig. 3.4. The systems under normal conditions.

attempt at present to specify the relations within the non-food sector in detail but the wage and employment level and the asset endowments will, of course, determine the incidence of starvation when famine occurs.

The essence of the problem then is that many of these regular links are snapped or operate at an altered intensity in famine times. Thus the labour/wage exchange link could snap totally and labourers fall on relief. Similarly the delivery of surplus food to traders could be much reduced and traders may have to rely on previous stocks. The non-food system becomes dependent on the traders and the public relief for their supply of

food and also for jobs. To illustrate this reversal of the normal pattern in
famine times, Fig. 3.5 describes a different pattern. Thus, there is no
delivery of surplus grain from the food production system and there is no
employment for the labourers in the food production system or for
employees in the non-food production system. Thus the public agencies
have to step in to augment the previous stocks of the traders and to provide
a relief wage in return for labour services to the workers in the food and
non-food sectors. For simplicity the food growers – landlords, farmers, and
sharecroppers – are assumed not to be buyers of grain.

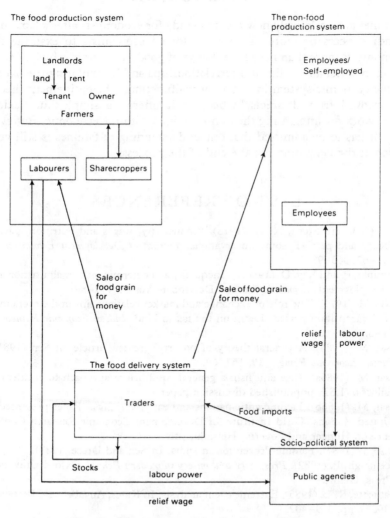

Fig. 3.5. The systems under famine conditions.

Of course, there are simplifications in all of the Figs 3.3–3.5. The relief system may not work as smoothly as the figures assume. Even the food production system may need to buy food. There is scope for further details, for example the allocation within households, migration from the non-food system to the food system of workers, etc. The purpose of these figures is, however, to convey the central features of the system as emphasized by the entitlement approach.

CONCLUSION

Famines are a relatively new topic of study for economists after a lapse of a hundred years or more. They have forced economists to examine the economy as more than merely exchange of goods and services by having to bring in social and political interrelationships and by exploring the nature of the economic system in a state of malfunction. The entitlement theory has proved fruitful precisely because it offered a simple but flexible framework for integrating the non-economic with the economic. But even here it has to be admitted that our understanding of famines is still very much at the beginning not the end of the process.

LIST OF REFERENCES

Bliss, C. J. and Stern, N. H. (1978). Productivity, wages and nutrition, part I, theory and part II, some observations. *Journal of Development Economics*, **5**, 331–62, 363–98.

Dasgupta, P. and Ray, D. (1986/7). Inequality as a determinant of malnutrition and unemployment. *Economic Journal*, December–March, 177–88.

Desai, M. (1972). The role of exchange and market relationships in the economics of the transition period: Lenin on the tax in kind. *Indian Economic Review*, **7**, 61–8.

Desai, M. (1984). A general theory of poverty? (review article on Sen (1981).) *Indian Economic Review*, **19**, 157–69.

Desai, M. (1986a). Rice and fish: a general equilibrium approach to entitlement failures. (LSE, unpublished discussion paper.)

Desai, M. (1986b). Famine anticipations and early warnings. (Paper presented at United Nations World Institute for Development Economic Research Conference on Hunger and Poverty, Helsinki, July.)

Dreze, J. (1987). Famine Prevention in India. In Sen and Dreze (1987).

Greenough, P. (1982). *Prosperity and misery in modern Bengal*. Oxford University Press, Oxford.

Heathcote, R. L. (1985). Extreme event analysis. In Kates, Ausubel, and Berberian (1985), pp. 369–402.

Jasnyi, N. (1972). *Soviet economists of the 1920s.* Cambridge University Press, Cambridge.

Kates, R. W., Ausubel, J. A., and Berberian, M. (1985). *Climate impact assessment.* Wiley, New York.

Koopmans, T. C. (1957). *Three essays on the state of the economic science.* McGraw-Hill, New York.

Lamb, H. H. (1982). *Climate, history and the modern world.* Methuen, London.

Lenin, V. I. (1971). The tax in kind. *Selected works,* Vol. 31. Progressive Publishers, Moscow.

Mitra, A. (1985). The Meaning of Meaning (review of Sen (1981)). *Economic and Political Weekly,* 17, 27 March.

Rangasami, A. (1985). Failure of exchange entitlement theory of famine: a response. *Economic and Political Weekly,* 20, 12 and 19 October.

Ravallion, M. (1985). The performance of rice markets in Bangladesh during the 1974 famine. *Economic Journal,* March, 15–19.

Sen, A. K. (1977). Starvation and exchange entitlements: a general approach and its application to the Great Bengal Famine. *Cambridge Journal of Economics,* 1, (1).

Sen, A. K. (1981a). *Poverty and famine: an essay on entitlement and deprivation.* Clarendon Press, Oxford.

Sen, A. K. (1981b). Ingredients of famine analysis: availability and entitlement. *Quarterly Journal of Economics,* 95.

Sen, A. K. (1986). Food, economics and entitlements. Lloyds Bank Review, April.

Sen, A. K. and Dreze, J. (1987). Hunger and poverty: the poorest billion. Proceedings of WIDER Conference on Food Strategies Research.

Sorokin, P. A. (1975). *Hunger as a factor in human affairs* (ed. T. Lynn Smith). University of Florida Press, Gainesville, Florida.

Srivinasan, T. N. (1983). Review of Sen (1981a) in the *American Journal of Agricultural Economics,* February.

Thompson, E. P. (1978). *The poverty of theory.* Merlin Press, London.

Wigley, T. M., Ingram, M. J., and Farmer, G. (1981). *Climate and history: studies in past climates and their impact on man.* Cambridge University Press, Cambridge.

6

1 Drawing the line: on defining the poverty threshold

MEGHNAD DESAI

For as long as there has been poverty, there have been attempts to question its existence, minimise its incidence or its adverse effects and curb any enthusiasm for its alleviation. People normally of a generous disposition become stingy when it comes to assessing minimum needs. Even advocates of poverty eradication programmes feel forced to be apologetic when accused of including 'frills' on their list of basic needs.

Measuring poverty is an exercise in demarcation. Lines have to be drawn where none may be visible and they have to be made bold. Where one draws the line is itself a battlefield. The process of moving a line a few pounds up or down gets bogged down in prolonged and futile controversy most reminiscent of a rugby game, where the ball moves hardly ten yards in the course of an afternoon.

Those who are suspicious of the notion of poverty insist both on there being a precise and clear definition of what poverty consists of and then on blurring the exercise by pointing to a diversity of needs, circumstances, tastes, propensities, etc. The notion of a poverty threshold, a demarcation line between the poor and the not-poor, is a fraught exercise for just such reasons. A simple threshold figure, easy to grasp and on which to base an anti-poverty policy, would be invaluable, but to be that it also has to be (nearly) universally acceptable. It is in the nature of the social perceptions of poverty in unequal societies that such simple figures are demanded only to be debated.

Any argument in favour of a poverty threshold has, therefore, to be wary of the exercise. The important thing is to make the basis on which the threshold is calculated explicit both in terms of what its constituent items are and why they are there. It should also be open about whose judgment it is that guides the inclusion or exclusion of these items. It has to be debatable and debated by the widest number of people. Only those definitions of poverty which appeal to the widest possible audience will stick.

1

The political dimension of poverty measurement

A poverty threshold is in many ways a political concept. But while this may always be said, it is the sense in which it is political that is important. The concern with poverty and its alleviation may have originated in the Judaeo-Christian notion of charity (I leave out for the moment other cultures such as the Hindu, the Islamic or the Buddhist). But its conceptualisation has changed with the political environment. The poor law enforcers were local gentry who, as rate-payers and voters, had a stake in the civil society of their times to the exclusion of those they were aiding. As industrial capitalism spread and enfranchisement progressed, the industrial workers (and their families) began to impinge on the politically minded not only because of their actual or potential voting power but also because of the increasing likelihood that the business cycle could deal adversely with them. Thus began the search for a separation of the deserving poor from the shiftless ones. Researchers and reformers like Charles Booth came from within the citadels of the civil society and wished to separate those who should be allowed within the keep and be protected from the incidence of poverty from those who were to be left outside.

The urgency of identifying the poor was made plain by the reverses that the British suffered in the Boer War. Their military vanity hurt, the nation's leaders began to look for possible causes of the deterioration of the nation's stock. The beginnings of the welfare state in the first decade of this century gave a new push to the venture Booth had begun.

The tradition of poverty studies of Joseph Rowntree and many others continued in this shifting perspective. The investigator, with the best of intentions, stood above and outside the world he (as these were almost always men) was surveying. Those he was studying were marginal economically and socially as well as politically. He could decide what the poor wanted or needed, sit in judgment on admissible needs and avoidable frills. The poor were the object of study but had no say in what constituted adequate standards for them.

Full political democracy was long in coming. Universal adult franchise was established in Britain in 1928, but its full effects on the political shape of the nation were felt only in 1945. By then, a 'people's war' had been fought and demands for an implicit contract between the rulers and the ruled about future provision had emerged. The tradition of the expert setting down the menu for universal provision remained. Beveridge relied on previous expert studies and nutritional guidance. But even with him, the distinction between insurance for those in work (the deserving poor) and assistance for those outside work (the indigent ones) remained.

2

This separation of working and non-working poor is fraught with contradictions. In a democratic society, there are no formal barriers placed in access to political rights — of voting, of participation in politics — except the qualification of having reached a minimum age — though, as Sue Ward's chapter shows, informally, low incomes inhibit even political activity. But economically we also live in a capitalist society — a society where allocation of incomes is, by and large, a market process only partially modified by non-commercial considerations. Thus, being in paid work is the predominant way of getting spending power. If normally in work, insurance schemes will provide you with some resources in unemployment or retirement. Work outside the market must be its own reward since no other reward is guaranteed for it. Those not in paid work are not only deprived of normal spending power but also lack the insurance entitlement that unemployed paid workers have. Their claim on resources as citizens is marginal and precarious. Thus supplementary benefit has always been much more stingily given them than unemployment benefit and is quickly withdrawn as soon as there is any hint that the recipient has access to some earned money — by cohabiting, for example.

Thus, political citizen rights have not been fully translated into economic rights. The effect is not abstract. Just as women were the last to get the franchise, they are also left to struggle for economic rights.

Principles for fixing a poverty threshold

A first principle of any discussion of a poverty threshold is, therefore, to start with the individual citizen and her/his rights to an economic entitlement. The entitlement is not a quid pro quo for work done in the past, ie, return of taxes paid, pension contributions made or wages underpaid. Rather, it is a right due to members of the political community to enable them to be full members. There are in every society a variety of non-paid tasks to be done — child-bearing and child-raising, taking care of the household, of the elderly, voting, canvassing at election times, participating in political marches, lobbies, giving blood, helping the disabled. Not all such tasks can be or are paid for on a one to one basis, yet they are essential for the continued functioning (reproduction) of the community as a community. The first principle, therefore, is that *economic entitlement to an adequate living standard should be such that citizens can take full part in the political community.* Not to give this is tantamount to a denial of political rights.

A second principle, however, directly follows from this. If economic entitlement is a passport right, who shall decide on the size of the annual income flowing as a 'dividend' from the entitlement? In

3

the past, it has been the expert opinion, whether individual or a government commission, which has determined the components of the poverty threshold. It is not the intentions (the well-meaningness) of the experts that are in doubt, but it is their *locus standi* in the matter. In a Bismarckian state, with limited popular participation, experts are appointed from above to devise plans to keep the poor docile. In the consensus state that Britain had for much of the twentieth century, the increasing degree of political participation did not affect the supremacy of experts in devising poverty thresholds. The only change was that the poor had perhaps better middlemen (middle-class men, too) to argue their case. But the poor could only assert their voice through agents, not directly. The political community also did not participate directly in the determination of the poverty threshold except through experts. Experts and agents were in *loco parentis* for the citizen.

The consensus state ended with the advent of the Thatcher government, not by accident but by design. Already, in the 1960s and 1970s, the effectiveness of the agents to argue successfully a case for the poor was in doubt since the poverty line continued to be depressed. In many respects, citizen groups learned to rely on direct action, locally or community based, in defence of their hospitals, schools, etc. The women's movement, where a coalition was built on only one common element — gender — taught us that it is possible to organise outside party political lines for a broad spectrum of issues.

It is necessary hence to extend this logic to the poverty debate. If, in defining a poverty threshold, we are looking for a level of living that will enable people to participate in community life, *it is the community which must determine* what the content of such a level will be. Poverty, it is often said, is in the eyes of the beholder, but this is to make it individual-subjective. What is more true is that poverty is determined by the norms and expectations of the community relative to whom certain individuals are poor. So it is social-subjective not individual-subjective. Therefore, our second principle is that *the level of the poverty threshold, ie, the specific contents of the level of living flowing from a citizen's economic entitlement, must be determined by the community.*

With these two principles in mind, the nuts and bolts of fixing the poverty threshold can be tackled. The first principle urges that we sever the connection between paid work and entitlement to a minimum income. It also tells us that the minimum is not related to physical survival — to subsistence — but to being able to perform a whole host of unpaid tasks which the community expects of its citizens and without which it will not function. But once we go away from a need-based poverty line (needs often being defined by experts and not by the needy), the question is how to make the

4

poverty line concrete. It is in this respect that the second principle tells us that it is the community which sets the limits which a poverty line must respect.

The community does this in two ways. First of all, the practice of day-to-day living (the reproduction of daily life) determines empirically what is required in a certain cultural/social context to live as full members of a community. It is the consumption practice — the style of living — that is the bedrock on which any poverty norm must be based. No expert can be trusted to determine this. Experts may be required to take statistically adequate samples to estimate actual consumption practice (eg, the cost of bringing up children in an inner-city environment), but they cannot be allowed to presume what is necessary and what is secondary to daily living. I shall expand below on what it is that the experts must sample; here let me stress that the experts must be subordinate and not superior to the community. They may be independent, they cannot be autonomous; they are servants of the community.

But there is another way in which the community determines the limits of the poverty line. It is the not-poor members of the community who must pay for the poor. There is nothing peculiar to the poor as a group that the community has to make a special dispensation for. While paid work should not be a precondition for income, the sum of all outputs produced for sale (including many public services) forms the pool to be shared out. No community for any appreciable length of time can consume more than it produces, but it can choose to share out what it produces in a variety of ways. Thus, in all societies, the children and the elderly, as well as those who are physically incapable of performing tasks which lead to paid work, are supported by those who produce. Transfer of resources across generations is thus the norm in any society. The way in which such transfers are made — either directly or via the exchange nexus — differs in different societies. The financing of the poor by the not-poor is a case of intra-generation transfer.

The size of the transfer from the not-poor to the poor is an issue over which there will be continuous debate. The feasibility of any poverty line as a guide for policy depends upon whether the community will willingly foot the bill. But, here again, it is easy to exaggerate the peculiarity of the poverty programme. Many public programmes (as well as many private acts) involve transfer from one section to another within the generation of the working population. Thus, adult education in universities, polytechnics and elsewhere is subsidised, as is much basic research. We consider the arts as suitable objects of subsidy. What is much more costly, but not perhaps so transparent, is the transfer to the well-to-do — tax concessions for home-owners, tax deductions for business expenses,

5

subsidies for businesses in various guises such as accelerated depreciation allowances. We also all pay collectively for diseases and accidents caused by the products of tobacco manufacturers, breweries and spirits manufacturers, and automobile manufacturers. There is longer-run damage done by manufactured food products which are injurious to health, by environmental pollution caused by 'wealth-creating' factories, by the noise and fumes of juggernauts whose manufacture is applauded for their greater cost effectiveness.

Living in a world of pervasive transfers, some in good causes and many in dubious ones, the objections that we hear about the difficulty of financing a welfare state or, even more narrowly, a poverty programme can only be political. It is easy to exaggerate the selfishness of individuals and natural to pretend that those who get generously rewarded in the marketplace deserve their rewards, inflated though these may be by tax concessions and hidden subsidies. But the ideology of associating income with prior performance of paid work is so strong that people will ask why should the tax-payer pay for able-bodied men and women, who should be able to help themselves?

It is from this broad perspective that the debate about the poverty threshold must be viewed. Ultimately at issue is who is to define the needs and the resources required for an adequate standard of living — is it the expert, is it the poor themselves or is it the community?

While individual workers such as Rowntree tried to single out the poor and examine their living standards, the practice now is to rely on questionnaires in which the poor as well as the not-poor are surveyed. Peter Townsend's large study of poverty[1] illustrates this transition to the community as a whole as the primary pool of data from which to define the poverty thresholds. But this still leaves the issue of which questions to include in the questionnaire, and who is to frame these questions. There is also the thorny problem of how to relate the responses to these questions to the definition of a poverty threshold.

As we shall see below, in the course of the debate between Peter Townsend and David Piachaud on the definition of a poverty threshold some of these issues were raised and answered. The Townsend-Piachaud debate also informed the next and the latest available poverty study conducted by Joanna Mack and Stewart Lansley on behalf of London Weekend Television (LWT).[2] As I show below, we are closer to the proper determination of a threshold now than at any time previously. It is also helpful that the two studies, although conducted fifteen years apart, reinforce each other in arriving at a similar measure of the threshold.

In what follows, I survey the Townsend-Piachaud controversy

first. Then I look at the LWT study. At the end, the implications of these studies for the nature of contemporary deprivation will be examined.

Townsend-Piachaud debate

Peter Townsend's *Poverty in the United Kingdom: a survey of household resources and standards of living*[3] marks a definite step forward in British discussion on poverty. The book incorporates a definition of poverty as relative deprivation, a spirited argument in defence of this definition and provides results from a questionnaire survey designed to measure relative deprivation. Far from taking the view that poverty is 'in the eyes of the beholder', poverty 'is understood objectively rather than subjectively'. The definition of relative deprivation is then explicit.

> Individuals, families and groups in the population can be said to be in poverty when they lack the resources to obtain the type of diet, participate in the activities and have the living conditions and amenities which are customary, or are at least widely encouraged or approved, in the societies to which they belong. Their resources are so seriously below those commanded by the average individual or family that they are, in effect, excluded from ordinary living patterns, customs and activities.[4]

Armed with this definition, Townsend proceeded to measure relative deprivation from answers to a questionnaire and related this measure to income. He concluded that there was a poverty threshold at 150% of the supplementary benefit (SB) level, below which families were deprived, and that the loss of each pound would increase deprivation sharply. Above that level, extra income reduced deprivation steadily.

This finding was criticised by David Piachaud,[5] who thought the attempt to fix a particular threshold level to be misguided. Piachaud also had several objections to the approach adopted by Townsend. Townsend had computed a deprivation index from answers obtained from the questionnaire and had calculated further an average value of the index for each of twelve income levels and then obtained a measure of 'the break' or the threshold from the relationship between the deprivation index and the income level.

Piachaud found Townsend's deprivation index 'of no practical value whatsoever as an indicator of deprivation'. He argued that for any income level, households showed a great deal of diversity in their score on the deprivation index, this diversity being an indication that the score of any household on the Townsend deprivation index is as much a matter of taste as an indicator of poverty.

7

There is thus no prior reason why many of the components of the deprivation index should bear any relationship to poverty. Townsend's index offers no solution to the intractable problem of disentangling the effects of differences in tastes from those of differences in poverty.

From these criticisms followed Piachaud's central proposition against Townsend.

The combination of two factors — that there is diversity in styles of living, and that poverty is relative — mean [sic] that you would *not*, in fact, expect to find any threshold between the poor and the rest of society. Townsend's hypothesis that such a threshold would exist is intrinsically implausible.

Piachaud thus poses quite boldly the central issues in the measurement of a poverty threshold. In what sense do Townsend's questions capture the notion of poverty? Is an answer to one of his questions purporting to measure deprivation a reflection of the investigator's tastes, of the respondent's tastes or of genuine poverty? Taking the questions at their worth, Piachaud asked whether, by compressing all his responses into summary measures of deprivation for twelve income classes, Townsend ignored information which may vitiate his conclusion. Was the method of locating a threshold objective or did it prejudge the issue?

The matter, as Piachaud said, 'is, alas, rather technical'. Indeed it is more technical than either Townsend or Piachaud allow for. But the substantive issue is important enough to pursue these technical questions further.

The deprivation index: a measure of tastes or of poverty?

Townsend asked sixty questions of his sample of 2,050 households (6,040 individuals). These questions cover a variety of aspects -- diet, clothing, household facilities, housing conditions, conditions at work, health, educational and environmental conditions, etc. The answers in a 'yes'/'no' form were correlated with income of the relevant unit. Now if the answer of 'yes' or 'no' to any question, eg, 'Have you not had a cooked breakfast?', were entirely a matter of taste, one would not expect any correlation between the income level and the answer. The poor as likely as the rich could answer 'yes' or 'no'. The evidence is, however, overwhelmingly against this supposition. As many as forty out of the sixty questions elicited a 'yes'/'no' pattern highly correlated with income. The correlation was significant at 0.001 level, indicating that there was only one in a thousand chance that the true relationship may reveal no correlation between income and the answers to this question, despite the

8

fact that the data showed such a correlation. The lower the income, the more likely it was that a 'yes' answer was found.

Townsend's deprivation index was based on twelve out of these sixty questions, all highly correlated with income. In Table 1, these questions are listed along with the proportion of the sample answering 'yes' (ie, 'deprived') and their correlation with income. They have to be seen not as markers indelibly stamping the respondent as 'poor' if he/she says 'yes', but as evidence that a 'yes' answer is more likely to be associated with a poor family than not. But it is not just the odd individual answer that matters. It is the clustering of several similar answers along with their common pattern of negative correlation with income that is an additional strength of the evidence. Together they improve the odds that a family scoring high (yes=1, no=0) on the index will be poor.

Table 1: *Townsend's deprivation index*

Characteristic	% of population	Correlation coefficient (Pearson) (net disposable household income last year)
1 Has not had a week's holiday away from home in last 12 months	53.6	0.1892
2 *Adults only*. Has not had a relative or friend to the home for a meal or snack in the last 4 weeks	33.4	0.0493
3 *Adults only*. Has not been out in the last 4 weeks to a relative or friend for a meal or snack	45.1	0.0515
4 *Children only* (under 15). Has not had a friend to play or to tea in the last 4 weeks	36.3	0.0643
5 *Children only*. Did not have party on last birthday	56.6	0.0660
6 Has not had an afternoon or evening out for entertainment in the last two weeks	47.0	0.1088
7 Does not have fresh meat (including meals out) as many as four days a week	19.3	0.1821
8 Has gone through one or more days in the past fortnight without a cooked meal	7.0	0.0684
9 Has not had a cooked breakfast most days of the week	67.3	0.0559
10 Household does not have a refrigerator	45.1	0.2419
11 Household does not usually have a Sunday joint (3 in 4 times)	25.9	0.1734
12 Household does not have sole use of four amenities indoors (flush wc; sink or washbasin and cold-water tap; fixed bath or shower; and gas or electric cooker)	21.4	0.1671

Source: Townsend, *Poverty in the United Kingdom*, p.250.
NB: The correlation coefficient measures the strength of the relation between income and the characteristic. The closer to 1 the stronger the relationship, the closer to 0 the weaker.

9

Thus, for each household, Townsend obtained a deprivation index by adding up the number of 'yes' answers. Two of the twelve questions relate to households where there are children and two are particularly relevant for adults. A household with adults and children could score as high as 12 on the index if it answered 'yes' to all the twelve questions, and for a household without children, the score could be 10. Obviously, therefore, household composition would determine the score as would other characteristics such as income, education, health, wealth, etc.

Townsend looked at the relation between the deprivation index for a household and its net income for each of fourteen different household types — two person households, four person households, single old age person, etc. It was after looking at these different patterns that he proposed a way of combining household type information with income information. This was to compute the SB entitlement for each household and look at its income as a proportion of its SB entitlement. All the households falling within a certain range, say 0-60%/SB level, were put together and their deprivation index was summarised by their *modal* value, ie, the value at which there was the highest number of households within that income range. For twelve income/SB proportions, twelve modal values of deprivation index were obtained. Thus, any one modal value could be summarising the experience of households of different types with different levels of net income but a common value of the proportion of income to SB level. (The modal values as well as the mean values of the deprivation index and the standard deviation of the index within each income/SB range are given in Table 2.)

Townsend then plotted these twelve modal values against the (logarithm of) income/SB level. The graph was 'included tentatively' and the index suffered from 'relative coarseness'.[6] But despite these qualifications, the graph fell conveniently into two lines, one for the five lowest income/SB levels and the other for the seven higher points. From this graph, Townsend concluded: 'As income diminishes from the highest levels, so deprivation steadily increases, but below the 150% of the supplementary benefit standard, deprivation begins to increase significantly. Above and below this point the graph falls into distinct sections.'[7]

Piachaud's criticisms

(a)   Tastes
There are a number of criticisms levelled by Piachaud against Townsend. The first concerns the status of the questions which go to make up the index. Is this a reasonable or an arbitrary set of questions? If a household (in 1968-9, we must remember) answered

10

Table 2: Townsend's deprivation index: some measures

Net disposable income last year as % of SB scales plus housing cost	y	Score on deprivation index									Total	Number	Mean	Mode	Standard deviation
		0	1	2	3	4	5	6	7	8					
600 or more	7	15	26	23	15	7	4	6	4	0	100	81	2.29	1	1.9226
400-599	5	5	25	35	16	13	4	1	2	0	100	101	2.35	2	1.9462
300-99	3.5	6	21	24	20	16	9	2	1	0	100	337	2.57	2	1.9423
250-99	2.75	7	19	22	22	14	8	5	1	0	100	517	2.62	2.5	2.0988
200-49	2.25	5	15	22	22	19	11	4	2	0	100	874	2.99	2.5	2.1702
180-99	1.90	3	17	18	19	17	15	6	3	2	100	506	3.29	3	1.7765
160-79	1.70	5	17	19	21	16	11	5	4	2	100	567	3.16	3	1.7845
140-59	1.50	1	8	16	18	17	16	12	8	3	100	523	3.94	3	1.8777
120-39	1.30	3	7	18	20	18	11	12	8	3	100	611	3.82	3	1.4098
100-19	1.10	0	3	10	14	19	15	17	12	9	100	420	4.74	4	1.5444
80-99	0.90	0	5	10	11	14	15	16	16	12	100	236	4.93	6.5	1.6479
Under 80	0.70	0	1	11	6	10	12	21	11	26	100	80	5.52	8	1.5099
		4	13	19	19	17	12	8	5	3	100	4,853	3.52		

Source: Townsend, *Poverty in the United Kingdom*, Table A.11, p.1001. Additional computations done by Dilia Montes of LSE.

11

'no' to the question 'Have you had a cooked breakfast most days of the week?', should this be taken as a sign of deprivation or just a sign that it did not like cooked breakfasts? Why should the fact that a household 'Has not had an afternoon or evening out for entertainment in the last two weeks' constitute deprivation rather than its habits, which may be stay-at-home? What in effect do the questions purport to measure?

My own response to this last question is that Townsend is trying to measure the community's *consumption practice* or living style. Going out for entertainment, having a Sunday roast, fresh meat with high frequency during a week, inviting friends or relatives for a meal or snack, all such events are what everyday life consisted of in the UK community in the late 1960s. If you consider day-to-day life as marked by these events — meals, going out, holidays, entertaining — then you need to define the typical or normal practice and locate people who, *for one reason or another*, are below the norm. Thus, having fresh meat four times a week would have been the norm and the first job is to find out those who do not have meat that often. The reason for their being below the norm may be either that they don't like meat that much (could be vegetarians) or that they cannot afford it.

Now Townsend did not use any method for separating out those who could afford but did not want from those who could not afford but did want. He relied on the overall negative correlation between the responses and income level as sufficient evidence for concluding (quite rightly) that, on average, given the large sample, it was reasonable to ignore the 'could afford but did not want' category. The correlations for all the twelve questions are quite highly significant and this gives him adequate support. It does not mean that if one took a particular household, you may not find that its high index was a result of peculiar tastes, but it is unlikely to be true in any significant number of cases.

There is, however, one qualification. For three out of the twelve questions, more than half of the sample could be classified as having not had the experience. When trying to capture typical or normal community behaviour, care should be taken to include only those questions for which the majority would be likely to be classified as non-deprived. Thus, even in 1968-9, 67.3% of the population did not have a cooked breakfast most of the week. While the answers were significantly negatively correlated with income, the correlation coefficient is quite low, 0.0559. This means that only a very small proportion (equal to the square of 0.0559 or about 0.004%) of the variation in breakfast habits was explained by income.

One way to get around this problem would be to give different questions different weights in the overall index. Thus, something that was enjoyed by 93% (cooked meat most days) should be given a higher weight (say 0.93) than something enjoyed by only 32.7% (cooked breakfast) which should get a weight of 0.327, ie, equal to the proportion in the community enjoying that experience.

Yet another qualification has to be made about these questions. They should relate to events which are universally enjoyed in the community. If certain groups (eg, old age pensioners) are likely to be precluded for reasons other than lack of income, then the index will distort. Thus single persons, old people and childless households, as well as the household type commonly thought to be typical — married couple with children — should be equally capable of and likely to enjoy the event contained in the question.

(b) *Variability*

The next serious objection Piachaud made has to do with the effect of averaging across all households within a certain range and then using the modal value or the mean as a summary statistic. How serious is this problem? We see that for the upper income ranges, the standard deviation is a much greater proportion of mean score than for the lower income ranges. This variation may be due to family size.

Any process of averaging means that variation around the average is being ignored. Townsend used the modal value, ie, the value recorded by most people within an income group. But there would be households below the modal value and some above. One way to allow for such variability is to compute a summary indicator capturing it. The standard deviation is one such indicator of dispersion around the average value. The larger the standard deviation relative to the mean, the more dispersion there is in the data and the less representative the mean of the underlying information.

In Table 2, the mode and the mean deprivation score as well as the standard deviation are displayed for each of the twelve bands of income characteristics; it is clear that there is much less variation among the scores of the low income families than for the rest. To be able to go without hot meals may be a 'luxury' the rich man can afford to indulge in or not as his taste permits — the poor have less freedom to manoeuvre in such matters. But we must take into account this variation in inquiring about the threshold.

Is there a threshold?

The central issue is about the existence of a threshold level of income, a demarcation level, below which one could say that families are most likely to be poor and above which it is less likely. Piachaud denies the existence of such a threshold and finds many faults with Townsend's procedure. While Townsend's method was

13

quite rough and ready, it turns out that doing regression analysis on Townsend's data confirms his conclusions.

The idea of regression analysis is to check if all the pairs of points on a graph (in this case value of deprivation score and the corresponding income levels) form a pattern, around a straight line or a curve. Could we say that they form a common pattern or two separate patterns? If they form two separate patterns, then we can locate the feature that separates them. They may separate due to the level of income. If so, we can locate the level of income — the threshold — which separates those above and those below in terms of the relation between the deprivation level and income.

A question before we locate separating patterns is to ask what sort of pattern is it? Is the relation between deprivation and income a straight line, indicating a fall in deprivation of so many points for each extra £100? Is it a curve, indicating a faster or a slower change in deprivation as income grows? It turns out that the best overall pattern is a curved line on the graph. Deprivation varies with the reciprocal of income. The lower the income, the higher is its reciprocal and the higher too is deprivation. (Income is defined throughout this discussion as income relative to SB entitlement.[8])

The reciprocal pattern between deprivation and income turns out to be different for the five lowest income levels from that for the seven higher income levels. For the lower levels, it is much steeper, ie, reduction in income increases deprivation sharply. For the higher income levels, extra income registers only a minor drop in what is already a low deprivation level. The two separate patterns explain the data better than a single pattern. There is thus a break in the relation between the mean (average) deprivation score and income and the break occurs at the value Townsend located — above 150% of SB level (details are in the paper mentioned in footnote 8).

There is a further check that we can carry out. The mean score is, after all, a single number to capture the whole distribution and much information is lost. We incorporate, therefore, the variation around the mean within each income level. If the diversity in the scores was due to tastes and not income, then using the mean may overstate the strength of the relationship. So I divided the mean score by the standard deviation within each income level. If the dispersion around the mean was truly random across each income level — ie, if tastes determined whether households scored low or high on the index — then the mean score divided by the standard deviation should be uniform across incomes. The strength of the relationship of the deprivation score with income should be weakened, if not totally obliterated, by this procedure if Piachaud was correct.

The results confirmed the existence of a relationship of deprivation index with income. They also confirmed the existence of a

14

threshold 150% of SB level. Thus the variability in the deprivation scores strengthens the threshold relationship. This is because, as we saw before, the standard deviation falls with income just as the mean rises. The coefficient of variation — the ratio of the standard deviation to the mean — falls with income. There is not much scope for the poor to indulge in diversity of consumption patterns, at least within the context of the questions asked.

Thus, we have reasonably strong evidence that for income above 140-160% of SB level, the relationship between deprivation and income is different from that for incomes at that level and below. The conclusion, then, is that despite the diversity in styles of living and the qualitative flavour of the questions used to compute the deprivation index, Townsend's conjecture about the existence of a threshold level of income, below which deprivation is more severely felt, is confirmed.

The LWT poverty study

The above exercise with Townsend's deprivation score based on twelve questions was originally carried out in September 1981, soon after Piachaud's critique appeared. The Townsend/Piachaud debate, as well as this exercise, influenced to some extent the next large investigation of poverty in the UK — conducted for London Weekend Television.' The LWT team commissioned MORI to conduct a survey on poverty. In all, 1,174 people aged 18 and over were interviewed in February 1983. The LWT survey asked questions about thirty-five indicators of styles of living (rather than sixty, as Townsend did), but care was taken to refine the questions to take into account some of the earlier objections. Thus it tried 'to see whether a degree of social consensus exists about what constitutes a minimum standard in Britain today'. The researchers let the respondents, ie, the *community*, decide which of their list of thirty-five items 'are necessary and which all adults/families should be able to afford and which they should not have to do without'. Thus, only necessary items could be included in the deprivation index. A majority of the respondents agreed that twenty-six of the items were necessities (see Table 3); more than two-thirds agreed that seventeen were necessities. Thus, it is possible, not to say desirable, to ask the community to choose which items are necessary and which are not.

Some of the LWT questions cover housing conditions (damp-free home, garden, indoor heating), environment (public transport), furniture as well as food and social activities. It is also striking how, except for the requirement of '3 meals a day for children', it is housing rather than food which ranks high in the community's definition of necessities. The notion of poverty for the community

15

Table 3: *Living standards in Britain* (%)

	Proportion describing items as necessities	Proportion lacking the item	Proportion lacking item as can't afford it
Heating to warm living areas of the home if it is cold	97	6	6
Indoor toilet (not shared with another household)	96	1	1
Damp-free home	96	10	8
Bath (not shared with another household)	94	2	2
Beds for everyone in the household	94	2	1
Public transport for one's needs	88	9	3
A warm water-proof coat	87	10	7
3 meals a day for children*	82	7	4
Self-contained accommodation	79	6	3
2 pairs of all weather shoes	78	15	11
Enough bedrooms for every child over 10 of different sex to have his/her own bedroom*	77	17	10
Refrigerator	77	2	1
Toys for children*	71	5	3
Carpets in living rooms and bedrooms	70	3	2
Celebrations on special occasions such as Christmas	69	6	4
A roast joint or its equivalent once a week	67	12	7
A washing machine	67	9	5
New, not second-hand, clothes	64	13	8
A hobby or leisure activity	64	21	9
2 hot meals a day (for adults)	64	18	4
Meat or fish every other day	63	17	9
Presents for friends or family (once a year)	63	8	5
Holiday away from home for one week a year, not with relatives	63	30	23
Leisure equipment for children, eg, sports equipment or a bicycle*	57	17	13
A garden	55	10	5
A television	51	1	—
A 'best outfit' for special occasions	48	20	13
A telephone	43	17	11
An outing for children once a week*	40	38	25
A dressing gown	38	14	3
Children's friends round for tea/snack once a fortnight*	37	34	15
A night out once a fortnight (for adults)	36	41	18
Friends/family round for a meal once a month	32	32	13
A car	22	37	24
A packet of cigarettes every other day	14	58	6

*For families with children only.
Source: Mack and Lansley, *Poor Britain*

is thus one of relative not absolute deprivation. Rowntree would hardly have considered any of the seventeen items with two-thirds vote as necessities.

The LWT study also distinguishes those things the family did not want from those the family could not afford. This is clearly a tricky distinction and answers may not always reflect true lack of income, since the deprived may learn to live with their deprivation. But at least those who said they cannot afford an item obviously would like it if they could afford it. The LWT team carried out a test of the correlation between 'don't have'/'want to have' response and income for each item and a parallel one for 'don't have'/'don't want' and income. For the first group, thirty-one out of thirty-five items showed a significant negative correlation with income, confirming that it was those with low income who didn't have an item because they could not afford it. For the second group, only eight items were significantly negatively correlated with income, thus showing much greater randomness in the 'taste' for certain items across income.

Thus, the issue of taste in measurement of poverty is dealt with better in the LWT survey. It is neither the standards and preferences of the interviewer nor of the particular respondent which define deprivation. It is the community which chooses which items to rank as necessities and which not. Even when people indicate they do not have an item, care is taken to ask further whether it is lack of resources or lack of desire for the item that is the root cause. But even within the thirty-five items, there are many which only a small proportion of people described as necessities. Avoiding these minority items, the LWT team made an index out of fourteen items, each of which 55% or more of the sample described as necessities (see Table 4).

The LWT data were grouped in twelve income classes similar to the Townsend data. For each level, mean deprivation score and the standard deviation were calculated. Once again, regression analysis indicates that the best pattern was the curvilinear one between deprivation and the reciprocal of income. In experimenting whether there were two separate groups of incomes, three alternatives were tried so as not to prejudge the threshold level. The bottom four and top eight groups, the bottom five and top seven, and the bottom and top six were three groupings tried and a test was carried out as to which separation was the sharpest.

It turned out that the bottom four formed a separate group from the top eight. The mean deprivation score of the bottom four was 2.025 and of the upper eight 0.3626. Thus the bottom four were four and a half times more deprived than the top eight groups. The overall mean was 0.9167. There is no doubt that this separation is statistically valid. Dividing the mean by the standard deviation

17

once again confirmed the results. The break in the LWT data occurs at 133% of SB level for a couple at current rates.

Table 4: *An index of deprivation (%)*

	Proportion describing items as 'necessary'	Proportion lacking these items	Proportion lacking as can't afford them
heating to warm living areas	97	6	6
public transport for one's needs	88	9	3
a warm waterproof coat	87	10	7
3 meals a day for children*	82	7	4
2 pairs of all-weather shoes	78	15	11
toys for children*	71	5	3
celebrations on special occasions like Christmas	69	6	4
roast/joint equivalent once a week	67	12	7
new, not second-hand, clothes	64	13	8
hobby or leisure activity	64	21	9
meat or fish every other day	63	17	9
presents for friends/family once a year	63	8	5
holidays away from home for one week a year	63	30	23
leisure equipment for children (bicycles, etc)*	57	17	13

*relevant for children only
Source: S Weir and S Lansley, 'Towards a popular view of poverty', *New Society*, 25 August 1983

Beyond the threshold: from analysis to policy priorities

A threshold level for poverty has thus been identified from two exercises — one with data for 1968/9 and the other for 1983. Allowing for objections about tastes, about variations within income classes, linear or non-linear relations, we confirm the existence of a threshold. The similarity of the gap between the threshold and the SB level in the two studies is also remarkable. An increase in SB level of between a third and a half is obviously needed — needed in the way need is defined by the citizens of Britain, by the community.

What would it mean to be below the threshold? In Table 4, we have the fourteen items which were in the LWT deprivation index and in the last column we have the percentage of people who could not afford these items. Of course, as the money falls short, different households might do without different items. This would be a matter of taste, of individual household circumstances, etc. But there is a way to the people's priorities from the sample responses. It can be assumed that any household would be extremely unwilling to admit that they go without something because they could not afford it. Thus, the smaller the percentage

18

in the last column, it is more likely that such an item has a high priority. Though not a fail-safe rule, this is a plausible hypothesis.

Looking at the table with this criterion in mind, we see the following hierarchy. The highest priority is toys for children, followed by three meals a day for children and celebrations (4%). The least urgent are holidays (23%), leisure equipment for children (13%) and two pairs of all-weather shoes (11%). Other deprivations are being cold (no heating in home, no warm waterproof coats), eating food you'd rather not (no roast/joint weekly, meat/fish every other day), having old rather than new clothes, etc. These are very basic freedoms being denied to citizens.

But who will provide the extra money? The LWT survey also asked this question. The majority of the sample thought all benefits — pensions, unemployment benefit, child benefit, as well as SB — were too low. What is more, '74 per cent are willing to pay an extra 1p in income tax to enable others to enjoy these necessities'.[10] What more need one say?

Notes and references

1   P Townsend, *Poverty in the United Kingdom: a survey of household resources and standards of living*, Penguin Books, 1979.
2   J Mack and S Lansley, *Poor Britain*, George Allen and Unwin, 1985.
3   As note 1 above.
4   As note 1 above, p 31.
5   D Piachaud, 'Peter Townsend and the Holy Grail', *New Society*, 10 September 1981.
6   As note 1 above, pp 261-2.
7   As note 1 above, p 261.
8   The details of this reciprocal relation are as follows. Full details of this analysis are contained in a paper by the author, 'Is Poverty a Matter of Taste? An econometric comment on the Townsend-Piachaud debate', available on request.

Income : deprivation equations
In each case the first equation is with the mean deprivation score (d) as the dependent variable and in the second equation, it is the mean dividend by the standard deviation (D) which is the dependent variable. R^2 gives the proportion of total variation in the data explained by the equation. The closer to 1 the R^2 is, the better the fit. Numbers in parenthesis are standard errors of the estimates. Roughly the smaller these are relative to the numbers below which they appear, the more confidence do we have in the strength of the relationship.

All twelve observations

$$d = 1.8104 + 2.7562 \,[100/y] \qquad \bar{R}^2 = 0.9609$$
$$\quad\;\; (0.12) \quad\;\; (0.17)$$

$$D = 0.9011 + 1.8028 \,[100/y] \qquad \bar{R}^2 = 0.8212$$
$$\quad\;\; (0.18) \quad\;\; (0.25)$$

Top seven income observations

$$d = 1.9128 + 2.3048 \,[100/y] \qquad \bar{R}^2 = 0.9213$$
$$\quad\;\; (0.11) \quad\;\; (0.27)$$

$$D = 0.7535 + 1.9854 \,[100/y] \qquad \bar{R}^2 = 0.6671$$
$$\quad\;\; (0.21) \quad\;\; (0.55)$$

19

Bottom five income observations
d = 2.4090 + 2.2323 [100/y] $\bar{R}^2$ = 0.8717
    (0.43)   (0.42)
D = 2.0188 + 0.7744 [100/y] $\bar{R}^2$ = 0.2604
    (0.51)   (0.50)

9   As note 2 above.
10 S Weir and S Lansley, 'Towards a popular view of poverty', *New Society*, 25 August 1983.

Story-telling and formalism in economics: the instance of famine

Meghnad Desai

Introduction

Economics as a discipline has been concerned
with issues of scarcity and allocation, of economic growth and the limits placed upon it and
of the capacity of an economy to achieve a
level of output consonant with the absence of
involuntary unemployment. Such might be the
very terse way in which one could encapsulate
the concerns of neo-classical, classical and Keynesian economics. These
three schools straddle what
one may call mainstream
economics, but they do not
exhaust economics. There
are various schools and
movements in economics
which exist at the periphery.
Sometimes they constitute
what Keynes called under-
ground economics – the
economics of cranks and
prophets, of the advocates
of a single panacea for all
ills – Silvio Gessell, Henry
George, Major Douglas,
Ezra Pound, Rudolf Steiner. There are others,
factions and tendencies which claim to speak
the language of technical economics, but with
different accents. The Marxists and the Austri-
ans are two such tendencies; others are the
political economy of James Buchanan, newly
respectable since his Nobel Prize, the neo-
Ricardian disciples of Sraffa merging into the
post-Keynesians; the institutionalists now
almost decimated and the German Historical

Meghnad Desai is professor at the Lon-
don School of Economics and Political
Science, Houghton Street, Aldwych,
London WC2 2AE, United Kingdom.
He has published on the economics of
famine and poverty.

School which has disappeared. Economics is at
once a narrow, single-paradigm subject and a
moving feast. As each generation of academic
practitioners attempts to put up barriers to entry
and introduce stringent criteria for admission to
the profession, popular concern with economics
especially among the practically minded creates
an open market for anyone with a cure for the
many economic ills that face us.

Thus, on questions such as inflation and
unemployment, poverty and hunger, the politician and the 'man in the
street' *know* the answer
must be simple and have
little patience as the professional economist demurs.
When now and then some-
one with a sound pro-
fessional reputation offers a
nostrum that appeals to all –
the Phillips curve, as a tool
for choosing inflation and
unemployment optimally,
the monetarist admonition to
set money supply growth at
x per cent, the Laffer curve
– their professional col-
leagues proceed to question and dissect the
argument pretty thoroughly. It is only when the
arguments work at the level of the profession
that economists grant the particular nostrum
their approval.

A recently advanced view of economists'
activity sees it as practising rhetoric.[1] In this
view, economists tell stories and the simpler,
more plausible the story, the better is it likely
to be accepted. The process is multilayered.

When economists tell stories to each other, these are detailed, full of technical arguments, sometimes of econometric evidence. When they address the public at large they simplify, appeal to intuition. But the simple story told to the politician must connect with the detailed story told to colleagues, otherwise the profession will shun the person. He (or very infrequently, she) may become the King's friend but will always feel defensive when entering the seminar room.

The problem is that the underground economists – the single-cure peddlers like Henry George, the eccentrics like Major Douglas or Silvio Gessell, the prophets like Rudolf Steiner, address only the larger public. They tell only the simple, abridged story. No matter how noble and appealing the story may be, the professional economist is always eager for details – the blueprint maps and the drainage charts behind the pretty façade. If these are lacking (and they almost always are), there is no hope of entering the keep of economics.

Keynes acknowledged the necessity of this multilayer communication when he began the preface to the *General Theory* by stating that the book was addressed to his fellow economists.[2] He had advocated his fiscal policy in the public domain to Roosevelt, with some success, but to his own government with none (Keynes, 1933, 'For Advocacy'). But the technical argument still had to be made in order for him to carry the profession with him and win lasting influence.

But even Keynes's influence, though lasting, has suffered in recent years, because the internal dynamics of the professional discipline is perpetually sharpening the theoretical tools, learning new mathematical languages, discovering new data sources. A story that has convinced one generation is re-examined by the next. In the course of re-examination it is amended, pruned and sometimes expurgated.

One story has been common through the 200 years of economics: the 'invisible hand' story of Adam Smith. The core of the theory is that individuals left to their own devices and free to pursue selfish gain with minimal interference from the state (or any supra-individual collectivity or coalition), will achieve a state of affairs such that cannot be improved upon except by making someone better off at the expense of others. Put formally, it is the theory that individuals and firms optimizing their respective objective functions (utility, profits), taking prices as given and beyond their influence will so act in buying and selling goods and services that the markets for all will be cleared. There will be no unsatisfied demand (backed by purchasing power) or excess supply (in the absence of rigidities in prices). Every action – purchase or sale in their absence – will match the desire of the individual. There will in particular be no involuntary unemployment. The competitive equilibrium is characterized by full employment of all rseources and is Pareto optimal in the sense that no one can be made better off (achieve higher utility or profits) except by making someone worse off involuntarily.

The invisible hand story told by Adam Smith was refined and restated without the rich historical frills by David Ricardo. Ricardo especially won the argument with Malthus who entertained the theoretical probability of a general glut. It was restated, but with a different value theory, by Léon Walras in 1874, who used formal mathematics. His argument appealed but his formal proof was inadequate. The story was told more formally in a new mathematical language by the mathematicians Abraham Wald and John von Neumann.[3] It was refined and restated in a pedagogically convenient way by Kenneth Arrow and Gerard Debreu in the early 1950s.

The simple Adam Smith story assumes a minimal state. The story in its simplest form has been adopted by advocates of a free market philosophy. Sometimes these advocates have not at all been enamoured of or convinced by the formal proofs. indeed some, like Hayek, think that the formal story completely misses the point of the way in which the market establishes a continuing equilibrium of supply and demand. They emphasize the decentralized nature of the process, the fragmented nature of the information available to any participant, and the spontaneous co-ordination performed by the price mechanism. It is possible to champion the free market without embracing the formal proof in its entirety.

On the other hand it is possible to tell the story formally, but not accept it as an infallible guide to social action. To many economists, general equilibrium is a method, an example of the holistic approach, but the details are 'such

The instance of famine in India: near Calcutta, Bengal, 1971. R. Depardon/Magnum.

stuff as dreams are made of'. They point to the many plausible grounds on which the 'real world' (itself a figment of the economist's imagination) departs from it. Thus market failures abound, equilibria fail to exist, or can be unique if they exist, or be unstable if they are unique. Kenneth Arrow is a good example of someone who has done the most in recent years to place the invisible hand story on a sound formal footing, but at the same time has pioneered a number of fruitful areas of investigation where market failures alert us to the limitations of the free market principle as a guide to action.[4]

Marx in the nineteenth century and Keynes in the present one are two major economists who sought to challenge the invisible hand theory in a fundamental way. Marx's argument is complicated and he never fully finished its statement in formal terms that economists could scrutinize. He also used the method of immanent criticism which continues to perplex us today, a method that made him adopt Ricardo's system completely before trying to destroy it from within. Thus many parts of Marx's theory read very much like the Smith–Ricardo classical political economy. These parts are also the more formally worked out ones, if not by Marx himself, then by economists who took up his battles. The critique of political economy, the vastly ambitious part of his work, remains a jigsaw puzzle with many missing pieces. Here the argument is tantalizing but elusive; as the prose sweeps one away the reader hankers after something he can cling to. The formal elements of Marx's theory – the transformation problem, the reproduction scheme – have, like classical theory, been cast in the various mathematical languages by successive generations (Morishima, 1973; Roemer, 1980. For an earlier generation von Bortkiewicz (1907, 1948).) The other parts have been the subject of endless debates: those economists who hanker after a semblance of formal clarity are beginning to make attempts to recast the jigsaw puzzle into a manageable alternative (Roemer, 1986).

Keynes, for a while, succeeded much better: he spoke the formal language and addressed his fellow economists. He questioned the proposition that the market left to its own devices unaided by a guiding hand can arrive at an equilibrium of full employment. He especially doubted that, once dislodged from such an equi-

librium as a result of some exogenous shock (e.g. war), it can return automatically and in a reasonably short time to a full employment equilibrium. It was not that an equilibrium did not exist, but that it may be neither unique (i.e. there could be a less than full employment equilibrium as well as a full employment one) nor globally stable (i.e. if dislodged from the equilibrium the economy would automatically return to it).

Technical issues aside, Keynes challenged the notion of scarcity. He showed that some individuals could be involuntarily unemployed, i.e. face want due to lack of income, despite a willingness to work while employers had idle productive capacity. Thus the poverty of the unemployed was not due to lack of resources to employ them, as for example may be the case in a developing country or in times of post-war reconstruction. There was unemployment in face of excess capacity. The price system, far from dealing with scarcity by making full utilization possible, was leaving some resources idle and others underutilized. The fact that prices could be positive in face of excess supply of labour and of capital services means that scarcity is not the reason for prices being positive. Such an argument is utter anathema formally as well as substantively to the 200-year old discipline of economics.

The battle concerning the adequacy of Keynes's story, regarding its detailed formal proof, was not joined till after the Walras story had been neatly packaged and delivered by Gerard Debreu in his *Theory of Value* (1960). Until then an uneasy compromise had existed. The theory of competitive markets was taught in microeconomics – in individual markets – but the Keynesian theory was taught in macroeconomics – at the level of the whole economy. There were a number of doubters as to the adequacy of Keynes's story, but they objected to the social message of governmental guidance to achieve full employment more powerfully than they could point to flaws in the formal argument. The major exception to this was Patimkin's *Money, Interest and Prices* which did not so much question Keynes's own proof but gave an alternative route by which the full employment equilibrium could be re-established (Patimkin, 1955, 1964).

The battle over Keynes's story reopened in

The instance of famine in Africa: Ethiopia, Tigrè province, 1985. S. Salgado Jr./Magnum.

the early 1960s with an attack on the adequacy of Patimkin's proof (Hahn, 1964). But it was also seen that for Keynes's argument to carry through at the general equilibrium level, a separation had to be made between voluntary plans and constrained outcomes, between demands and purchase, supply and sale (Clower, 1965). It was soon clear that, if the Walras story was formally correct, the Keynes story was incomplete, either because they were substantively about different worlds (e.g. with money, uncertainty and time present in one, but not in the other) or because Keynes's story was logically faulty.

The 1970s saw the initiative very much in the anti-Keynesian camp. While the early detractors of Keynes – Hayek, Haberler, Viner – had posed doubts but no counterproofs, the current generation of new classical economists – Lucas, Barro, Sargent – purported to give formal arguments as to why Keynes's story was

logically incomplete. The polemical argument had been started by Friedman, but the formal *coup de grace* had to be delivered by Lucas. At present, the battle see-saws with Keynesians pointing to the descriptive irrelevance of new classical economcis, and the new classicals claiming rigour to be on their side. Keynes's story can be rescued by pruning, some would say bowdlerizing it. This is done in the literature on fixed price equilibria (Malinvaud, 1976). The full story threatens to become like Marx's, a jigsaw puzzle with missing pieces unless a counterargument to the new classical story emerges soon.

The entitlement approach to famine

This introduction has been provided because recent theorizing on the economics of famine

The instance of famine in France: distribution of bread in 1662, in front of the Tuileries Palace, Paris. Roger Viollet.

has similarly questioned the notion of scarcity. The seminal work in this respect is Amartya Sen's *Poverty and Famine* (*PF* hereafter, Sen, 1981). A famine would, after all, be thought of as a classic example of pervasive scarcity serious enough to cause death. Sen's main message is that famines can occur (and have historically occurred) without there necessarily being a shortage of food. Thus, just as involuntary unemployment can occur in the face of excess capacity and unsold commodity surpluses, famines and 'unnatural' deaths can occur in face of available food stocks. Sen's theory has led to arguments within economics precisely along the lines that such a phenomenon cannot occur systematically as long as the markets are left free to adjust and reach equilibrium. Thus it has been argued that, in the absence of market failure due to the violation of one or other assumption underlying competitive market equilibrium, Sen's argument must be either logically incomplete or trivial (Srinivasan, 1983).

PF was preceded four years earlier by Sen's study of the Great Bengal Famine of 1943 (Sen, 1977), in which he carefully examined the question of food availability during this famine in which 3 million people died. He shows that in terms of the total physical availability of food grains, 1943 was a normal or even better-than-normal year. Starvation occurred not because there was not enough food overall, but because a number of socio-economic groups could not obtain as much food as they previously could, and that they were entitled to. Their food entitlements shrank (a) partly due to the sudden rise in food price when the military authorities in Calcutta requisitioned grain for the army and civilians engaged in war-related work; (b) partly because there were no markets for what they had to sell since food absorbed the bulk of the budget of most consumers; and (c) because they were unable to produce as much as they normally did. But it was typically those in the rural areas far from the primary food producing activity who suffered most. People in rural non-food agricultural production (jute growing), non-agricultural food production (fisheries) and non-food, non-agricultural production (village blacksmiths, barbers) experienced a greater incidence of starvation than agricultural labourers who worked in food production. Thus, while in 'normal times' the agricultural labourer had a smaller food entitlement (because of lower income) than the non-agricultural producers (say, fishermen), the labourer's food entitlement was safer than the fishermen's when food prices rose. All those who were engaged, in one way or another, in food production activities which yielded them direct income in food were insulated against the price rise. All those who had to buy food suffered an entitlement loss whatever they had to offer in exchange.

Entitlements in Sen's view are mediated through a network of legal and property relations: 'market forces can be seen as operating *through* a system of legal relations (ownership rights, contractual obligations, legal exchanges, etc.). The law stands between food availability and food entitlement. Starvation deaths can reflect legality with a vengeance' (*PF*, p. 160). A private property system may permit certain entitlements which a socialist economy would not. Slave-owning societies permit some entitlements, while denying others (i.e. the slave's own entitlements) as compared to those where slavery is prohibited. In a private property economy, ownership entitlements crucially determine exchange entitlements. Other societies may have arrangements which disarticulate this intimate connection between ownership and exchange entitlements. But the legal context can also be changed as a result of political action. Thus a welfare state will grant certain minimum income entitlements merely on the basis of citizenship or residence. Such income entitlements are independent of ownership or any other endowment except birth in a certain community.

Sen, in *PF*, works out the definition of entitlements in the context of four famines. Besides the 1943 Great Bengal Famine, he covers the Bangladesh famine of 1974, the Ethiopian famine of 1972–4 and the Sahel drought and famine of 1969–74. In these communities he examines the entitlements of a number of socio-economic groups. Thus, in Ethiopia,

nomadic pastoralists, farm servants and dependants, tenant cultivators, small land-owning cultivators, urban daily male labourers, women in service occupations, weavers and other craftsmen and occupational beggars are the eight groups listed (*PF*, p. 100). The point is that droughts or a rise in foodgrain prices hit these groups unevenly, but do so systematically much more severely if the group is non-food producing. The pastoralists in Ethiopia suffered a loss in their entitlements due to (a) fewer and leaner cattle to sell due to drought (quantity effect); and (b) a higher relative price of grain to animal products (price effect) (see *PF*, Table 7.7, p. 108). Implicit in these two effects there is a general effect of shrinking markets for non-food products because of lower effective demand caused by high food prices.

In the Bengal famine, fishermen were the main non-agricultural rural group affected. They were prevented from fishing freely due to the seizure of their fishing vessels as a war-time precautionary measure but also because, for other reasons, their catch was small. But while rural non-food, non-agricultural groups suffer entitlement loss, urban groups are paradoxically always looked after much better. Governments have traditionally been more afraid of urban civilian unrest, especially in the capital, and have made provision for urban workers and similar groups. Grain storage facilities are also better in towns than in rural areas. Thus groups not directly growing food grain migrate to the towns. But they find that in towns the long-time resident groups, such as urban workers, have safer entitlements than the migrants. When entitlements collapse it is not enough for groups to migrate where they may be food. Spcial action is needed to restore entitlements.

This is typically the task of relief agencies. It is not sufficient, in the logic of Sen's model, merely to convey food to where there is famine. It is more improtant to give the people purchasing power to enable them to buy the food. Thus people want their food entitlements restored, not just 'enjoy' better food availability. It is now well established that the practical measures adopted in India during the nineteenth century which formed the Famine Code did precisely this. They started relief work to provide entitlement for people so they could buy the food grains specially brought into the area. Famine

Relief thus involves more than food supplies. Sen's theory does not, however, imply that food imports are irrelevant or unnecessary for famine relief. They are not sufficient, only necessary, but food availability decline is neither necessary nor sufficient to precipitate a famine (see Desai, 1984, 1987 for details on some of these points).

If one were then to examine the socio-economic phenomenon of famine, one could see it as a chain of interrelated system blocks. The food production system is pivotal since it feeds the producers engaged in it and everyone outside it by providing surplus to the food delivery system. The non-food production system, rural or urban, sells inputs and final goods to the food-production system and buys food from the food delivery system. The simultaneous interaction between these systems in normal times is depicted in Figure 1. (This and the subsequent figures are taken from Desai, 1987). The production systems are subject to the exogenous influence of the nature system which embodies

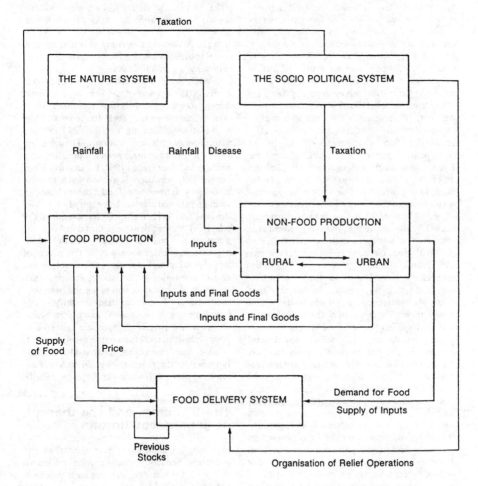

the ecology and weather variables. Both the food and the non-food systems are affected by it. The affecting variables may be rainfall – amount, timing, location – or livestock disease. Although land use and resource use patterns by the production systems affect the ecology in the long run, in the context of a famine, the nature system must be taken as given. The socio-political system – the state, the political system, the kinship structure – constitutes another by and large exogenous variable operating upon the production system as well as the food delivery system. The socio-political system extracts taxation from the economic system in return for certain benefits. But taxation can take a variety of forms, e.g. compulsory requisition in war conditions. A civil war constitutes a major exogenous shock emanating from the socio-political system onto the economic system. By challenging the established legal system, a civil war puts all entitlements at risk and makes exchange uncertain and sporadic. Of course, the economic system has a feedback effect upon the socio-political system. But again, in the time frame within which famines occur and relief can be organized, the socio-political system can be taken to be exogenous. This is not to say governments may not fall. Ethiopia is a prime example of the abdication of the previous government caused by the revolution whose effectiveness is attributed to famine conditions.

Within each of these economic systems one can identify groups of people, e.g. landlords, tenants, owner-cultivators, landless labourers in the food production system. In normal times there are transactions within the systems and across them. These are depicted in Figure 2a. I have simplified the non-food system to incorporate employers, the self-employed and employees. The normal flows of sales and purchases are delineated and the triangle of interaction between food production, food delivery and non-food production is the core of the economy. The socio-political and the nature systems act as exogenous blocks. During famines, the pattern is changed as can be seen from Figure 2b. There is little surplus for the food production system to deliver and it also ceases to buy from the non-food system. Anyone not paid directly in food becomes dependent on the socio-political system which now acts as a relief agency. It generates jobs and imports food to make it

possible for the non-food system groups and any deprived groups in the system to obtain food.

The contrast between Figure 2a and Figure 2b then summarizes the socio-economic roots of famine. Of course, the initial shock could come from the nature system or the socio-political system. The latter often fails to provide relief even after a famine has occurred and international relief measures become necessary, as was the case during the Civil War in Russia and has been more recently the case in the Sahel and Ethiopia. The capacity of a socio-economic system to cope with the tasks of relief is a complex issue about which we do not know enough. A comparative study of 'relief competence' is urgently needed, but it could also raise very sensitive political issues.

While Sen put forward the theory of entitlements in the context of famines, it is a much more general approach since it embeds economic relationships in a legal framework. Thus market transactions are not the only nor the natural set of economic relations. They are one among a variety of arrangements for allocating entitlements (see Desai, 1984, for details). Thus Louise Tilly has used Sen's approach to look at conflict surrounding food (bread) riots in seventeenth- and eighteenth-century France and Britain (Tilly 1971, 1985). She has examined the effects of 'adventitious' circumstances – wars, speculation, business cycles outside food-producing agriculture, as well as the effects of long-run structural changes – the development of capitalism, division of labour, and proletarianization of workers as well as the rise of centralized states – on entitlement shifts. The establishment of a national market in grain, an important part of Physiocratic laissez-faire policy, changed local food entitlements in eighteenth-century France drastically and led to many riots against the removal of grain from certain regions by traders (*entraves* as they were called).

The Sen story and the theory of general equilibrium

In posing an alternative view of scarcity and allocation, Sen has, of course, invited criticisms. It is said, for instance, that for such shocks to have any marked effects they must be unanticipated and short-lived. To the economist, used

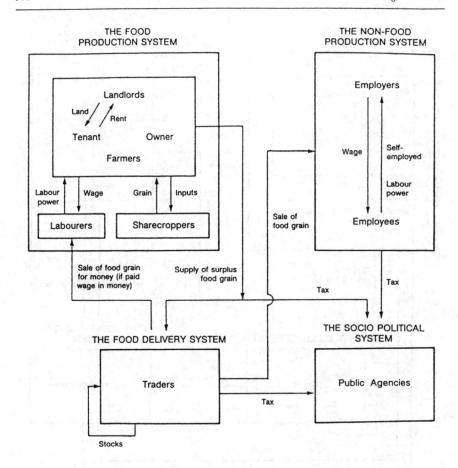

FIGURE 2a. The system under normal conditions.

to methodological individualism and Walrasian competitive theory, the idea of a persistent failure on the part of individuals to obtain what they want, is anathema. Just as no involuntary unemployment can be allowed in the pure model but must be supported by some departure from the assumptions of the model, so one must rule out involuntary hunger and starvation. Such phenomena, if observed, must be attributable to insufficient endowments or artificial barriers

to free movements of grain and labour put up by the state. An optimizing individual, in the face of anticipatable harvest failure, would make insurance arrangements – store grain, buy a plot of land where he could grow food, etc. Famines arising despite rational behaviour on the part of all economic agents is something that is hard for the economist to swallow.

Thus Sen told a story which is very appealing and has been a powerful stimulus to further

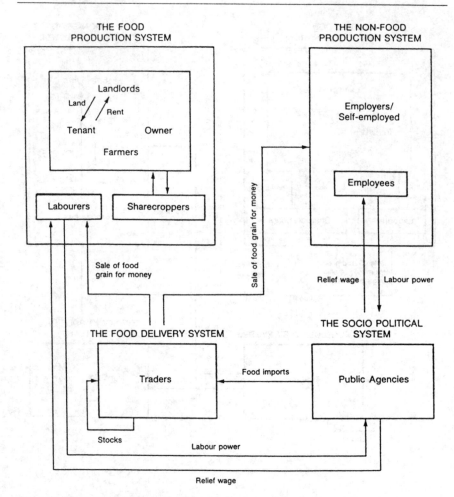

FIGURE 2b.   The system under famine conditions.

analyses of famines and hunger as socio-economic processes. His message is that famines are not natural, but socio-economic phenomena. His approach has been to spell out his story partly in formal terms, but much more in descriptive historical studies: the argument within the economics profession is about the detailed formal underpinning – the general equilibrium model underlying the attractive story. Those who have questioned the Sen story (e.g.

Srinivasan, 1983) are asking for detailed micro-foundations which obey the rules of Walrasian general equilibrium theory. In the pure Walrasian case, entitlements are assumed to be secure in a trade-independent way, i.e. the possibility of starvation death due to an inability to buy sufficient food in exchange for whatever one has to sell is ruled out (see Sen citation of Koopmans, 1957, *PF*, p. 172). The theorist does this to rule out awkward problems in the formal proof construction, just as the theory rules out the possibility of bankruptcy for firms. Such ruling out is not done with any idea that such things do not happen in the real world, but that they are either too unimportant to worry about (they happen rarely or in a negligible proportion of cases) or that they introduce complications which require further elaboration. Thus, for instance, if one were to introduce minimum subsistence for consumers as a necessary condition for equilibrium, discontinuities enter and make mathematical proofs difficult.

But what for general equilibrium theorists is an anomaly or a curiosity to be ruled out is the central problem to be investigated in famines, i.e. precisely the fact that minimum subsistence quantities are necessary for survival, but impossible to obtain for a sizeable number of people. The pure economic model of competitive equilibrium cannot handle this any more than it can handle the phenomenon of involuntary unemployment. To rule it out or to minimize its importance by labelling it as an anomaly does not make the problem go away. It may, however, influence policy adversely. We have recently witnessed governments in many OECD countries following the logic that employment is automatically determined by the private economy and not by government action. This is to say, in effect, that there is no involuntary unemployment. It would be equally likely that, in famine relief policies, an attitude could be taken that famines are merely temporary aberrations due to the obstruction of relative price movements by some natural or political factor. Following such logic, relief operations could be thought unnecessary, irrelevant or even counterproductive if they prevent the free movement of relative prices. Thus, while economists tell stories, these stories have real consequences. It is necessary to examine them not only for their appeal and elegance in underpinning detailed formal structure, but also for the real life policy choices they entail.

Conclusion

Sen has expanded the agenda for economic theory firstly by focusing attention on an urgent and long-neglected problem in modern economic life. He has also done this, not by reducing non-economic phenomena to an economic framework, but by stretching the economic framework to accommodate and respond to non-economic considerations (in a narrow technical definition). He has made us look at social relationships and legal frameworks as contexts within which production, trade, exchange and consumption are carried out. His approach has already been fruitful in studying famine, hunger and conflicts over food as the large literature attests (Tilly, 1985; Sen and Dreze, 1987). It can only be hoped that it will be extended to other examples, historical and contemporary, of conflicts over resource allocations.

Notes

1. McCloskey (1985). In what follows, the interpretation of the McCloskey thesis is entirely mine. I do not claim to be reporting his views in any detail.

2. 'This book is chiefly addressed to my fellow economists. I hope that it will be intelligible to others. But its main purpose is to deal with difficult questions of theory, and only in the second place with the applications of this theory to practice.' Preface to *The General Theory*, Keynes (1936) (1973), p. xxi.

3. See E. Roy Weintraub's fascinating account of this episode (Weintraub, 1983).

4. It is impossible to give a complete list of Arrow's contributions. His recently published collected works run to six volumes and he is still active. Of the many ideas he has contributed market failure due to asymmetric information, adverse selection, uncertainty, have each yielded a large literature. His proof of the impossibility of deriving a social welfare function which satisfies a minimal set of consistency conditions from individualist utility functions spawned the entire field of social choice. See Sen (1986).

References

ARROW, K.J.; INTRILLIGATOR, M.D., 1986. *Handbook of Mathematical Economics.* Vols. I–III. Amsterdam: North-Holland.

BORTKIEWICZ, L. von, 1948, 1967. 'Wertrechnung and Preisrechnung im Marxschen System'. *Archiv für Sozialwissenschaft und Sozialpolitik*, July 1906, July and September 1907.

CLOWER, R., 1965. The Keynesian Counterrevolution. In Hahn and Brechling, 1965.

DEBREU, G., 1960. *The Theory of Value.* New York: Wiley.

DESAI, M., 1984. A General Theory of Poverty. *Indian Economic Review.*

DESAI, M., 1987. The Economic Aspects of Famine. In B. Harrison (ed.), *Famines.* Oxford: Oxford University Press.

HAHN, F.H., 1964. On the Problems of Proving the Existence of Equilibrium in a Monetary Economy'. In Hahn and Brechling, 1965.

HAHN, F. H.; BRECHLING, F.P.R., 1965. *The Theory of Interest Rates.* London: Macmillan.

HARRISON, A.B., 1987. *Famines.* Oxford: Oxford University Press.

KAPLAN, S., 1976. 'Bread, Politics and Political Economy in the Reign of Louis XV'.

KAPLAN, S., 1977. Lean Years, Fat Years. The Community Granary System and the Search for Abundance in Eighteenth Century France. *French Historical Studies*, pp. 197–230.

KEYNES, J.M., 1933. The Means of Prosperity. In *Collected Writings of John Maynard Keynes.* Vol. IX, pp. 335–66.

KEYNES, J.M., 1936. *The General Theory of Employment, Interest and Money.* London: Macmillan.

KEYS, A.; BROZEK, J.; HENSCHEL, A.; MICKELSEN, O.; TAYLOR, L., 1950. *The Biology of Human Starvation.* Minneapolis.

KOOPMANS, T.C., 1957. *Three Essays on the State of the Economic Science.* New York: Wiley.

MCCLOSKEY, D.N., 1985. The Rhetoric of Economics. *Journal of Economic Literature*, June, Vol. XXI, No. 2, pp. 481–517.

MALINVAUD, E., 1976. *The Theory of Unemployment Reconsidered.* Oxford: Blackwell.

MENKEN, J.; TRUSSEL, J.; WATKINS, S., 1981. The Nutrition Fertility Link. *Journal of Inter-Disciplinary History*, pp. 425–41.

MORISHIMA, M., 1973. *Marx's Economics.* Cambridge: Cambridge University Press.

PATIMKIN, D., 1955, 1964. *Money, Interest and Prices.*

POST, J.D., 1976. Famine, Mortality and Epidemic Disease in the Process of Modernization. *EHR*, pp. 14–37.

ROEMER, J.E., 1980. A General Equilibrium Approach to Marxian Economics. *Econometrica*, March, Vol. 48, No. 2, pp. 505–30.

ROEMER, J.E., 1986. *Analytical Marxism.* Cambridge: Cambridge University Press.

ROTBERG, R.I.; RABB, T.K., 1985. (eds.), *Hunger and History: The Impact of Changing Food Production and Consumption Patterns on Society.* Cambridge: Cambridge University Press.

SEN, A., 1977. Starvation and Exchange Entitlement: A General Approach and its Application to the Great Bengal Famine. *Cambridge Journal of Economics*, Vol. 1, No. 1.

SEN, A.K., 1981. *Poverty and Famine: An Essay on Entitlement and Deprivation.* Oxford: Clarendon Press.

SEN, A.K., 1986. Social Chocie Theory. In Arrow and Intrilligator, op. cit., Vol. 3, pp. 1073–181.

SEN, A.K.; DREZE, J., 1987. Hunger and Poverty: The Poorest Billion. Proceedings of the Food Strategies Research Conference, Helsinki, forthcoming.

SRINIVASAN, T.N., 1981. Malnutrition: Some Measurement and Policy Issues. *Journal of Development Economics*, pp. 3–19.

SRINIVASAN, T.N., 1983. Review of Sen (1981) in the *American Journal of Agricultural Economics*, February.

TILLY, L.A., 1971. The Food Riot as a Form of Political Conflict in France. *Jl & H*, pp. 23–57.

TILLY, L.A., 1985. Food Entitlement, Famine and Conflict. In Rotberg and Rabb, op. cit., pp. 135–52.

WALTER, J.; WRIGHTSON, K., 1976. Dearth and Social Order in Early Modern England. *Past and Present.*

WEINTRAUB, E.R., 1983. On the Existence of a Competitive Equilibrium: 1930–1954. *Journal*

of Economic Literature, March, Vol. XXI, No. 1, pp. 1–39.

[8]

RICE AND FISH

Asymmetric Preferences and Entitlement Failures in Food Growing Economics with Non-Food Producers

Meghnad DESAI*

London School of Economics and Political Science, London WC2A 2HD, UK

An entitlement approach to understanding famines has been proposed by Amartya Sen. This paper seeks to provide two analytical 2×2 general equilibrium models which display sufficient conditions for famine situations to occur without invoking market failure. The conditions are that preferences as between the two goods be asymmetric and that there be complete specialisation in endowments/production. Under these conditions, prices fail to play an allocative function despite absence of market failure.

1. Poverty and famine

Peasant economies are typically poor. Their main activity revolves around growing, storing and consuming food grains. But even the simplest peasant economy contains sufficient differentiation to contain a non-food growing sector. The non-food growing sector is usually dependent on the food growing part but not vice versa. The availability of food in every way shapes the social relations in a peasant economy.

The typical poverty of peasant societies makes them especially liable to the occasional famine, i.e., a situation where the availability of food from being the dominant concern becomes the sole preoccupation of all parts of the society. It has been observed however that there is an asymmetry in the incidence of starvation deaths as between different parts of the peasant economy. Thus, the non-food growing sector suffers disproportionately relative to the food growing one. Sen, who has most eloquently argued this and given ample evidence of this, relates this to the 'food entitlements' of the individuals. He argues that those individuals who have to *purchase* food have

*This is a much revised version of my earlier paper 'Rice and fish: A general equilibrium approach to entitlement failures' [Desai (1986)]. I am grateful to Monojit Chatterjee (University of Dundee) and Peter Skott (University of Aarhus) for saving me from sloppy errors. Chuck Blackorby (UBC) and David Donaldson (UBC) made a crucial input to section 3 in 1980. Julian Le Grand and Jim Gordon, my colleagues at LSE, also made helpful suggestions. Amartya Sen with whom I have discussed this problem over many years has been patient with my dilatoriness in finishing this work. At the final stage comments by an anonymous referee and by Manfred Holler improved the paper very much. To all, my thanks. All errors are acknowledged to be mine.

a more precarious exchange entitlement to food relative to those who *grow* and have *direct* access to food. These 'non-food' individuals suffer from adverse terms of trade since what they wish to sell falls in price relative to food, and they also experience an adverse quantity effect since they have less to sell if there is a drought. Such individuals often sell edible items – livestock products, fish – but not being sellers of food grains, they are in an asymmetric position vis-à-vis food producers [Sen (1981)].

Such asymmetry is not the same as inequality. In terms of their wealth holding, evaluated at 'normal' prices, some of these individuals may be better off than individuals within the food-growing sector. It is also not related to what Marx would call the social relations of production. Thus a landless labourer working in food growing, although not owning 'means of production', may have a more secure food entitlement than an owner of cattle which are the means of production in the livestock sector. [See Sen's examples of the Sahel, op. cit. ...].

In his book Sen makes two further, fairly strong, points. First, that this precariousness of food entitlements is not a case of market failure in the sense normally understood. In his theory, markets clear but fail to ensure that everyone gets a minimum food entitlement. Second, he claims that a decline in food availability, e.g. a harvest failure, is neither a necessary nor a sufficient condition for the entitlement failure to occur.

These claims are contentious [see Srinivasan (1983) for a sceptical view of Sen's claims]. If there is no market failure, then relative price movements should lead to optimal outcomes. The food purchasing power of non-food seller's income may decline if there is a sharp fall in terms of trade but that is hardly novel. Such declines can have serious consequences only if there are minimal quantity requirements in an individual's consumption set. But while this may be factually true, in analytical terms such minimum requirements typically lead to existence problems in equilibrium theory. This is well known since Koopmans' (1957, p. 59) elegant exposition of this issue. For existence of equilibrium, trade independent security has to be assumed. Sen in recognising this calls this 'a very exacting assumption' [Sen (op. cit., p. 173)]. Obviously, if we are in a situation of non-existence of equilibrium, then this is market failure. Thus, the first of the two strong claims needs to be re-examined. This is the task of the next section where we set up a two individual two good model and explore the conditions under which existence of equilibrium and entitlement failure can be reconciled. Our example shows that an asymmetry in the preferences between the two goods combined with complete specialisation in production (endowment) produces an outcome which *while an equilibrium exists, relative prices fail to play an allocative role.* This is only a sufficient outcome; its necessity remains to be demonstrated.

But the second contention of Sen is equally problematical. If there is no decline in food availability and/or no rise in the price of food, how can entitlement failures in food occur? We take up this question in section 3. Again a two individual two good model is set up. Once again there is an asymmetric preference structure which leads to the outcome that food buyers are in a weaker position vis-à-vis food sellers even when equilibrium can be shown to exist. Once again only sufficiency can be claimed for the result. The very simplicity of our model and the elementary nature of the mathematical tools used urge caution before claiming too much. But at least there are two examples here supporting the prediction of entitlement failures.

If such examples are at all typical, an issue arises as to whether peasant economies generate endogenous responses to correct such outcomes. Thus, if entitlement failures are endemic rather than accidental, how could they persist? There should be some institutional mechanisms to insure against their recurrence. This issue is taken up briefly in the course of the paper. While no analytical models are developed, various institutional arrangements in peasant economies – bonded labour, for instance – make sense in the light of our modes. Phenomena such as the caste system and land hunger also can be reconciled with our models.

Before we go into the formal set up of our models a few caveats are in order. Although the theory of entitlements was our starting point, nothing in our arrangement hinges on a precise definition of entitlements. Thus a person's food entitlements could be thought of as the *maximum* quantity of food he could purchase with all the marketable assets at his disposal. This would be the *unconditional stock* entitlement. We could also adopt the Hicksian definition of income by saying that it is the maximum quantity of food a person can purchase, leaving their initial wealth unchanged. This would be the *unconditional flow* entitlement. There is also the amount a person could purchase given that other people are purchasing/withholding food simultaneously. This would be a general equilibrium or conditional entitlement view. In his book, Sen seems to take the unconditional flow definition (see fig. 5.1) in as much as it is a partial equilibrium view. We do not take up the question of assets in our models but do take a general equilibrium view [see, however, Desai (1988) for a treatment of real balances]. Thus, it is the conditional food entitlement that is studied here. But to reiterate, we do not need this definition in any way.

In order to bring out sharply the asymmetry in our example, our non-food commodity is taken to be an edible one (fish) in the first model. In the second model it can be any non-food consumable, but personal labour services is an especially appealing illustration. Again nothing hinges on the commodity chosen to illustrate the non-food sector.

2. The minimum quantity model

Against this background, let us set up a simple general equilibrium scheme. There are two persons – a farmer and a fisherman. The farmer produces rice and the fisherman catches fish. Although a fish is edible, we take it to be non-essential in consumption. The fisherman stands for the class of non-food producers who have to *purchase* food and cannot get it directly as the farmer can. We ignore the inputs and treat each person's output of rice and fish as exogenously given. Labelling rice as X_1 and X_2 and the individuals as farmer (A), fisherman (B). We posit for each of them a utility function of the Stone–Geary–Klein–Rubin type with an asymmetry in their preferences, i.e.,

$$U_i = (X_{1i} - X_{1i}^*)^\alpha X_{2i}^{(1-\alpha)}; \qquad i = A, B. \tag{1}$$

In (1), the asymmetry arises from imposing $X_{2i}^* = 0$. The asymmetry is across commodities not across agents. Both the agents have identical utility functions. Thus both individuals need a minimum quantity of rice X_{1i}^* before they can derive any utility from consumption. Notice that both goods are required; $X_{2i} = 0$ implies $U_i = 0$. It is possible to allow for α to differ by i as X_{1i}^* does but we shall not pursue that.

Each individual maximises utility subject to the income constraint;

$$\max U_i = (X_{1i} - X_{1i}^*)^\alpha (X_{2i})^{1-\alpha}, \qquad i = A, B, \quad \text{subject to} \tag{2a}$$

$$P_j \bar{X}_{ji} = \sum_j p_j X_{ji}, \qquad j = 1, 2, \quad i = A, B. \tag{2b}$$

$\bar{X}_{ji}$ is total output (endowment) of the jth good of the ith individual and Pj its price. Since there is complete specialization, we need not sum the outputs (endowments) over the two individuals. In addition to the income constraint on each individual, we have the overall constraint

$$\sum_i X_{ij} = \bar{X}_{ji}, \qquad j = 1, 2, \quad i = A, B. \tag{3}$$

This simple structure is sufficient to demonstrate the consequences of an asymmetric position in the market as between the two producers. To begin the equilibrium price ratio is defined as:

$$\frac{P_1}{P_2} = \frac{\alpha}{1-\alpha} \frac{\bar{X}_2}{(\bar{X}_1 - \sum X_{1i}^*)}. \tag{4}$$

Note that a necessary condition for the existence of an equilibrium price ratio is $\bar{X}_1 > \sum X_{1i}^*$. If there is a serious famine and rice output falls below $\sum X_{1i}^*$, the minimum quantity of rice necessary to sustain the economy, then the mechanism of relative prices should be deemed to have been suspended. In that case, there are no trading possibilities for the fisherman by which he can buy any rice.

Let us however examine the cases where there is more than the minimum of rice and hence the equilibrium price ratio is finite and positive. If we now derive the demand curve for rice for the two individuals, the basic asymmetry emerges clearly. Thus the farmer's demand curve for rice is:

$$X_{1A} = X_{1A}^* + \alpha(\bar{X}_1 - X_{1A}^*), \tag{5}$$

i.e. the farmer's demand curve for his own product is *independent of relative prices*. This is a consequence of the fact that the farmer produces the commodity which is the pivotal one, and he does not need to buy it. The fisherman's demand curve for rice is:

$$X_{1B} = X_{1B}^* + \alpha \frac{(P_2 \bar{X}_2 - P_1 X_{1B}^*)}{P_1}. \tag{5a}$$

The fisherman needs to go through the market to obtain rice.

Given the structure of the problem, note that there is nothing the fisherman can do to obtain the rice he needs. Producing more fish or less does not help him. While the farmer is insulated against the market, the fisherman needs the market but cannot in any way influence the outcome. This is especially so if the farmer's minimum needs for rice X_{1A}^* is very high relative to the fisherman's.

In particular, let us concentrate on the possibility that while there is sufficient food, i.e. $\bar{X}_1 > \sum X_{1i}^*$, the fisherman may fail to obtain enough rice through the market, i.e. $X_{1B} < X_{1B}^*$. This involves working out the condition under which in eq. (5a)

$$P_2 \bar{X}_2 - P_1 X_{1B}^* < 0.$$

Using (4) we get that if

$$(1-\alpha)/\alpha < X_{1B}^*/(\bar{X}_1 - \sum X_{1i}^*), \tag{6}$$

then $X_{1B} < X_{1B}^*$. Eq. (6) says that the lower the intensity of preference for fish in the two people relative to rice, the more likely it is that the fisherman will starve. The more the farmer needs rice, the smaller will the denominator be on the right-hand side of (6), and again the more likely is the fisherman to starve. The only way out for the fisherman is to lower his need for rice, in as much as he cannot obtain more rice. The fisherman's starvation set is all allocations $X_{1B} < X_{1B}^*$.

An alternative way of expressing (6) is to write

$$\bar{X}_1 < \left(X_{1A}^* + \frac{X_{1B}^*}{1-\alpha} \right) > \sum X_{ij}^*. \qquad (6a)$$

The right-hand side inequality ensures that there is enough food to meet subsistence needs since $\alpha < 1$. The left-hand side inequality is equivalent to requiring that the farmer's vertical offer curve does not lie in the interior of the fisherman's starvation set. To say (6) or (6a) holds is to imply that the offer curves do not intersect.

But although the equilibrium allocation of rice in eq. (5) and (5a) with the price rates given by (4) does not involve market failure, it is still a peculiar equilibrium. The fisherman may find himself 'enjoying' a level of utility equal to $-\infty$, but that is the outcome of optimisation. Why then should he voluntarily accept such a degenerate situation? It is here that the combination of asymmetric preferences and complete specialisation bites hard. Since both goods are normal, i.e. the consumer wants positive quantities of both of them, we cannot stay at his initial endowment point. But since he has also to obtain more than a minimum amount of rice to be better off, he has to trade in the hope of obtaining that much; from his experience in good times, the fisherman has come to rely on trade but in bad times the reverse is the rule. Only if one gave an extra weight to choice as such would the fisherman prefer $0 < X_{1B} < X_{1B}^*$ to $0 = X_{1B}$.

It is the asymmetry between the two goods, i.e. the restriction that $X_{2i}^* = 0$, which creates the degeneracy. In absence of that any move off the initial endowment point is welfare improving. But the asymmetry brings the paradox that for the fisherman, all points between $X_{1B} = 0$ and $X_{1B} \leq X_{1B}^*$ are not welfare improving. If, after some time, the fisherman resorts to trade to improve himself, he will be worse off. He has the choice not to trade but then he may only find out his position ex post – after trade and not *ex-ante*.

But notice also that a *second* important point which arises concerns the way to relieve the incidence of starvation. The favoured policy for famine relief is to correct the maldistribution of purchasing power rather than provide food directly. This is a much emphasised conclusion of his analysis by Sen (1986). It is also codified in the Indian Famine Code whereby relief works were started to create the purchasing power for people to be able to buy the food. In our analysis, this policy will not work. Giving the fisherman purchasing power is not enough since the normal operation of the relative price mechanism is suspended. If the actual total output of rice and the parameters in eq. (6) are such that the fisherman could get less than X_{1B}^*, then the relief strategies have to be based on *making food available outside* *the market mechanism* to the fisherman. This explains the historic practice of maintaining food reserves especially in towns where the non-food producers flock to seek food. It also provides some rationale for the suspicion with which free movements of food grain were regarded in the famine prone regions of France in the eighteenth century, and such suspicions are still entertained [see Tilly (1985) for a study of the French history in this respect]. If grain cannot be brought in from the outside, e.g. from stocks accumulated in the past, then in that case only taxation in kind or direct requisition of food will enable the non-food producer to obtain food. The 'authorities' could either seize all output $\bar{X}_1$ or what they calculate to be surplus above minimum requirement $(\bar{X}_1 - X_{1A}^*)$ and distribute it so that both get at least X_{1i}^*. They may alternatively levy a tax in kind on the farmer and distribute the rice collected to the fisherman. Such arrangements have been tried in the past. The post-revolutionary Russian government tried a policy of compulsory requisition of food grains from the farmers to feed the army and the urban civilian population. But this ran into problems of concealment of food grains by the farmer. A more foolproof system of 'tax in kind' was adopted as part of the New Economic Policy.

If we can ignore cheating or adverse incentive effects of taxation for the moment, then the tax rate to be imposed on the farmer can be worked out fairly simply. Thus taking (5) and (5a), let us propose a tax rate ζ such that

$$X_{1A} = X_{1A}^* + \alpha(1-\zeta)[\bar{X}_1 - X_{1A}^*]. \tag{7a}$$

Thus a tax of ζ proportion of surplus food is levied on the farmer. This is then given to the fisherman,

$$X_{1B} = X_{1B}^* + \alpha \frac{(P_2 \bar{X}_2 - P_1 X_{1B}^*)}{P_1} + \zeta(\bar{X}_1 - X_{1A}^*). \tag{7b}$$

To ensure that the fisherman will have the minimum he needs, we set ζ such that

$$\alpha(P_2 \bar{X}_2 - P_1 X_{1B}^*) + P_1 \zeta(\bar{X}_1 - X_{1A}^*) = 0. \tag{8a}$$

An alternative way of obtaining ζ is to proceed via total food balances. The fisherman gets what the farmer lets him have,

$$X_{1B} = X_{1B}^* + (\bar{X}_1 - X_{1A}) = [1 - \alpha(1-\zeta)](\bar{X}_1 - X_{1A}^*). \tag{8b}$$

Solving either of them, we get

$$\zeta = 1 - \frac{(\bar{X}_1 - \sum X_{1i}^*)}{\alpha(\bar{X}_1 - X_{1A}^*)}. \tag{9}$$

The proportion of the surplus rice in the economy as a whole $(\bar{X}_1 - \sum X_{1i})$ to the farmer's extra demand for rice when not taxed $(\bar{X}_1 - X_{1A}^*)$ is the crucial quantity in (9). A surplus generating system by its productivity $(X_1 - \sum X_{1i}^*)$ or the farmer's frugality in rice consumption X_{1A}^* will lead to low if not zero taxation.

Again we can interpret (9) in the light of (6a) above. Thus rewriting (9) as

$$\tau = \left(\frac{1-\alpha}{\alpha}\right)\left[\frac{(1-\alpha)^{-1}X_{1B}^* + (X_{1A}^* - \bar{X}_1)}{(\bar{X}_1 - X_{1A}^*)}\right]. \tag{9a}$$

The numerator on the right-hand side comes from the left-hand side inequality of (6a) and we now see τ as the amount necessary to make the offer curves intersect which they did not before.

This example then illustrates a general equilibrium model where asymmetry in preferences leads to an equilibrium outcome where relative prices fail to play the role they should. The two agents in the economy are in an asymmetric power situation with the person who has to go through the market to obtain his food being the less powerful person. But while this example confirms Sen's observation of the asymmetric outcomes for food and non-food producers, it does not confirm his policy prescription for famine relief, that famines should be tackled by distribution of purchasing power through organising work schemes rather than by direct food handouts. In a world like this, it is the physical availability of food for the non-food producers which alone can avert starvation. So it points to a rationing scheme, or requisitioning of food by taxation.

3. The model with unequal weights

Our second example is also a general equilibrium model. There is again an asymmetry between the two goods, one of which is more important than the other. The necessary or important good is rice. The less important one could be thought of as fish or as labour power sold and bought for consumption. Thus the seller of labour services has an own demand for leisure, whereas the buyer hires him for personal services. This way of characterising labour services obviates the need to specify the production function which would be necessary to derive the demand for productive labour. It simplifies the algebra without losing our point.

Again there are two individuals. One rice farmer and the other a servant (or fisherman). Let the goods be again X_1 (rice), X_2 (personal services), the prices p_1, p_2 and individuals A, B. The utility function now is a Cobb–Douglas form modified to incorporate asymmetry:

$$U_i = X_{1i}^{\alpha}(\beta X_{1i} + X_{2i})1 - \alpha, \qquad i = A, B. \tag{10}$$

If $\beta = 0$, then the two goods are symmetric. Otherwise (10) tells us that the individuals can have utility even when they do not consume X_2 but they must have X_1.

Assume once again complete specialization. It is straightforward to derive the demand equations:

$$X_{1A} = \alpha \frac{p_1 \bar{X}_1}{(p_1 - \beta p_2)}, \tag{11a}$$

$$X_{1B} = \alpha \frac{p_2 \bar{X}_2}{(p_1 - \beta p_2)}, \tag{11b}$$

$$X_{2A} = \frac{p_1 \bar{X}_1[(1 - \alpha)p_1 - \beta p_2]}{p_2(p_1 - \beta p_2)}, \tag{11c}$$

$$X_{2B} = \frac{\bar{X}_2[(1 - \alpha)p_1 - \beta p_2]}{(p_1 - \beta p_2)}. \tag{11d}$$

The demand equations bring out the importance of the asymmetry parameter β. Its presence puts a lower limit on the range within which relative prices can vary. Thus, it is clear that $(p_1/p_2) > \beta$ is a necessary condition for $x_{1i} > 0$. For X_{2i}, note that given that condition is fulfilled, $X_{2i} > 0$ requires further $(p_1/p_2) > \beta/(1 - \alpha)$. Since $0 < \alpha < 1$, it is the latter condition that is binding. This is also clear from the equilibrium price ratio

$$\frac{p_1}{p_2} = \frac{\beta}{(1 - \alpha)} + \frac{\alpha}{(1 - \alpha)} \frac{\bar{X}_2}{\bar{X}_1}. \tag{12}$$

The structure of the preferences thus puts a limit on how high the price of X_2 can be relative to that of X_1. No such limit exists for X_1 relative to X_2. Thus, the value $\beta/(1 - \alpha)$ is the lowest (P_1/P_2) can fall to even in the unlikely event of complete withdrawal of the X_2 supply. Thus, suppliers of X_2 cannot gain from the price effects more than they lose from the output effect. On the other hand, they can see their entitlements of X_1 shrink drastically if (p_1/p_2) were to rise.

A collapse in the purchasing power of X_2 sellers can happen without any diminution of the output of food. Personal circumstances such as sickness, disability or temporary loss of working ability (pregnancy) can cause diminution in labour supply. If X_2 is a commodity such as fish or livestock products, a sudden epidemic (mercury poisoning of fish, cattle disease) can decimate the supply. This drop in supply fails to raise the price sufficiently to compensate the suppliers due to the asymmetry in demand.

Thus we clearly have

$$\frac{d(p_2 \bar{X}_2/p_1)}{d\bar{X}_2} = \frac{\beta}{1-\alpha}\left(\frac{p_2}{p_1}\right)^2 \tag{6a}$$

i.e. there would be no change if $\beta = 0$.

In this example, food supply need play no role at all in causing starvation among the non-food producers; any event causing a drop in the supply of what they sell will be sufficient to do so. In a world like this, traditional famine relief such as creating earning opportunities is effective because the issue is the collapse in the purchasing power of the non-food suppliers. Thus, a drought may reduce the opportunities for hired agricultural labour as well as the supply of many non-food products. In this case the point is to augment the output of X_2 by generating a demand for it at a price that will enable the X_2 suppliers to purchase food. This will also prevent the food price from falling too much.

4. Conclusion and some institutional implications

We have shown in the course of our two examples that rigorous general equilibrium foundations can be provided for the case of entitlement failures. In each case there is an asymmetry in the utility function which generates an asymmetry in the market position of the participants. This asymmetry does not arise from market failure in the normal sense of the word. Markets clear; but despite price taking behaviour on the part of individuals and market clearing there is a limit to which relative prices vary. In one case, one side of the market is rendered independent of relative price movements, leaving all the adjustments to output variations to be borne by the other side. In another case, output reductions have asymmetric effects on the relative prices and hence purchasing powers of the two sides.

One major question which arises from our static general equilibrium exercise is whether such outcomes can repeat themselves or will people seek devices to insure themselves against them. Take our first case. If the rice output were to drop, the fisherman could starve. If this is an unanticipated shock then there is nothing much he can do about it. But if this were an economy with a repeated output shock, there will be a response. One well documented institutional response is public granaries. As long as harvest failures are periodic, stocks can be built up to be used in lean times. The biblical story of Joseph in Genesis testifies to this as it also illustrates the plight of shepherds in times of drought.

The possibility of a private insurance market is the more intriguing one. In 'good times', the fisherman should be able to exchange his 'rice savings' for a promise to deliver rice in 'bad times'. The rice merchants in analogy with the goldsmiths who pioneered banking will take in the rice saving deposits of the fisherman in exchange for promises to pay. If rice is storable then there will be a demand for such rice deposits, i.e. fishermen willing to pay in. We would then need to work out the conditions for the supply of such liabilities to be issued. The ubiquitous non-existence of private insurance markets in food grains tells us that this could be a fruitful area of further investigation.

But there are other institutional responses. Note that in both our examples there is complete specialisation. It would be optimal for the non-food producer to hold a mixed portfolio of food and non-food activities. (Or as rather succinctly put by Patrick Minford, 'The fisherman's daughter will marry the farmer's son'!) One consequence of this is land hunger which is observed in many peasant societies. Another is the premium on jobs connected with harvest operations which give an individual access to food. The drift into such jobs was recorded during the Bengal famine [Sen (1981)]. In medieval England, many crimes were recorded in the manor rolls which had to do with stealing the standing crop or the threshed corn [Thomas (1971)]. The frequently observed practice of the head of household working in the city but returning to help the family at harvest time is another.

There is further speculation worth entertaining in this regard. Complete specialisation is socially enforced in the caste system. This would imply that it was sustained by a 'social contract' whereby the food producing castes guaranteed the non-food producers' regular food supply. This would keep the non-food producers in their caste occupations. Such a system is sustainable only as long as the food supply can be augmented in line with population. Historically this was most probably the case in India, the home of the caste system, until the middle of the 19th century. Once population growth outstrips food availability, land hunger becomes strong as the non-food producing castes attempt to ensure their food supply. They may not directly cultivate the land but lease it out to sharecroppers. They can thereby ensure their food supply.

Our second example also points to some interesting implications. Thus groups with only labour services to sell in peasant societies can only hope to survive by becoming attached or bonded labour. They need to become complementary rather than substitutes to food production. These arrangements can be sustained as long as food availability is stable. Once the (shadow) price of food in terms of unskilled labour rises, farmers may end bonded labour and hire seasonal labour.

One further implication of our second example is not so much with peasant societies but with the question of gender and household labour. The complete specialisation paradigm whereby A earns 'the bread' and B performs the personal services for A is a stylized model of intra-household distribution of resources on which much has been written [Brannen and Wilson (1987)]. But this must be pursued elsewhere.

References

Brannen, Julia and Gail Wilson, 1987, Give and take: Studies in resource distribution (Allen and Unwin, London).

Desai, Meghnad, 1988, Economic aspects of famine, in: G.B. Harrison, ed., Famines (OUP, Oxford).

Koopmans, T.C., 1957, Three essays on the state of the economic science (Wiley, New York).

Sen, A.K., 1981, Poverty and famine: An essay on entitlement and deprivation (Clarendon Press, Oxford).

Sen, A.K., 1986, Food, economics and entitlements, Lloyds Bank Review, April.

Srinivasan T.N., 1983, Review of Sen, 1981, in The American Journal of Agricultural Economics, Feb.

Thomas, K., 1971, Religion and the decline of magic (Penguin, London).

Tilly, L., 1985, Food entitlement, famine and conflict in: Rotberg and Rabb, eds., Hunger and history: The impact of changing food production and consumption patterns on society (Cambridge University Press, Cambridge).

[9]

HOMILIES OF A VICTORIAN SAGE:
A REVIEW ARTICLE ON PETER BAUER

Meghnad Desai

I. Introduction

Peter Bauer has been for many years the *bête noire* of all those who wish to promote aid to the Third World. This has not daunted but rather sustained him through the 1950s and 1960s when he fancied himself as a voice in the wilderness. Now of course with the Right resurgence and the Thatcher-Reagan experiments, the climate has changed. Peter Bauer's hour has arrived. If the present collection‡ which follows his earlier *Dissent on Development* is any sign, he does not lack platforms and opportunities to expound his views. But now, far from being a distant, ignored voice, his is very much the Establishment view. The time has come therefore to take Peter Bauer and his arguments seriously. Indeed, in some ways it may be overdue. The climate today is different from the heady days of UNCTAD 1964 or even the 1974 UN Declaration for the New International Economic Order. Cancún has collapsed and the Brandt Report, with its insistence on the mutual benefits of aid for the donors and the receivers, has fallen on deaf ears. The arguments presented in this book are germane to this new climate if they have not actually brought it about.

Through the 1950s and 1960s Peter Bauer's writings frequently aroused anger, if not apoplexy, but little reasoned criticism. He was ignored, dismissed, but not answered. (I know of only one considered critique of his views and this was by Nicholas Stern in 1975.) This lack of criticism has led to the impression that in some way Peter Bauer's views are unassailable and that his opponents are forced to ignore them. Since he writes with great vigour and style, and keeps to the same theme through many years, readers may conclude that he has disarmed his critics. But, as we have seen in the case of Milton Friedman, while infinite repetition wins influence, it does not necessarily vouch for the truth of the principles so repeatedly asserted.

The present book has three sections. Section one is on Equality and discusses egalitarianism and the class structure in Britain. Section two, of major interest to the readers of this journal, is titled 'The West and the Third World' and recapitulates Bauer's views on aid, development, colonialism, commodity agreements etc. But though disparate, they are woven together by a uniform view of how economic development takes place in developed as well as less developed societies in the past as well as in the present. Since he believes his view is the correct one, Bauer then derives great pleasure from criticising economists who either do not hold this view or do not maintain a consistent view. This comprises section three on 'The State of Economics'. It will be sufficient for my purposes to concentrate on section two but I shall refer to other sections as need arises. I shall list the main propositions of Bauer's uniform view of economics and then examine them.

‡ Peter Bauer, *Equality, the Third World and Economic Delusion,* London: Weidenfeld and Nicholson, 1981.

II. Bauer's Uniform View

1) All societies except very primitive subsistence ones are bound to contain 'substantial differences in economic performance and therefore in incomes among individuals and groups with access to the same physical resources, including land.... Such differences could not be explained if ... physical resources were a decisive or a major determinant of economic achievement' (p 43).

2) Those groups who are better off in any society relative to other groups in the same society or in other societies have arrived due to 'sustained effort, the adoption of improved methods and the reinvestment of income' (p 45).

3) Natural resources or physical capital does not explain differences in development.

4) Population size or growth is not an obstacle to development. Indeed, Bauer argues this in chapter 3, 'The Population Explosion – Myth and Realities', with a passion that is positively Maoist. If people choose to have children this is because they calculate that, on balance, children are a benefit not a cost. Excessive population will correct itself by modification of family formation behaviour on the part of the people themselves.

5) Income, even if measured accurately, is not a good index of economic welfare, and hence, inequality in measured incomes should not be a consideration of policy. Income differences as between countries have even less meaning and are distorted by problems of definition and measurement.

These general propositions derive from a largely qualitative, market-oriented theory of economic development. Their use and extension in interpreting the historical experience of under-development and development are then made by Bauer in various controversial assertions:

6a) The impact of the West on its colonies was not harmful but beneficial. The exposure to trade and international commerce benefited these countries, many of which were very primitive before the contact.

6b) The possibility of development in these countries without external aid is witnessed by the enrichment of certain trader groups in West Africa, of the Chinese and Indians in South East Asia and East Africa. These communities grew by the application in their private lives of proposition 2 above.

7) Not only can the West not be blamed for the past but, even in the present, Western countries are not exploiting the Third World. They do not, for example, gain by adverse terms of trade of primary producing countries. Prices are set by the free competitive markets and no one sets them. Nor can commercial rates of bank loans be high since they are set by competition and paid willingly by borrowers.

8) Foreign aid is a government-to-government transfer and not necessarily a transfer from a rich person in the First World to a poor person in the Third World. Its benefits are limited to the extent that the same amount does not have to be borrowed at commercial rates. Its use is made mainly in unproductive channels to benefit the governments but not the people of the Third World.

9) While the benefits of foreign aid are at best limited to the extra interest charges saved, its harmful effects can be very deep. Aid has politicised economic life in the Third World, made the governments of the Third World arbitrarily powerful, and encouraged them to adopt statist, interventionist policies which are inefficient. In particular by controlling

free trade, internal and external, the state hurts those groups which enriched themselves by self help.

10) The donor countries are blackmailed into giving aid to the extent that LDCs think they are statutorily entitled to aid. The Third World countries share only one unifying characteristic – they all receive and clamour for aid from the West. The Third World is a creature of aid. Myths of underdevelopment and of western guilt for Third World poverty were created by the aid lobbies aided by academic hucksterism and wooly-minded liberalism. This makes aid into an issue above politics but aid harms the donor countries.

Propositions 6 to 10 are argued in various places in section 2 and especially in chapter 5, a long essay entitled 'Foreign Aid and Its Hydra-Headed Rationalisation.' There is much more in this and other essays in this section which is pertinent to development than I can summarise. Before I proceed to examine it in detail, I may mention some conclusions of Bauer's on aid which are pertinent.

11) Aid should be largely given via voluntary agencies (e.g. OXFAM) which receive voluntary contributions from citizens of the First World and who channel it directly to groups in the Third World without the intermediary of governments. Governments should only give relief aid for earthquakes etc. This minimises politicisation.

12) The best help that the First World governments can give is to reduce barriers they have imposed against exports from the Third World. Costs of adjustment to groups thereby affected in the West can be met from a diversion of foreign aid to domestic recipients.

13) Aid, if at all to be given, should be given in the form of untied cash grants. It should be given bilaterally not multilaterally and the donor country should see to it that the recipient is a friendly country following liberal economic policies.

To counter Bauer's views on economics and economic development, one will have to go into the various levels at which he conducts the debate. His theoretical perspective is that of the classical *laissez faire* theorist of the nineteenth century. Free trade is an engine of growth, and free movements of capital and labour are the best way to promote this economic growth. Market prices are competitively determined and the economic benefits of an activity are best measured by the measurable profitability (yield) accruing from it. In most cases, credit will be available in international capital markets at a price which is an alternative measure of the benefit.

This is a world of breathtaking simplicity. The entire corpus of literature which deals with the gap between social and private returns in economic activities beginning with nineteenth-century French writing through Pigou and the subsequent developments of project appraisal, cost-benefit analysis is ignored. There are no gaps in Bauer's view worth speaking of between private and social return and, if a government cannot borrow money privately to finance a project, this is *prima facie* proof of its undesirability. To finance such a project by domestic taxation would divert resources from more efficient use; to do so by foreign aid can be even more deleterious since those who bear the cost – the foreign taxpayers – cannot protest directly. One has to be neither a Marxist nor irrational to demur at such a simple view. Simple though this view is, its appeal derives from its political message which is that those who have money got it by dint of merit and effort and those who do not only have themselves to blame for it. To aid the unfortunate by transfers, whether domestic or international, takes away from the worthy (rich) to give to the unworthy (poor).

Thus nineteenth-century economic theory is firmly wedded to nineteenth-century

Victorian morality (though without its prudishness) in Bauer's works. He points out that 'official aid does not go to poor people, to the skeletal figures of aid propaganda' (p 111). Further 'the policies of most Third World governments are not designed to relieve poverty' (p 111). But even if they were so designed, it would not do much good. The poor in the Third World are poor because they 'tend to be materially unambitious'. What is more, they 'are unlikely to possess the aptitudes and motivations for economic achievement to the same extent as those who are more prosperous, which is why relief of poverty and promotion of development differ radically as objectives, or indeed are largely at variance' (p 113). So Third World governments are at fault for not directing the money to relieve poverty but if they did they would be harming development anyway! But the voluntary nature of poverty is not just a feature of the Third World. In the very first essay, 'The Grail of Equality', Bauer endorses the same view of even the First World. 'A disproportionate number of the poor lack the capabilities and inclination for economic achievement, and often for cultural achievements as well' (p 20).

The view then clearly is that development occurs through voluntary efforts of enterprising individuals who grab economic opportunities and are willing to work hard. Bauer has arrived at this view from his previous studies of West African and Malayan economics. Here again the pull of nineteenth-century history on him is evident. The spread of capitalism to the farthest corner of the world via Empire and trade was a notable achievement of the nineteenth century, celebrated as much in *The Communist Manifesto* as in countless tomes extolling *laissez faire* policies. The period between 1815 and 1914 was characterised by expansion of population, trade and incomes in Western Europe and the US. There was free trade which was guaranteed (paradoxically) by the dominant position of Britain through much of this period. Technological innovations meant falling transport costs as well as other costs of production. Much capital flowed to the peripheral parts of the First World from Britain and much labour moved from poorer peripheral countries to other parts.

This was the period in which the colonies of Britain, France, Holland and Belgium, but especially of Britain, were integrated into world capitalism. Some had a developed pre-capitalist economy (e.g. India) which underwent traumatic structural change. The impact of market forces here was not entirely benevolent nor was it unaided by the political power of the colonial government. Other economies which had a less developed precapitalist economy experienced an end of self-sufficient production systems and growth of modern activity. The net effect of the imperial experience is still a matter of controversy and not as settled as Bauer claims.*

Whatever the net benefit, it is clear that there was substantial growth of commercial activities in the British colonies. Some groups benefited from this growth and it is these

---

* I am thinking here of the Indian experience with which I am acquainted and not of Africa which I do not know in detail. The debate about nineteenth-century Indian economic history continues. One phase of it is available in Dharma Kumar (ed) *Towards A Reinterpretation of Nineteenth Century Indian History* (Delhi, 1970). I have challenged Morris D Morris' contention that the disappearance of the traditional Indian textile industry is explained purely by demand and supply factors in Desai, 'The Demand for Cotton Textiles in Nineteenth Century India'. *Indian Economic and Social History Review*, December 1971. See also recent articles in C Dewey and A Hopkins (ed) *The Imperial Impact: studies in the economic history of Africa and India* (London, 1978).

groups that form the basis of Bauer's optimism about the development capabilities in the Third World. But the interwar period witnessed a slowing down of the growth of the world capitalist economy. The dominance of Britain in trade and growth was already being challenged by the US and Germany even as early as the 1880s. (It may also be noted that during this crucial period of early growth, there grew up an economics literature in these countries challenging the benevolent assumptions of English *laissez faire* doctrine, as, for example, in the work of Friedrich List. The struggle to escape under-development thus naturally provokes a challenge to the traditional economic theory as we witness again today.) The interwar period was marked by slow growth, protectionism, falling prices of raw material exports relative to manufactures etc. It also witnessed substantial declines in mortality rates and hence the demographic bulge in the Third World. (The population of India grew rather slowly in the nineteenth century but doubled between 1921 and 1951.) The problem of Third World poverty and stagnation arose then since there were limited opportunities for other groups to enrich themselves as the pioneering groups had done in the nineteenth century. The pioneers, now rich, sided with the foreign powers; the nationalist movements everywhere mobilised the other articualte groups – native industrialists struggling against metropolitan competition, peasantry suffering from declining product prices and fixed revenue demands, the urban educated elite impatient for economic betterment. These groups were frustrated by the sluggish growth of the world economy. They of course blamed their condition on the proximate source – the foreign rulers. They also noted that the pioneering rich were collaborating with the foreign rulers.

Nothing in Bauer's writings gives one a feeling that he either recognises the force of growing nationalism from the interwar years onwards, or that he likes what he sees of it. The nineteenth-century market economy operated smoothly due to a whole host of peculiar circumstances. At home in Britain franchise was limited and the costs of the *laissez faire* policies – cyclical unemployment – were borne by those not yet enfranchised. Internationally, Britain dominated as the major manufacturing power with monopoly control in many lines and as a major exporter of capital. The Third World had no political independence. The costs of the *laissez faire* policies could be thus privatised. The growth of franchise in the developed world following the First World War (Britain introduced universal adult franchise only in 1928) and the growth of nationalism in the periphery meant that the costs of economic change could not be so easily shifted on to the poor. They now had the vote in the First World. The aspiring groups who were frustrated in the interwar period came to power in the various countries upon the end of Empire. Their resentment against the market mechanism was not all irrational prejudice nor was their displacement of the pioneering rich totally perverse. In many cases this displacement had racial aspects which Bauer frequently points out – the Chinese in Malaysia, Asians in East Africa. But in each case it was the attempt by new aspiring groups to use the levers of the state to further their position.

Economic nationalism in the Third World was then the important force the First World had to contend with. Bauer dates the growth of aid from President Truman's Point Four programme but this is surely a slip. The origins of the wooing of the Third World are in the rivalry between the US and European Imperial powers, especially Britain, during the Second World War. Partly from anti-imperialist idealism and even more from naked self-interest, the Americans sought to muscle in into the old colonies as European power slipped.† What Peter Bauer considers a massive waste of resources is hardly that. The aid when given has never amounted to much in terms of the incomes of the donors (until their recent economic sufferings) and was a small price to maintain open access to the markets and resources of these countries. Aid programmes in the US had, until recently, the support of a coalition of bankers, corporations with international branches (now universally, though mistakenly, labelled multinational corporations) as well as liberal opinions comprising academics, trade unionists, etc. Self-interest was never absent from these calculations and, indeed, could not have been.

The growth of trade and incomes in the First World countries through the Keynesian quarter-century (1950-1975) was explosive. In fact this meant that the First World was able to develop rapidly without the need of the Third World as a market for its products and for supplies of raw materials only to the extent that technical progress had not found substitutes for these. (Of course, one has to remember that the First World itself is a major producer and exporter of primary products.) So in the Keynesian quarter-century, the markets of the Third World were of peripheral importance for the First World. But the reverse was not the case. A developing, industrialising Third World needed access to First World markets. The growth in First World trade with the Third World was much slower than that of intra-First World trade. It is this that explains the thrust behind UNCTAD 1964 and the NIEO 1974.

This historical background to the changing relationship between the First and Third World is entirely missing in Bauer's perspective. Thus, when he defines the Third World as a creature of aid (p 87), he is not only making a dramatic simplification, it is an error. The notion of the Third World, as indeed the original French label for it, is a creature of the Cold War and predates the emergence of foreign aid as a major phenomenon. (I date the growth and institutionalisation of foreign aid not so much from the Point Four programme as from the late 1950s when US involvement in India and Africa grew substantially.) It was the Cold War which first defined the Third World, which to a large extent was non-aligned, and it was through the conferences of non-aligned nations in Bandung, Cairo and Belgrade that the Group of 77 grew in cohesion.

Bauer finds that donors do not exercise control over how funds are used by recipient countries or he finds that government-to-government transfers dominate disbursals and this for him represents an inefficient use of resources. But his narrow economic perspective is to blame for this. Whatever the declared objectives of the donors, aid is a weapon in international economic diplomacy where donor countries are trying to promote their political-military objectives as well as the interests of their citizen corporations. Of course, it would be more efficient to have separate loans for separate ends but the mixture has the advantage of imparting a certain moral ambiguity to the transaction which all sides find advantageous. The international perspective also makes clear that the doctrine of national sovereignty – local autonomy over economic policy – has to be respected at least formally. Aid is not a purely economic transfer. This is why each sectional interest wishing to promote aid – military, trade, humanitarian – finds aid dissatisfying and seeks to push it one way or another. The sum total is pervasive frustration which then gets mobilised by the anti-aid lobby.

† See Christopher Thorne, *Allies of a Kind*, Oxford: OUP, 1979, for a superb historical account of US-British jockeying for position in Asia during the War.

For whatever Bauer's fear about aid becoming a permanent burden, the truth is there has been a major reversal in the attitude towards aid and the Third World in general in the 1970s, and the 1980s promise no reversal. As the NIEO 1974 declaration came soon after the OPEC price rise, the First World, faced with uncertainty about raw material prices, was willing to humour the Third World for a while. Shrewd analysts in the First World such as Fred Bergsten saw that the point of conceding NIEO was to ensure adequate raw material supplies for economic and military emergencies. But the OPEC habit did not spread to other metals and the First World sought to sabotage any proposal for a multi-commodity stabilisation scheme just to make sure that the OPEC habit did not catch on. They also suffered a relative decline in actual growth as well as expectations about growth and prosperity. Having in their prosperous period not needed the Third World and now facing an erosion of their industrial base due to Third World competition, they find it hard to be persuaded by the insistence of the Brandt Report that the Third World's prosperity is a precondition for the First World's prosperity. Indeed, it is debatable whether the First World needs the Third World for restoration of its prosperity. What it needs is a co-ordinated reflation programme which will generate mutual trade and prosperity. If this Keynesian solution is difficult to implement it is not due to any factor connected with the Third World.

The reluctance of the First World to continue aid is thus a result of a whole complex of factors – a feeling of relative impoverishment, some let-up in the Cold War, the receding danger of an OPEC-type cartel in other commodities. This leads to two conflicting reactions. One is to say, as Bauer says, that aid has been misused anyway by the Third World or that it is irrelevant to development. Since aid has gone to many countries in different amounts over many years, instances of misuse or small yields can be found. After all it was with the connivance of the First (and the Second?) World that Bokassa, Idi Amin, Pol Pot, Somoza and other spectacular instances happened. But there is also evidence that there has been rapid growth in some less developed countries which are now called newly industrialised countries (NICs). There is some fear that these countries threaten the industrial base of the First World countries and many left-wing groups, especially in Britain, are tying themselves in knots over this problem.

What is at issue is that the actual experience of economic development in individual Third World countries is not explained simply in terms of size and use of aid, nor is the experience anything like as dismal as Bauer's articles suggest. For him, all state intervention is counter-productive by definition, but the emergence of NICs is another demonstration as the growth experience of US, Germany, Russia and Italy in the nineteenth century was, that classical and neoclassical theory of efficient allocation fails to provide lessons for economic growth. Policies such as tariffs, protection, import substitution, planning, inefficient in terms of static neoclassical theory have proved to be useful for growth. They have distributive consequences but so does a *laissez faire* policy. To understand the dynamics of growth we need different paradigms.

[10]

Is state control necessary for economic development in the Third World?

The necessity for state control for economic development has always been a hotly debated subject. Even as early as the 19th century, Britain and France could be said to have taken differing views on it. Laissez-faire prevailed in Britain while it was a late and reluctantly imported ideology (despite its French origins) in 19th century France. Countries which embarked upon the course of development later in that century – Germany, Italy, Russia – all admitted an active role for the state. Once a certain stage of development had been achieved then again laissez-faire tendencies could raise their heads.

For the Third World Countries, an era of development commenced at the end of the Second World War. In the two decades following, many countries went through the anti-colonial revolutions. Some of these were directly ruled by metropolitan countries (such as India) and others only indirectly so. In each case the programme for development had to be launched by the new state. The new state provided the impetus not only by way of mobilizing savings and choosing investment projects but also by creating a new legal structure of property rights – land reform and redistribution, buying out or confiscation of foreign capital, setting up of national-ized industries and networks for credit to agriculture and industry. The new state initiated changes in education and health provision, and introduced rudiments of a welfare state – trade union legislation, child care and care for the elderly, public housing, etc.

These first attempts by the new states for development had their critics. Those on the political Right clamoured for a more open economy i.e. open to foreign capital. They argued that industrialization programmes for the Third World countries were inefficient since they wanted to preserve and deepen the old patterns of commodity trade. They raised the bogey of deficit finance and inflation. They opposed foreign aid programmes, commodity price stabilization programmes and indeed all forms of fiscal and monetary policies to encourage development.[1]

There was also a criticism from the Left. There was no debate, there could be none, in the few countries which had experienced socialist revolution as part of or in consequence to their national liberation struggles. China, Cuba, Vietnam and Algeria were countries in this category. They took it for granted that the state alone was the force for economic growth. Thus the debate about the role of the state, its necessity, or desirability took place in the countries which were 'intermediate regimes'.[2] These regimes were neither developed capitalist democracies nor were they workers' states. They were democracies to some extent but whatever their form of government, they were all subject to popular pressures. They had a native capitalist as well as landlord class, a small urban educated middle class and a mass of petty bourgeoisie as well as rural and urban workers.

In the intermediate regimes, a left critique was mounted. It was said that the pace of industrial development and social transformation was much faster in the socialist countries. To emulate them, a much greater degree of state ownership and control was required. Obstacles to rapid development caused by multiparty politics or by openness of the economy had to be removed. China, Cuba and the early Soviet experience were all held up to be models for all Third World countries. Frequent comparisons were made for example of the development programmes of India and China to the detriment of the former.

Such was the climate in the 1950s and 1960s and even to some extent in the early 1970s. At that time there was a liberal consensus in the developed capitalist countries which promoted aid programmes designed to fill resource gaps opened by development plans. The climate for intergovernmental aid was favourable and the criticisms from the Right and the Left could be ignored.

The climate has now changed radically in this regard. In developed countries as well as in the Third World, the necessity for state control of the economy is challenged. Indeed, the presumption is that everywhere the Market forces work best and that the agencies set up by the state in various countries are inefficient, as well as inequitable. The state is no longer accepted as a benevolent agent of economic progress but is viewed with suspicion as the prime culprit for the persistence of poverty and inequality.

This is the background against which I shall re-examine this old question of the necessity of state control for economic development. To some extent, it is a great paradox since the initial impetus for development has succeeded in establishing many Third World countries as fully fledged industrialized countries: the Newly Industrialized Countries (NICs) are the most visible examples of this. But not only the NICs have progressed. The group of Third World countries which are grouped as oil importing experienced a rate of growth of manufacturing value added faster than the developed countries in the 1960s and especially in the 1970s. Their share of world trade in manufacturing below 20 per cent before 1960 is now nearing 50 per cent. By any account the last two or three decades of industrialization programmes undertaken by the Third World countries have borne fruit.[3]

The reason for the reopening of the debate about the role of the state is the stagflation suffered by the developed countries in the 1970s. To some extent, the US war efforts in Vietnam were financed by generating a balance of trade deficit and flooding the Eurodollar markets with America's IOUs. This accelerated the incipient pressures for wage and price rises in the OECD countries which were enjoying a prolonged period of full employment and economic growth for the first time in the history of capitalism.[4]

By a strange twist of logic, all the ills of inflation and unemployment were blamed on domestic fiscal and monetary policy. The idea gained ground that it was the uncontrolled expansion of money supply which had caused stagflation. Monetarism was the name given to this idea, which was only the old quantity theory of money revived. On the back of this doubtful proposition about the monetary causes of inflation, a whole host of anti-state ideas entered popular discussion. The macro-economic policy problems were used to cast doubt on all actions of the State in the economic sphere.

The upsurge of monetarism in the advanced country was also reflected in the policy prescriptions of the IMF and other international agencies towards the Third World. From the advice of the 'Chicago boys' in the post-Allende Chile to the pervasive influence of the IMF monetarist prescriptions in the various indebted countries, a systematic attempt was made to scuttle the active participation of the State and increase the scope of domestic and foreign private capital.[5]

At the time when this concerted attack by economic ideology and international financial bureaucracy was undermining the case for State intervention, there were parallel developments on the 'Left' which fuelled this attack, perhaps inadvertently. Ever since the early works of Marx and Engels, there has been an anti-statist tendency on the Left. Lenin codified the Marxist aversion to the State in his *State and Revolution*. The exigencies of the civil war and the need to accelerate economic development in the Soviet Union changed Lenin's perspective and his writings on economic policy never returned to this anti-statist stance. Thus, in his defence of the New Economic Policy in the pamphlet, *The Tax in Kind*, he brings out clearly that *state capitalism* is a progressive development beyond private capitalism. Lenin saw the transition to socialism as a very long drawn out process taking generations and thus state capitalism becomes in his view a vital step in the long transition to socialism.

Subsequent developments in the Soviet Union accelerated the process of statization beyond the limits laid down in NEP. This move towards statization led to acrimonious political debates and the exile of Trotsky and the Left opposition as well as the defeat and purge of Bukharin and the Right opposition. In ideological defence of the increased statization and collectivization, it was claimed that socialism was already established in the USSR. The long transition period envisaged by Marxists until then was telescoped into a few years. Socialism, far from being a goal of human liberation and freedom from want, became synonymous with controls and scarcity.

Stalin's industrialization policy succeeded at least in making the USSR strong enough industrially to fight a long and successful war against Nazi Germany. The functional efficacy of planning and State direction of economic activity was thus established but the political case for Stalinist economics remains weak since its popularity has never been great. In the aftermath of the Hungarian Revolution but especially in the wake of a series of workers' revolts in GDR, Poland, Hungary and Czechoslovakia, it was clear that the hold of orthodox socialist ideology was precarious. The revival of Trotskyism in Western countries opened up again the issue of socialism in one country.

It was as part of this ideological debate on the Left that State capitalism became almost a word of generalized abuse and contempt. Lenin's notion of State capitalism derived from the central direction of a capitalist economy in wartime Germany and combined it with a different political framework of a workers' state. But as the very nature of the Soviet state became an object of debate in the 1960s and 1970s, State capitalism became a suspect. This debate had little effect in the Soviet Union and Eastern Europe but it weakened the case for State intervention in the Western economies. Thus, any and all State activity – nationalization, the welfare state, Keynesian fiscal policy all came under a general attack from the Left. In some instances, Left attack on fiscal policy was no different from the monetarist attack.[6]

In the bloc of Socialist countries, there was a parallel but significant erosion of the State's activities. The qualitative shift beyond NEP in the USSR had been the collectivization campaign. The difficulties of Soviet agriculture highlighted by Khruschev gave a clear impression that while State intervention may work in industries, in agriculture it was an obstacle. Most Eastern European countries avoided collectivization; agriculture stayed private. The marketed output from small privately-owned plots was seen as crucial to keeping food prices down. It seemed in agriculture that private ownership was a significant element in motivation. Since these farms were typically small and employed little or no hired labour they could be seen as an exception to the 'profits equals surplus value equals exploitation' catechism. There came to be a significant literature on agrarianism, peasantism which traded its roots as far back as the Russian populists and Chayanov. Peasants were claimed to be an exception to Capitalist or Marxist logic.

Agrarianism has always had its romantic appeal. A small farmer operating in a capitalist market context is a different species from the peasant that the Narodniks dreamt about. But while the romantic ideology reconciled many Left intellectuals with peasant private holdings, the efficiency displayed by small farmers and their evident prosperity in many economies undermined the case for State's role in the economy.

The idea that private property ownership is vital to economic motivation is a crucial point here. Many schemes for workers' control, workers' ownership, profit sharing derive their edge from this connection. It was in this context that the Chinese experience of rural economies seemed to make the opposite point. The communes were not collectives. The Chinese transformation of landlord/tenant farmer conditions into rural communes spanning many villages seemed to provide a combination of high motivation and efficiency with a cooperative ethos and without the need for private ownership. In the early 1970s, the Chinese experience in agriculture seemed to be a new and potent weapon in the armoury of Socialists. It was the subsequent developments in the Chinese economy which dealt a crucial blow to the case for non-capitalist economic policies.

China under Mao Tse Tung (Mao Ze Dong) was regarded for sometime as having combined collectivist economic planning without forfeiting popular participation and support. Indeed the developments during the Cultural Revolution were thought to be a salutory correction to the tendency of such economies to become bureaucratized. Politics was put in command and tremendous popular energy was released which was harnessed to strengthening collectivist behaviour. The introduction of tripartite revolutionary committees for management of factories, the attempt to overcome the city-country contradiction by sending urban cadres into rural areas, the harnessing of popular enthusiasm for productive purposes in the Tachai experiment all these seemed to be a challenge and supersession to the Stalinist bureaucratic methods.

The course of the Chinese economy in the decade since the death of Mao has been remarkable. Although such reports and recantations must be treated with caution, it would seem that far from helping the economy the popular uprisings during the Cultural Revolution were disruptive. It would also seem that the uprisings were not spontaneous but manipulated by one faction in the ruling party against another. We now know that despite the great success in the agricultural front, China suffered a major famine in the early 1960s whose effects were kept concealed. The Left tendency which dominated from the mid-1960s to the mid-1970s was bereft of popular support and could be easily supplanted. Above all, China has renounced many of the practices which were thought to be her unique contribution to Socialist economic policy. The much heralded connection between voluntary collectivism and economic efficiency was denounced by Chinese leaders as hollow. China, while still practising planning and continuing with communes, is a leader in preaching the virtues of market discipline and the benefits of private property and material incentives. In reversing it previous attitude towards foreign capital and indeed seeking it eagerly, China is now cited as yet another salutary example of the follies of overzealous 'socialist' policies.

This shift on material incentives and on foreign capital has also occurred in Poland, Hungary and to some extent the USSR. The indebtedness of these countries to Western banks has increased in the wake of the strenuous efforts by the banks to recycle petrodollar deposits. Attempts to overcome the structural weaknesses of their economies by modernization with the help of foreign loans by, for example, Poland ran into the problems that market economies often face. When the economy was hit by an international recession and had to squeeze more surplus out to be able to meet the debt burden, the lack of popular support for the ruling élite became transparent. Real wage cutting by deflation is an option that democratic governments in capitalist countries have found less difficult to implement than Poland has.

The case of state action for economic development thus needs to be argued again. Our view of the nature of the State has changed. It is no longer enough to mouth platitudes about proletarian democracy and the vanguard party. The State has to be run by a government that can demonstrate genuine popular support. Failing this, the State ends up merely representing an élite which runs an economy where the sacrifices for accumulation fall on the people while privileges are protected. Growth alone is no longer sufficient as a goal. The types of goods produced, the distribution of income among the citizens and the quality of life they are able to lead have all moved up much higher on the agenda. A government which lacks popular support is bound to end up with a wrong list of projects and priorities, is likely to waste resources and worsen the conditions.

The nature of the State – the character of the ruling élite and the content of the economic programme that is pursued are both likely candidates for close questioning. At the same time, popular discontent with centralized bureaucracies has been rising. Many of the most significant political movements of recent years have occurred outside the party political framework. These movements have been built upon local, autonomous groups fighting on a terrain they know and linking up in larger units only slowly. National politics and civil service have found these movements an annoyance. The movement of the US black people against discrimination starting in mid-1950s, the anti-Vietnam war movement, the feminist upsurge, the anti-nuclear crusade, the Solidarity movement in Poland – these are but few examples. These movements point to the need for State action at the decentralized level in order that many of the benefits of development accrue to the common people.

It is by establishing islands of local autonomy with sufficient access to resources that local groups lock into the economic process. The market process which is avowedly decentralized is impersonal as well as dominated by large agglomerations of economic power. Large corporations are often in collusion with governments which only further enhance the feeling of helplessness of the people. Thus even when the state may play a beneficial role in economic development it is at a different level of politics than was accepted previously.

It is this desire for local, *palpable* autonomy that explains the continued appeal of nationalism. Across the world in a number of countries, various regional, ethnic, religious, linguistic minorities (or even oppressed majorities) aspire to nationhood, to break away from whatever larger units they are part of. Basques (Spain), Bretons (France), Sikhs (India), Tamils (Sri Lanka), the somewhat weaker nationalist aspirations in Scotland, Wales and Northern Ireland, the Quebecois in Canada – examples could be multiplied. There seems to be in all these movements the desire for a state on a small enough scale so that the community comprising the state will be homogeneous. If such a movement succeeds (as it did in the case of Bangladesh), it obtains a state where the centralist/decentralist issues operate with lesser intensity. The desire for autonomy and for homogeneity is accorded high preference compared even to conventional economic rewards as the Sikh issue in India illustrates. People are willing to trade economic betterment for autonomy.

The anticolonial movement which established a number of independent nation states was the originator of such movements. At that time the colonial masters argued that foreign rule brought peace and prosperity and that independence will only lead to chaos. The breakdown of economic mechanisms accompanying decolonializaton has never however been sufficiently serious to deter the demands of other communities for independence. Thus the state as such may yield economic benefits but the desire seems to be for a certain type of state despite economic costs. Once such a state has been achieved, the terrain of debate shifts to specific kinds of economic demands and if these are ignored, the State may face further disintegration.

It is clear therefore that the connection between the State and economic development can no longer be taken for granted as it was in the 1950s. Nor can we succumb to the simplicities of the conservative ideology which argues for dismantling of the State from the economic arena. A qualitatively different relationship has to be arrived at. In the space left at my disposal, I wish to sketch the main ingredients of such a relationship.

1. The necessity of State control for economic development must be contingent upon the demonstrable benefits to be derived from such developments.
2. If benefits from development programmes are in the future and the sacrifices have to be made at the present, the sacrifices have to be made politically visible and the share of different groups in the society has to be made equitable

as a priority of government policy. This is especially required of the ruling group which chooses the development strategy.

3. No economic cost benefit calculus can be regarded as a technical or expert, government planning exercise. Forms of democratic discussion and referenda have to be organized to obtain and renew popular support for such policies. Thus politics should be in command as the Chinese said but politics does not mean politicians or the ruling party but the democratic political process.

4. Economic development has to be interpreted very broadly. It cannot be measured merely in terms of some income construct but must be related to making easier the day to day reproduction of social life, to grant a little extra autonomy in people's lives by releasing the constant constraints of scarcity.

5. In order to allow democratic participation in the definition of what constitutes economic benefit, spatial decentralization has to be used as a crucial variable. This may create homogeneous political communities.

6. The growing size of economic units, the pervasive nature of externalities and the internationalization of economic life argue for the non-viability of small political units. There is a tension between decentralization and agglomeration. To be able to contain the adverse effects of large economic units, a large political unit is required. This tension is unlikely to be easily resolved. Forms of confederation are one answer but other means of resolving this tension will have to be found.

Notes

1. All these tendencies are reflected in Peter Bauer's work, though other authors could be cited. See Peter Bauer, *Dissent on Development*; see also M. Desai, 'Homilies of a Victorian Sage' in *Third World Quarterly*, April 1982.
2. The phrase was coined by Michael Kalecki. See for example K.N. Raj's discussion of the economics of an intermediate regime in *Economic and Political Weekly* (India), Annual Number 1973.
3. See UNIDO: First Global Report (forthcoming April 1985) for the data on which this conclusion is based.
4. See P. Armstrong, A. Glyn and J. Harrison, *Capitalism since World War II: The making and breaking of the great boom* (Fontana, London, 1984).
5. See, N. Howarth and J. Roddick, 'Labour and Monetarism in Chile 1975–80; *Bulletin of Latin American Research*, October 1981.
6. See, Ernest Mandel, *The Second Slump: A Marxist Analysis of the Recession in the Seventies* (NLB, London 1978). See my review in *Economic Journal*, June 1979.

[11]

Indian Economic Review, Vol. XIX, No. 2

A General Theory of Poverty?
A Review Article

MEGHNAD DESAI

In any year nowadays between half a billion to three fourths of a billion people are living in starvation conditions. At the same time it has to be admitted that in the years since the end of the Second World War we have witnessed a more sustained growth in output of almost all goods than at any other time in the history of mankind. Population has grown, life expectancy has increased and at the same time incidents of catastrophic mortality in any part of the world have attracted sympathy.

It is in this wider context that we must look at Amartya Sen's new book.[1] Obviously its main concern is with understanding poverty in general but especially famines in particular. As its subtitle makes clear Sen offers a theory of entitlement which explains why some groups suffer from deprivation—not only relative deprivation but deprivation absolute enough on occasions to lead to starvation deaths.

Needless to say this is an important book. As one would expect, it is lucidly written. Sen not only proposes a theory of entitlements but also tests it out in four studies of famine conditions — the Bengal famine of 1943 and the Bangladesh famine of 1973-1974, the Ethiopian famine of 1972-74 and the Sahel famine of 1973 and 1974. As an essay in theory and an essay in applied economics, one ought to read this book. My main worry is however that in concentrating on famines and poverty, the much more general implications of the theory of entitlement are likely to be missed. In this respect Sen has been very self-denying. He refuses to extend the logic of his theory to the general corpus of economic theory. I would like in this review to point out some of these implications, though they are my own interpretations and not the author's.

To begin with I shall expound the theory of entitlements as contained in Chapters 1, 4 and 5 of this book and in Appendices A and B. The theory of poverty, contained in Chapters 2, 3 and Appendix C though very important, I shall only briefly touch upon. In Section 2, I shall summar-

---

[1] Amartya Sen : *Poverty and Famines : An Essay on Entitlement and Deprivation*, Clarendon Press, Oxford (1981).

ize the four applications of the theory of entitlements. Many questions are
raised here such as the one on famine mortality taken up in Appendix D
which I shall ignore. I shall review the four studies as exercises in (contemporary) economic history writing which are models of what cliometri-
cians (or any other economic historian) should be trying to do. In the
third section I take up the implications of Sen's theory for the theory of
economic development. In the fourth section I shall look upon the theory
of entitlements as a critique of and an alternative to Walrasian general
equilibrium theory. The last section will relate to Marxian value theory to
which I believe it also offers a useful new approach.

I. THE THEORY OF ENTITLEMENTS

Each person, no matter how poor, has some endowments. They may consist of personal attributes—age, sex, race, height, weight and more elusive
personal qualities charm, beauty etc. In terms of economic measures every
person has at least their capacity for work—their labour power—unless too
young or too old or infirm or severely handicapped. Others may have
additional endowments land, money, durable goods, financial assets etc.
There are certain legal rules which define what can and what cannot be
owned. Thus a slave does not have any endowments which he can call his
own except the personal attributes which may have made him more
marketable. Serfs were not free to dispose of their labour power as they
chose. Modern societies do not permit slaves as part of one's endowments.

Given the endowments, there are various ways of converting them into
goods and services which constitute consumption baskets.[3] Some endowments can be directly traded into goods e.g. money is such a universal
solvent. Others have to be put into a production process—seeds or
ploughs—so they can yield output—things—which can be converted into
other goods. Labour power has a dual status in this scheme. It can be
directly sold for wages which can be converted into consumption goods.
It can also be engaged into a production process along with other inputs
which will yield output which again can be sold. All these exchanges
whether of labour directly or of labour and inputs via output presume a
market and they all are mediated via money in almost all modern economies no matter how 'less developed'. There also has to be sufficient
demand for these 'vendible commodities' (to use Adam Smith's expression)
for one to be able to obtain other goods for it.

---

[2] I leave out of consideration investment goods or financial assets which can also be
purchased as does Sen. The extension to such goods will be straightforward except
that it may lead to dynamic considerations of which more below.

A General Theory of Poverty

Now given one's endowments there are various ways of converting them into goods. If I have land, I could sell it outright and live off the sum of money with or without additional interest earned by investing the capital sum. I could alternatively rent the land out and live off the rent. Or I could give it to a sharecropper for half the output though I may also have to provide some of the inputs. I may lastly cultivate the land myself with or without hired labour.

Thus, from the ownership of one asset—land, there are various possibilities each of which will convert into a basket of consumption goods. Selling the land or renting it at a money rent will yield me sums of money which I could trade for consumption goods at the prevailing retail prices. If however I have let it for a rent in terms of a portion of the output, the situation is similar to sharecropping and to own cultivation. I have to *sell* the output and then buy consumption goods with the money revenue earned from the sale. Here again it is crucial for the probability of my experiencing starvation whether I grow edible or nonedible crops. For the former at least some portion of the output can be directly consumed and the price does not enter into the question. For nonedible crops there has to be a sale before there can be a purchase.

Now all the various combinations of consumption bundles I can obtain for my land traversing these routes is what Amartya Sen calls my 'exchange entitlements'. If I owned only my labour power, then I have the choice of working for a wage as an agricultural (landless) labourer, or as a nonagricultural labourer or perhaps as a sharecropper. The labourer and the sharecropper are similar because they own nothing but their labour power. They may turn out to have different exchange entitlements however.

In 'normal' times, the wage of the worker will be enough to provide subsistence, if not more. Thus the subsistence bundle is within his exchange entitlement. The same, let us assume, is true for the share cropper, the tenant and the landlord. Now if for some reason—drought, war, black-market hoarding—the price of grain were to go up, some of the participants will find their entitlements shrinking. This may be so drastic that they may not even get a subsistence bundle. They may starve.

Amartya Sen spends a considerable part of his essay trying to combat the food availability decline (FAD) explanation of why famines and starvation deaths occur. According to FAD, it is because available food falls short of the population's need for food that deaths occur. A famine is an obvious instance it would seem of food shortage leading to starvation deaths. Sen points out that food shortage can arise without food supplies (output plus net imports plus stocks) declining i.e., demand may go up due to special reasons. But even where available food declines, the question of who starves and why, is not answered by FAD. This is because FAD is too aggregative an explanation; decline in per capita food availability not only hides the usual income inequalities but very significantly it also ignores uneven changes in entitlements.

Take as an extreme case two landless labourers one paid money wages, and one paid in kind. Let us assume that the wage is fixed before the harvest ex ante at Rs. 1000 for the season, or 100 kilos of grain. If the rains fail or due to some other reason harvests are very low, the output will be below expectations. If this is a widespread phenomenon, grain prices may rise. If 50 kilos is subsistence bundle, a price rise of grain of more than 100% would push the worker paid in money wages below the subsistence line. Thus his exchange entitlements shrink due to *relative price changes*. The worker paid in grain will be that much safer (assuming the employer does not arbitrarily renege on the contract to pay him 100 kilos).

Take now a sharecropper and a worker paid in money wages. The sharecropper let us say may normally expect 150 kilos of grain—one half of normal output of 300 kilos. Again if output were to be anywhere lower than 100 kilos due to, say drought, then the sharecropper would be pushed below subsistence. So he will suffer not so much from relative price change as from a *pure quantity change*.

Take lastly a cattleman. The nomadic herdsmen of the Sahel raise livestock and take it from one place to another for grazing. They sell cattle or dairy products to buy grain. A drought would mean decline in cattle output (in terms of weight) and/or in dairy output. If in addition grain prices have also risen, then a cattleman would suffer relative price loss (grain more expensive in terms of dairy products or meat) and from output loss (leaner cattle/less milk). His entitlement of grain would thus shrink due to both these reasons and he will be doubly vulnerable as it were to starvation.

Thus whatever the macroeconomic dimensions of food shortage, the microeconomic incidence of starvation would depend on how individual households are placed in terms of their endowments and through these endowments in their exchange entitlements. To some extent these endowments relate to ownership of the means of production as in the case of share-cropper/labourer but they also depend on *access* to the means of production. But here again—ownership or access to the means of production are not sufficient to define the likelihood of entitlement loss though they may serve to determine the class to which an individual belongs. If you have two modes of production coexisting, say a nomadic one with livestock as the principal means of production and an agricultural one, the class portion of a rich cattle owner does not render him immune from entitlement loss if the cattle/grain price ratio changes. Thus entitlement leads to a more complex classification than simple class analysis.

In general, one is here talking about changes in potential real income when relative prices change in an unanticipated (unanticipable) fashion. Real income is here income in the sense of Hicks—maximum potential consumption flow, or equivalently ex-ante income conditional upon prices and interest rate expectations, i.e., income as potential yield of wealth. Sen is concerned with situation where *realised* (ex post) maximal consumption bundles may fall due to unpredicted price changes. These unpredictable and unpredicted price changes are also noninsurable ones since the entire economy suffers from the random shock and not just an individual. Only a purely external agency—food aid or Royal granaries as in the old days—can relieve the problem.

But of course one is not talking of income and consumption bundles in the abstract. Starvation and famines have to do with food shortages. So grain acquires prominence in everyone's consumption need at such times. Normal consumption habits collapse to basic food needs which acquire top priority. So grain and its price become pivotal. Hence it is the expost real income in terms of grain which is the crucial variable in predicting susceptibility of an individual to starvation.

This does not mean that the theory proposed in this essay is fitted only to the economics of famine. The notion of entitlement is quite general since it provides a way of relating real income changes to systematic information about ownership and access to assets. The pivotal commodity may be grain in famines but the economic experience since 1973 could be interpreted in terms of oil becoming a pivotal commodity. Nonoil producing economies suffered entitlement losses when oil prices rose and these were *ex ante* unpredicted and unpredictable losses. The consequences of this entitlement loss in terms of inflation and rise in unemployment are even now only dimly understood in terms of the conventional economic analysis.

But entitlement losses may arise from noneconomic forces just as well. Entitlements are after all defined within a certain legal, property right context. Changes in political regimes do lead to sudden shifts in entitlements. Thus the changes brought in the Bengal countryside when the East India Company got *Diwani* rights and unleashed their agents in local trades is one example of a drastic change in entitlements. The abolition of slavery in the post Bellum American South is another example which could be similarly analysed, where the entitlement sets of the ex-slaves and of the slaveowners change in unpredicted fashion. From the abolition of serfdom through the Stolypin reforms, the October Revolution and the collectivisation campaigns, the Russian peasantry witnessed multiple changes in their entitlement sets. (Thus it may even be possible to speculate that as a result of collectivisation, their entitlement sets shrunk though their real consumption may have gone up compared to before. But this is pure conjecture.)

II. CASE STUDIES OF FOUR FAMINES

In Chapters 6-9, Sen studies four specific cases of famines where he is able to contrast the prediction of his exchange entitlement theory compared to FAD. Of these the two Bengal episodes the famines of 1943 and 1973/4 would be of most interest to the readers of this Review. But the two case studies of Africa—Ethiopia and Sahel also raise interesting issues.

In each case, what is impressive is the prodigious amount of primary material digging Sen has done. To have gathered district level wage data in 1943 Bengal or gone through the Calcutta Municipal Gazette for all the weeks of 1941-43 for the prices of rice and fish (rohi fish as well as whole fish) in the College Street Market of Calcutta would be hard work even if one had known where to look. When it comes to districts of a certain region of Ethiopia and the calculation of real income loss suffered by Ethiopian pastoralists by calculating Sorghum-sheep or Maize-Camel exchange rates, one has to admit that this essay is a robust combination of theory and application. This has to be said because it would have been easy enough to stop at a theoretical critique of neo-classical theory and propose exchange entitlement as an alternative formulation. But this theory has arisen in course of explaining real phenomena and the application have not just been thought of afterwards to embellish the theory.

In each case, Sen calculates first whether available food supplies went up or not during the years when starvation deaths occurred. This is quite a tricky set of calculations. The Bengal 1943 study is a model of its kind where corrections are made to official output series, imports of grain are accounted for and stock carryover allowed for. In the case of Sahel, there is even a discernible drop in food supply though Sen argues that exchange entitlement offers better predictions.

In each case, when it comes to looking at the incidence of starvation, it is clear that the farther away from direct food cultivation a group is i.e., the more markets it has to go through to convert endowments into actual consumption, the more liable to starvation it is. Thus, cattlemen of Sahel and Ethiopia, the fishermen of Bengal or tradesmen suffer more than agricultural labourers who suffer more than share-croppers and peasant cultivators. One response is for people in nonagricultural occupations to throw themselves into agriculture related jobs e.g., husking paddy in Bengal.

Such a response is easy to understand but as I shall show below difficult to predict ex ante in a neo-classical model. What is more it fits very well with what we know of behaviour in other societies with scarcity. Thus in medieval England, many of the crimes recorded in the court rolls had to do with grain theft e.g., gleaning which the marginialised poor resorted to at harvest time. In later years in seventeenth century England, those whose exchange entitlements had shrunk due to the enclosure of common lands resorted to various forms of crime to sustain themselves. Even the incidence of witchcraft in these years in rural England can be interpreted as a sort of blackmail resorted to by some of the marginalised poor (Keith Thomas; Religion and the Decline of Magic, see the concluding chapters). It is thus clear that the new perspectives offered in this book will be an important addition to the historians 'toolbox as well as the economists'.

III. Economic Development and the Theory of Entitlements

The theory of economic development whether in the classical theory or in its revived form in the post 1945 years had its principal focus the nation state and its prosperity. (Adam Smith's book was after all titled the Wealth of *Nations.*) This focus on the nation state is understandable from many points of view. Nationalism was a powerful ideology and it seemed then one could talk of the nation as a single unit. In terms of narrow material interests this emphasis on national development helped the elite group which had led the independence movements since they benefited from the development process first. There was also in the strategy of import substitution the quasi rent to be earned by the local producers while promoting the national interest.

Thus the measurement of economic development was in terms of aggregate of per capita growth of real output. It was argued that before one could redistribute income, a country had to experience growth of output. In the Fifties and Sixties this growth was reasonable but not rapid enough to transform the economies of the developing countries. When growth faltered, various obstacles mainly international were blamed by the governments of these countries. In a sense the North-South dialogue is a way for the countries of the South to shift blames outside their own countries.

But even in days of growth, the status of the very poor did not improve. Only in the late Sixties and early Seventies, the problem of poverty of certain groups in the total population of a 'poor country' began to be discussed seriously. To begin with the debate, in India for instance, was about the *number* of poor : whether this had gone up or down over the development years. This is the headcount measure as Sen calls it. (But the very act of counting heads of the poor in a 'poor country' obviously means that there are differences among the poor as to the extent of their poverty.) Sen developed this measure of poverty further by concentrating on the income distribution within the group designated as poor by some head count measure. This measure is discussed in nontechnical terms in Chapters 2 and 3 of this book and the technical details are in Appendix C.

The Sen measure of poverty is now well known and as the extensive bibliography in this book shows it has been applied to calculate poverty indices for many countries (see especially Chapter 3, footnotes 22 and 23, p. 37).

The problem however is not only one of measuring poverty but of explaining its origin, its persistence and of proposing solutions to it. The question of economic development in the sense of a rising per capita income becomes a separate one from the question of the structure and morphology of poverty. This is the question opened up by Sen's book and although he does not go into the general problem of the causes and the persistence of poverty, his book offers a beginning.

The problem is in one sense that of aggregation. As we learned in the debates about capital theory, it is impossible to define a malleable aggregate without begging any important questions of the relation between prices and income distribution. As with capital so with income. When economic growth takes place, the increment may be measured as percentage growth of this malleable lump called GNP but such a measure gives the illusion that this increment is available for the government to dispose of as it pleases. But growth actually takes place in many small concrete activities: many prices change as well as quantities. The growth which is measured has already accrued in these price and quantity changes in the exchange entitlements and thereby in the actual incomes of certain sections of the community. These sections have already in a sense appropriated these gains and concretised them into commodity purchases—new tin roof, a transistor radio, jewellery or new apartments. These gains are not lying around to be redistributed at the will of the government. Those who have gained will resist taxation or redirection of these gains. Taxation, rationing or other attempts to mobilise resources through banking or money creation will have to act through price changes, open or hidden. What Sen's account shows is that these price changes will affect different people's entitlements further. What can be shown using his theory is that many of the policies adopted for resource mobilisation change prices in ways which affect the poor adversely. Those with small endowments cannot benefit from these policies. What they need is a direct quantity change in their endowments rather than an indirect change through price manipulation. One way to alter the exchange entitlements of the poor would be of course to change property rights. The efforts to ameliorate rural poverty in India as against China (except until the recent shift in Chinese policies) were differently successful because the rural commune in China altered property rights and exchange entitlements more thoroughly than land reform did in India. Tenancy reform, Zamindari abolition, relief on rural indebtedness helps those who own or have access to land in some way. It cannot affect the landless or those who have very small amounts of land. Thus the rural poverty problem is untouched if one only touches the cultivators.

IV. A CRITIQUE OF GENERAL EQUILIBRIUM THEORY?

In one sense general equilibrium *analysis* is a method, an approach. It is obviously better to be able to take a total view of the problem to appreciate the complex relationships among the constituents of a system. From that point of view, this book uses a general equilibrium approach. But there is also in Walrasian general equilibrium *theory* the attempt to assert that markets clear automatically and that the working of the price mechanism not only leads to equilibrium outcomes but that such an outcome has some desirable (economic welfare related) properties. In what sense then can one say that the theory of exchange entitlements (EE) differs from the Walrasian general equilibrium theory (WGE)?

It could be argued by proponents of WGE that Sen's EE theory is a mere storm in a teacup. They could say that all Sen argues is that when the price of grain goes up due to decline in food availability (supply shift) or hoarding (demand shift) the real wage in terms of grain goes down. This is quite straightforward. They could then add that in some cases this real grain wage could be so low as to cause starvation if one further assumes that there are no substitutes for grain (which in WGE terms is an unwarranted restrictive assumption).

This would be a caricature of EE and a simplification which robs it of its real interest. The point of EE is not that real grain wage goes down when grain price goes up but that different groups even within the grain producing sector (to say nothing of those outside) experience differential effects depending on their endowments and their position in the structure of production. Endowments relate to ownership of assets and the position in the production structure relates to the access to means of production. Contrary to market intermediation bringing smooth and beneficent outcomes, it is those who do not have to go through a purchase or sale to convert their income into consumption who are least vulnerable to a decline in real grain wage. The direct producer of grain, either as landowner or sharecropper and the worker who receives a grain wage are safer than he who receives money rent or money wage. As for the sectors other than the grain producing sector, each additional link in the chain between production of goods (or services) and the purchase of grain increases the chance of a decline in grain wage.

The usual proofs of the existence of equilibrium in WGE rule out by assumption the possibility that an individual's income may be so low that he may starve. They rule this out for the same reason that they rule out the possibility that firms may go bankrupt. Such likely outcomes pose difficult technical problems and restrict the generality of the results obtained. In empirical economics, it is quite useful to allow for such lower limits to consumtpion. The Stone-Geary Linear Expenditure system allows for the possibility of there being certain minimum required amounts of each commodity in the utility function. If actual consumption of any *one* of the many commodities falls below the minimum then the consumer is assumed to derive no utility from consumption. In a way Sen's theory can get by with a specific instance of LES which will say that a certain commodity (food grain) alone has this property that a minimum amount of it is required. In normal times this minimum is not a binding requirement but at certain critical times, this commodity regains its crucial position if its price rises so high that normal money income cannot buy this minimum amount for a substantial minority of the population. This result is systematically derivable from the behaviour of the relative price of the goods produced by this minority to the price of grain. Thus, the *terms of trade* of different sections become important.

But there is also an additional effect. The terms of trade are affected not only by the absolute price of grain going up. Ignore for the time being the sharecroppers and others paid directly in grain. If the price of grain goes up and the real grain wage falls, what happens in the economy? In a neoclassical model the employment in grain production will go up and if the same real wage is to prevail everywhere, the number of employed elsewhere should shrink or the price of other products adjust to restore a real product wage in each sector to a profitable level. But not only does agricultural employment not go up due to adverse output effects but the prices of other goods collapse even as the price of grain goes up. This is because having spent a larger part of their income on grain purchase, consumers cannot buy other goods—fish, barber's services, entertainment, etc. Thus the real wage in terms of the product of these activities moves *up* while real grain wage moves *down* and total employment goes *down*. The equilibrating mechanism does not work automatically since effective demand problems arise *as a consequence of* supply shortages in grain.

There is neither the space here nor is this the occasion for taking into account further refinements of EE or counter objections of WGE. In normal equilibrium, the various incomes derived in grain or money or other goods whether as wages or profits equalise across sectors and in a WGE world it makes no difference how you receive your income. If particular individuals experience random shocks to their income these cancel out with other people's grains. But in famines an entire economy experiences a shock which is uninsurable against. Within the economy various groups gain or lose differentially but the whole economy suffers a loss of output. The analogy of this with the effect on particular national economies of an oil price rise is obvious.

One aspect of EE where we can criticise Sen is in its lack of dynamics. The endowments which we start with obviously have arisen from previous accumulation behaviour and a single outcome like famine will affect future endowments. Even in his exposition of the EE theory in Appendix B, Sen takes a static view when he takes the proportion of income spent on grain by different groups as fixed. These proportions will depend on the prices that prevail and cannot be taken to be independent of them. Indeed while in normal times a household will spend only a fraction of its income on food (say half), when grain prices rise this fraction may go up even as high as to absorb all income. Thus the h_i of Sen's equations (B15-B23) cannot be taken to be constants, although assuming constancy aids the exposition.

V. EE Theory and Marxian Theory

There are many Marxian undertones in Sen's exposition. Thus in his first chapter he mentions modes of production and there seems to be a connection between exchange entitlements and modes of production. Little subsequent use is made however of the modes of production concept. Again by placing the questions of ownership, of property rights and of income distribution in the centre of his argument, Sen evokes but does not explicitly use any of the Marxian concepts.

To a certain extent this selfdenial is understandable as Marxian economic theory is hardly a neat and well finished body of economic theory one can confront. Marxian economics is not so much a broad church as an Indian bazaar where many hawk their wares without guarantee either of quality or of price. But more important than this consideration, the EE argument is in some ways broader and in other ways narrower than Marxian theory. It is narrower because of its lack of dynamics and nothing more needs to be said about that. It is its positive message for Marxian economics that we can concentrate on.

In a sense EE deals with differentiation within a class—the class of workers which consists severally of rural and urban workers, agricultural workers and nonagricultural workers, of landless labourers and sharecroppers. There is a large literature on class differentiation especially within agriculture in the writings of Kautsky, Lenin, Mao and others. The difference between sharecroppers and landless labourers may be small in some sense but may become important in face of systematic changes in grain prices. If one has a labour theory of value as a tool for analysis of these differences, many nuisances may be missed out because the crucial difference here is between ownership and access to means of production. This is because although one may grant the logic by which surplus value is produced in the production process, the division of the vendible surplus (in money or in commodity form) is not a straightforward business. In the classic Marxian model, all surplus accrues to the owner of means of production and wages equal the exchange value of labour power. But the actual division of surplus depends not only on relative strengths of different classes but also on their position in the production (labour) process. This is why access to means of production makes a difference to the sharecropper as against the landless labourer. This difference has not been entirely taken on board in the analytics of Marxian value theory although there are some elements in John Roemer's recent work on social classes which take this into account. (Roemer (1983)).

It is only by an enlarged definition of social relations—relations in terms of the means of production—which takes into account hierarchial gradations in the production process and the relative position of different groups that we will be able to accommodate these stratification outcomes systematically. Although Sen does not adopt a Labour theory of value, this approach offers a sufficiently detailed framework for doing this.

But in a sense the concept of a mode of production is a limited one for our purposes. All the societies Sen analyses and most that we are interested in studying are social formations—mixtures of overlapping modes of production. Attempts to label them uniquely as feudal, semi-feudal, colonial, asiatic or capitalist are futile. It is precisely because of the coexistence of the nomadic and the agricultural modes in the Sahel that despite their superior class position as owners of cattle within the nomadic mode, the cattlemen are marginalised with respect to the agrarian economy in times of high grain prices. This is much as merchant capital was predatory on old feudal aristocracy in the century of the Great Inflation. The relative positions of different groups in a social formation can be analysed in terms of their endowments but only by translating these endowments via exchange i.e. prices into entitlements that their changing relationships can be understood. Here again the currently available Marxian value theory is too blunt an instrument for analysing such problems. Labour is for example not as crucial an input in a nomadic mode as it is in the capitalist one. One may as well for the time being taken on the price theory in Sen to model these complexities.

VI. Conclusion

To conclude, this is a fascinating and important book. There is much more to be done to absorb, understand and extend the analysis proposed by Amartya Sen. It should prove to be one of the most original and fruitful books in economics published in recent years.

REFERENCE

Roemer, John, (1982), *A General Theory of Exploitation and Class*, Harvard University Press, Cambridge, Mass.

[12]

Consumption and pollution

Introduction
Within the context of this interdisciplinary conference on the topic of the consumer society, this paper has certain clearly defined tasks. It attempts to report the current state of thinking and research in economics on the relationship between consumption and pollution. Consumption has occupied a central place in economic theory since the days of Jevons and the marginalist revolution. This has been reinforced by the development of Keynesian theory and reflected in the change in government economic policies in the developed economies. It is only in recent years that the environmental consequences of economic activity in general and the high level of mass consumption in particular have come under public criticism and academic scrutiny. I shall relate how some recent rethinking in the theory of consumption, which proceeded independently of the environment debate, provides a way of examining this question of consumption and pollution within the context of established economic theory. I shall then outline a second tendency which uses the tools of economic theory but outlines the importance of certain constraints ignored hitherto by economists but a matter of commonplace knowledge in the physical sciences. This approach attempts to set up a quantifiable model of the environmental consequences of economic activity. I shall illustrate this approach by some numerical calculations carried out by investigators in North America. These researches lead to certain fresh ways of thinking about the end of economic activity and the determinants of the quality of as well as the standard of living.

The place of consumption in economic theory
Economists take it as a 'self-evident truth' that consumption is the end of all economic activity. Accumulation of wealth, economic growth, and increasing productivity are all seen ultimately as justified if they promise a higher level of consumption per capita in the future than the 'society' enjoys in the present. Elementary textbooks as well as advanced contributions on the subjects of growth and welfare can be cited in support of this view (see Dorfman, 1964, p. 43). Models are formulated for individual as well as society's behaviour where the goal is to maximize the utility of consumption in the current period and/or some discounted sum of utility over time.

This utilitarian bias in much of modern economic theory is rarely explicitly debated. Society's welfare is seen to be a function of the welfare of the individuals in it. Individuals' welfare is measured by the utility they derive from consumption of goods and services. There are several ways of relating individuals' separate choices to society's choice, but the one most frequently chosen for pedagogic purposes is a *laissez-faire* criterion where decentralized decisions about their separate welfares by atomistic individuals are said to achieve the highest social welfare (however see Sen, 1970).

For our purposes the essential part is that an individual's welfare is measured by the utility he derives from consumption of goods and services. If the individual has more of everything then he is clearly better off by these standards. If he has more of some things but less of others then a tricky problem of weighting his gains and losses arises. But it is always assumed that the individual will always want more goods – there is no satiety in the economist's world.

The measurement of social welfare by economic welfare and of the latter by the individuals' consumption level is easily translated into one of the objectives of economic growth being a rising level of consumption per capita. From an aggregate point of view, consumption, or at least consumer expenditure, is an easily predictable and stable function of income. In Keynesian theory, since employment is constrained by effective demand, the higher the consumer expenditure, the higher is effective demand likely to be. Whereas investment decisions may be unpredictable and subject to the changing state of expectations, consumer expenditure is a large and stable proportion of income. A policy for full employment has to rely as much on maintaining consumption at a high level by a combination of built in stabilizers and deliberate changes in tax rates etc. as on encouraging investment demand.

Thus, on theoretical grounds for measurement of economic welfare and policy considerations of maintaining a high level of employment, a high level of consumption occupies a central place in economics.

It would be an easy task to point out that the identification of welfare with economic welfare and of the latter with consumption level of individuals is an extremely narrow view of the way societies behave. Maximizing the utility of consumption can be seen as society's goal, if at all, only in recent years and in developed countries. Societies put survival of population much higher in the list of priorities as can be seen in experience of countries during war-time or temporary disasters such as earthquakes, floods, famines etc. Welfare may depend on provision of public goods, consumed in common by all – street lighting, museums and art galleries, safety in the streets etc. Quality of life may depend on whether society is competitive or cooperative, whether the distribution of income and power is grossly inequitable, and whether there is a hope of betterment in the near future. Such considerations are not unknown in economics but they impinge on the economist's thinking only if they can be formally analysed within the models thrown up by the paradigm. Such bias may be inhibiting of innovative thinking but it is held in the belief that such an approach alone can yield usable results. For the purposes of this paper, I shall try to relate the developments within the economics mainstream to deal with the problem of consumption and pollution.

Goods or the things that goods do

The first extension of consumer theory in economics that was pursued independently of the concern with pollution, casts doubt on the basic notion that consumers derive utility from goods and services (see Lancaster, 1966 pp. 132–57). In this extension, goods are seen as ways of satisfying certain needs and the utility is derived from the characteristics which goods possess than the physical nature of the goods themselves. A need may be satisfied by several goods in different combinations and with varying efficiency. If I am a commuter, utility is not derived so much from consumption of a car ride or a ride on the public transport. My need for transport services can be satisfied by a combination of walk, car ride, public transport in the following possible combinations (and many more):

1. walk to the train station – ride on train – walk to the office
2. car from my home to the office door
3. car ride to the train station – ride on train – walk to the office.

These combinations satisfy my need for transport but they have different characteristics of convenience, time taken, exercise provided, aggravation due to congestion etc. They also have different environmental consequences. If they all satisfy the need for transport, public policy may seek to encourage 1 or 3 against 2.

The technology linking goods to characteristics is crucial in this extension. The technology can be changed by introducing new goods and services, by altering the number of characteristics produced by available goods (e.g. increasing the inconvenience of commuter car traffic by imposing parking restrictions) or by using old goods in new combinations (e.g. food taken out, as against eating out or eating a home cooked meal). Introduction of a track for bicycle riders in urban traffic will increase the safety of bicycle rides to work etc.

By concentrating on the tasks performed by goods rather than the goods themselves, this approach emphasizes that welfare and utility depend on certain needs being satisfied adequately rather than on having more goods. Utility can be increased as much by public transport in combination with local car rides as by car rides all the way. The purchase of cars and their manufacture may suffer as a result, the decline in car production may lead to a decline in GNP, but the reduction in consumption of car services may lead to a higher level of utility obtained by the transport need being satisfied with more desirable characteristics and fewer undesirable ones.

In the original article outlining this approach, Kelvin Lancaster pointed out a peculiarity of the technology of consumption. In developed economies, we have many goods satisfying the same need in varying combinations. In poorer countries, one good may be used in several different ways to satisfy many needs. The important consequence here is that poorer societies tend to throw away very little but use all the different parts of a good (the flesh of the banana as well as the banana skin, the coconut shell as well as its inside) economically. This minimizes pure waste and also uses the good much more intensively. Developed societies not only throw away a great part of the goods – wrapping, packaging, all but the best parts of fruit, vegetable, and animals, and they tend to have goods performing identical functions but different only in superficial characteristics, just think of the many brands of toothpaste, cars, brands of food, television sets etc. It is thought to be a measure of the high standard of living enjoyed to have such duplication since it is said to provide choice.

Thus, this approach moves away from the fetishistic emphasis on goods and more goods. It helps to bring out the good and the bad characteristics generated by consumption activity. If cars 'produce' convenience of door to door transport, they also produce noxious fumes and noise. The technology also depends on the number of people engaging in the same activity. Thus, congestion is not produced by a single car driver but by many of them undertaking the same activity simultaneously in the same location. This aspect of the technology (its 'non-convexity' to give its technical name) was not brought out by Lancaster but his approach lends itself to such generalization where the interdependence of consumers, all seeking their highest utility in isolation from each other, is brought out. Hitherto, such interdependence was thought to be a special case, an exception in the model to be patched up quickly. The locational aspects of consumption activity can also be brought out since the same activity – playing your radio at its loudest – has different consequences whether you are doing it in a crowded train or on the moors.

A major shortcoming of this approach to consumption and the more traditional economic view of consumption is that it equates consumption of a good as the end of a process. Consumption is total disappearance, analagous to evaporation without any physical consequences. The residue left behind after consumption, such as garbage, rubbish, air and water pollution, empty non-returnable bottles, and abandoned old cars, is somehow not taken as a part of economic activity. The second approach I shall outline is more the environmentalist approach and emphasizes these consequences.

Consumption as transformation of goods into garbage

When discussing the role of constraints on economic behaviour, economists mention scarcity of resources in a general way, but even the physical constraints thought to be relevant have been shortage of machine capacity, limited supply of land, or skilled labour etc. The environmentalist approach or the Materials-Balances approach makes the dependence of the economic system on the natural system explicit (see Ayres and Kneese, 1969 pp. 282–97; Kneese and Bower, 1972). This is done by emphasizing the law of conservation of matter as a binding constraint on the economic system. Figure 1 summarizes this dependence.

Economic models concentrate on the production-consumption cycle indicated by F. Production simultaneously generates income and output which in turn are expenditures of the consumption sector which also provides labour input for production.

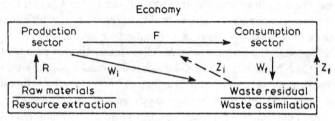

Source: Kneese and Bower, 1972, p. 14.

Figure 1   The economy and the environment

Production also uses raw materials extracted from the environment some of which are exhaustible in a more absolute sense than others. The world's reserves of metals, known and unknown, is in some absolute sense exhaustible whereas our supply of agricultural products is limited by the relative exhaustibility of soil fertility. The relation R then emphasizes the input of the environment with the production sector. Some resources, such as clean air and water, are unpaid for, of course, but this can be taken into account explicitly.

Much more important are the environmental outputs of the production sector (W_i) and the consumption sector (W_f). These are waste materials which are the transformed versions of the goods. They can be calculated by knowing the material weight and the chemical composition of these goods. These outputs accumulate as waste materials and tax the limited assimilative capacity of the environment. The unpaid for part of the raw materials is small but the waste output is largely generated as a 'free' good (which is a rather costly 'bad').

The two broken lines outline the possibility that some of these waste materials could be recycled back into the production sector (Z_i) and the consumption section (Z_f). The system as a whole – Economy and Natural environment taken together – must satisfy the law of conservation. Ayres and Kneese (1969) who first formalized the Materials-Balance approach, say the following:

> In an economy which is closed (no imports or exports) and where there is no net accumulation of stocks (plant, equipment, inventories, consumer durables or residential buildings) the amount of residual inserted into the natural environment must be approximately equal to the weight of basic fuels, food, and raw materials entering the processing and production system, plus oxygen taken from the atmosphere. [In addition, we must include residuals such as NO and NO_2 arising from reactions between components of the air itself but occurring as combustion byproducts.] This result, while obvious upon reflection, leads to the, at first rather surprising, corollary that residuals disposal involves a greater tonnage of materials than basic materials processing, although many of the residuals, being gaseous, require no physical 'handling'. (Ayres and Kneese, 1969, pp. 284–5)

(The interpolation in square brackets is part of a relevant footnote to this statement.)

By highlighting residual production as an inevitable and equiproportional consequence of economic activity rather than a small byproduct, Ayres and Kneese show that consumption and pollution are interlinked. At the same time, they show that one of the major reasons for our concern with pollution is the limited assimilative capacity of the environment (the spaceship Earth). They do not examine in addition (at least not in the study cited here) the consequence of increasing residual production on the quality of life, through the effect, say, of air pollution on health.

Operational implications of the two approaches

The approaches I have outlined above rather sketchily are designed to be operational and have been applied to practical problems. The mathematical structures of these approaches are quite similar. Lancaster's approach uses a technology matrix to describe the characteristics produced by the goods and services. Consumption activities are also combinations of goods. The linearity of the relationship makes the computation of the 'costs' of consuming a certain package of characteristics explicit. The total expenditure incurred in any consumption activity can then be seen either as the sum of expenditure on the goods consumed or the (shadow) price paid for acquiring a certain combination of characteristics. Using this method, Anderson and Crocker (1971, pp. 171–80) have been able to estimate the impact of atmosphere pollution on the price of houses in St. Louis. In buying a house, one not only buys so many rooms of specified size but also certain neighbourhood characteristics, proximity to transport, schools of a certain quality and atmospheric pollution of a certain standard. While it is clear that pollution will tend to lower prices and be associated with other social characteristics of slum housing, it can now be shown how much weight these factors have in house buying activity. This approach then also makes explicit that the burden of environmental deterioration falls mainly on the poorer sections. Many public statements to the contrary notwithstanding, better environment is not just a middle-class luxury. The incidence of pollution is regressive.

The Materials-Balance approach also employs the notion of a linear technology by explicitly using the input-output method. The input of raw materials into the production process is described by a matrix of constant coefficients relating the material requirements per unit of output. This is added to the conventional input-output table which covers only the goods explicitly paid for. The output of the process is then also expanded to include normal goods as well as residual waste. The material inputs from the environment (which are unpaid for) such as land, air and water appear also a residual waste output in their processed form. Thus, clear air is processed through production and consumption units, say, nitrogen oxides, carbon monoxide, sulphur dioxide, particulates etc.

Peter Victor (1972) has applied a generalized version of the Materials-Balance approach to calculate the total amount of land, air, and water pollution generated by economic activity in Canada. His Economic-ecological Input-Output Table can be schematized as follows:

Table 1   The Economic ecological input output system

	Economic commodities	Industries	Final Demand	Totals	Ecological commodities
Economic commodities		A	B		G
Industries	D				F
Primary Inputs		H			
Totals					
Ecological commodities	S	R			

Source: Victor, 1972, p. 56.

The table bordered by the heavy line is the conventional input-output matrix used in economics except that distinction is made here between commodities and industries producing them. Matrices A, B, D, and H are therefore capable of being calculated and are available from normal economic sources. The pollution consequence is seen in the ecological input matrices S and R which describe the data of environmental inputs in two different ways by the commodities in which they get embodied and by the industries using them. Similarly, consumers' wastage is described by the matrix G which is the consequence of final demand for economic commodities by consumers and the matrix F which describes the pollution generated by industrial activity.

Victor has calculated the pollution costs using information for 1961. Thus, the ecological impact of agricultural activities (livestock, fish, grain etc.) is mostly in terms of use of water inputs, production of discharged water, solid and liquid animal waste. Calculating the relative ecological costs in terms of air pollution alone, Victor identifies coal and petroleum and coal products as the two highest among all commodities. These high ecological costs, he concludes, are 'almost entirely because of the costs associated with consumption not production. Ninety-five per cent of the total ecological costs of petroleum and coal products ... are attributable to the consumption of these products' (Victor, 1972, p. 197).

Based on his detailed input-output calculations, Victor also gives an estimate of reduction in air pollution of transferring 50 per cent of the passenger car transportation in Canada to some form of public transport. The major reduction is, of course, in the consumption of petroleum products and the consequent reduction in pollution. But this reduction turns out to be of the order of about 7.68 per cent only. Since the technology of public transport is similar to that of private transport, this result clearly points out that we need to change the technology of production and consumption of transport vehicles, whether public or private if we are to get a real reduction in air pollution. This is not to deny that there may be other desirable environmental consequences of such a shift from private to public transport – reduction in congestion, fewer accidents, preservation of inner city areas, etc. The question remains what policies can secure a reduction in pollution.

Policy choices in reducing pollution

To begin with, let us say that a major lesson from the above discussion is that reduction of pollution is a matter of changing the detailed composition of goods produced and consumed and the technology of producing them rather than of any general cutback in income levels. In other words, this is a question of microeconomic rather than macroeconomic policy. A simple plan for zero growth of GNP is not enough. Much of the debate concerning the conflict between growth and pollution has involved naive macroeconomic projections implying more of the same. However, the price weights used in calculating GNP are frequently and rightly criticized as inadequate guides to social decision-making, especially in environmental matters. A zero growth in GNP, as conventionally measured, can lead to increased pollution as likely as to the opposite. The outcome will depend on the mix of goods produced. Therefore, we should reject any simple notion of conflict between growth and pollution, it merely clouds the issue and misdirects public energies.

Once this false dichotomy has been got out of the way, we can discuss ways of reducing pollution. The following are some of the possible ways of doing this:

1. Changing consumers' tastes and preferences in favour of goods which pollute less – by propaganda, exhortation, early education, as in the case of cigarette smoking and cancer. Economists have not discussed this aspect very much because they build their theories on assumptions of consumer preferences being given. A lurking regard for consumers' sovereignty is clear here but the task of reconciling consumers' sovereignty and interdependence of consumers in cases such as congestion, has to be faced. It has been pointed out that an agreement – a social contract – by all, not to consume polluting goods may secure a higher level of individual welfare for all compared to a selfish pursuit of maximum welfare in isolation (Sen, 1973).

2. Making the polluter pay. A tax on emission of pollutants and an effluent charge are among the schemes designed to levy the costs of pollution where they originate. In economic theory, pollution is treated as a particular instance of the general problem of externalities. Such externalities indicate that the private cost of production (or consumption) diverges from the true social cost and leads to excess production (or consumption). One way to tackle this problem would be to charge this difference where its incidence is appropriate and thereby reduce pollution by reducing production (or consumption) back to its social optimum. The imposition of polluter charges restores the economic system back to the condition that is much favoured by the economists. Decentralized decision-making by consumers and producers is re-established since the new prices (including polluter charges) reflect the true opportunity costs of economic activity. The bias towards price manipulation through taxation rather than through quantitative restrictions is pervasive in economic theory. It is believed that the pricing mechanism is a more efficient and inexpensive way of achieving control of pollution. A classic statement of this position is in the *Minority Report* to the *Third Report of the Royal Commission on Environmental Pollution* (1972). Professor Beckerman and Lord Zuckerman argue forcefully for price incentives in pollution control. 'Whilst recognising the many limitations on the price mechanism as a means of achieving all society's objectives, notably those concerned with income distribution or the provision of public goods, as a means of achieving the appropriate levels of output of other goods (and "Bads") the price mechanism is likely to be more efficient, and hence cheaper, than the use of direction' (p. 76).

The *Minority Report* (p. 77) further argues that 'as far as the choice between charges and some crude direct regulation system is concerned, such empirical evidence as exists confirms our view that the former must be cheaper and hence imposes a smaller burden on the economy'. They do not cite such evidence but once again take this as self-evident. The problem of computing such charges is immensely complex. To overcome the complexity of levying charges for different pollutants at different locations and various times of the year, some have suggested pollution licences and emission licenses which would be sold to firms and be allowed to be traded under certain conditions.

Montgomery (1972, pp. 395–418) has put forward a theoretical model which recognizes the complexity of imposing charges and argues for pollution licenses.

However, we have an important piece of evidence in this country that points to a third way of controlling pollution – that of legislation.

3. By legislation against certain polluting activities: Economists have not studied the contribution of legislation to the environmental problem. They prefer some variant of taxation and charges which leave the decentralized decision-making untouched. Governments have, on the other hand, shown a preference for detailed legislation to regulate and control activities they believe are likely to be socially harmful. While it would be interesting to debate this issue of the proper sphere of government activity theoretically, I would like to suggest that the experience in control of air pollution by the Clean Air Act of 1956 and of 1968 demonstrate the effectiveness of legislation in control of pollution. As far as I know, there has been no study of the economic impact of this Act or of the reasons for its success. But the dramatic reduction in air pollution in Great Britain since the passage of the act in 1956 suggests that this is a powerful instrument. It is also noteworthy that in recent legislation regarding emission of pollutants by cars, the US government has taken a similar approach of setting standards by legislation and enforcing them rather than levying charges. Therefore the question of charges or legislation in control of pollution remains open and further studies are needed of the interaction of the legislative and economic mechanisms. It may be that a detailed piece of legislation, followed up by an enforcement machinery, is a way of imposing the appropriate (shadow) price where proper distinction is made of the type of activity (household consumption or factories), location (urban areas or rural areas), by use (type of fuel) etc. Such legislation can then be a surrogate for a system of charges and deserves to be studied in greater detail by lawyers and economists.

The interaction by consumption and pollution is a complex thing, but I hope I have shown that it can be systematically tackled with available analytical techniques and policy instruments. Once our attention is shifted away from availability of goods and towards the services that the goods provide and the characteristics they generate, we can begin to evaluate and appreciate the changes in quality of living as well as in its standard.

References

Anderson, R.J. and T.D. Crocker, (1971), 'Air Pollution and Residential Property Values', *Urban Studies*, **8** (3), 171–80.

Ayres, R.U. and A.V. Kneese, (1969), 'Production, Consumption and Externalities', *American Economic Review*, **59** (3), 282–97.

Dorfman, R. (1964), *The Price System*, Englewood Cliffs N.J.: Prentice Hall.

H.M. Government, (1956), *Clean Air Act.* Ch. 52. London: HMSO H.M. Government (1968), *Clean Air Act*, Ch. 62. London: HMSO.

Kneese, A.V. and B.T. Bower (eds) (1972), *Environmental Quality Analysis: Theory and method in the social sciences*, Baltimore: Johns Hopkins.

Lancaster, K. (1966), 'A New Approach to Consumer Theory', *Journal of Political Economy* **74** (2), 132–57.

Montgomery, W.D. (1972), 'Markets in Licenses and Efficient Pollution Control Progams', *Journal of Economic Theory*, **5** (12), 395–418.

Sen, A.K. (1970), *Collective Choice and Social Welfare*, San Francisco: Holden-Day.

Sen, A.K. (1973), *Behaviour and the Concept of Preference*, Inaugural Lecture at London School of Economics. *Economica*, **40** (159), 241–59, August 1973.

UK The Royal Commission on Environmental Pollution (1972), *Third Report*, (Cmnd 5054), London: HMSO.

Victor, P. (1972) *Pollution: Economy and environment*, London: Macmillan.

[13]

Poverty and capability: towards an empirically implementable measure

Introduction

The starting point of most indices of poverty is to determine a threshold level of some crucial variable(s). If the individual economic unit – an individual or more typically, a household – is found to have a value below the threshold, the unit is classified as being poor. This variable has been defined variously as income; total expenditure; expenditure on a subset of commodities, especially, food; minimum amounts of one or more commodities – food, clothing, housing; minimum amounts of some measurable characteristics of commodities such as nutritional characteristics of food items, amenities provided by housing etc.; utility level derived directly from consumption data or indirectly from income and prices etc. All these measures are commodities/consumption oriented. Townsend has attempted to compute an index of relative deprivation by aggregating the responses to a number of questions concerning consumption as well as the living and working environment translating the deprivation index into a measure of a threshold level of income. This has been subject of a debate which I shall come to later, but for the present sufficient to say that this measure is a much broader *social* measure than the more frequent commodity/consumption measure which is more an *economic* measure.

The economic measures themselves are sometimes put in two groups. One is the poverty line (PL) method where the attention is focused on determining Z the level of income (expenditure) which is taken to be the minimum required for adequate living. The other approach is the (dis)satisfaction of basic needs (DBN) as it is called in Latin American poverty studies. Here the emphasis is on getting a minimum list of satisfiers of basic needs which the individual economic unit may or may not have. In a typical DBN study, these different needs are not added up; dissatisfaction of any one of them classifies the household as being deprived. (I discuss the way of translating DBN into PL and vice versa in my paper, 'Methodological problems in the measurement of Poverty in Latin America'). In this paper, I shall take the PL as the typical economic measure.

Absolute vs. relative views of poverty

The main issue is the basis for determining the poverty line. Should this contain only minimal subsistence quantities of a limited number of commodities or should it be related to overall standards of living of the society in which the poor live? This is the debate about absolute vs. relative deprivation. Many people who refuse to admit that there is any poverty in the advanced capitalist countries would define a subsistence standard in terms which are either time invariant ('today's so-called poor are much better off than the Victorian poor'), or space invariant ('Britain's

poor are rich compared to those of Burkina Faso') or both. Either way, the absolutists are absolutists in the space of commodities.

Another way in which one can be absolutist is in the space of needs. Thus, it is
possible to take the view that a few needs constitute the basic living level; and that
this level can be translated in commodity/income terms differently in different
countries but that these money income sums represent a comparable if not identical
level across countries in real terms. Marx took the view that it is the unbounded-
ness of needs which distinguish human beings from animals. The fewer the needs
which can be met the closer to an animal existence one leads. (See for a fascinating
discussion on these issues Heller, 1976; Springborg, 1981; Soper, 1981.) Thus in
the space of commodities there is a relativism in money terms and in the space of
needs there is absolutism. The issue again comes up whether these needs should be
time and/or space invariant. Should they differ from one individual to another and,
if so, on what criteria?

The social approach to poverty measurement that Townsend implemented takes
a relativistic view of poverty. But the poverty level is defined not in terms of
goods nor of needs but in terms of resources required for social interaction i.e.
for being a fully participant member of the society in which the person lives.
'Individuals, families and groups in the population can be said to be in poverty
when they lack the resources to obtain the type of diets, participate in the activities and have the living conditions and amenities which are customary, or at least
widely encouraged and approved in the societies to which they belong. Their
resources are so seriously below those commanded by the average individual or
family that they are, in effect, excluded from ordinary living patterns, customs
and activities' (Townsend, 1979, p. 15). Thus the measure is relative in the needs
space as well as in the commodity space. In as much as the measure was implemented only for one society (UK) its comparability across countries is an issue
not addressed. In principle, for each country, we would have to investigate the
social practices and norms to measure the resource requirements for being non-
excluded. Thus the measure may in principle be non-comparable across countries. In as much as historical change takes place modifying customs and norms,
the same non-comparability would apply across time. But besides these philosophical problems, there are some mundane measurement issues regarding
Townsend's measure which we shall come to later.

In his Geary lecture, 'Poor Relatively Speaking', Amartya Sen (1981) attempted
to clarify the absolute/relative distinction. Thus, his view is that there is some space
in which the poverty level has to be defined in absolute i.e. time and space invariant
terms but this is not the space of commodities. But what shall this space be?

In his Hennippman lectures, 'Commodities and Capabilities', he has argued that
this space is the space of capabilities (Sen, 1985). This was then extended beyond
measurement of poverty to the notion of the standard of living itself in his Tanner
lectures, (Sen, 1987). The concept of capabilities led to a lively discussion by John
Muellbauer (1987) and Bernard Williams (1987) (among others) at the Tanner
lectures (Hawthorne, 1987). It is in the light of their discussion that I wish to take
up the problem of empirically implementing a poverty measure based on capabilities. In the course of doing this, it would be useful at a later stage to take a detour

and examine the similar problems of implementing other measures of poverty, especially that of Townsend.

Capabilities, commodities and functioning

The three crucial layers in Sen's theory are capabilities, functioning and commodities. In the background to these are material characteristics of goods, personal characteristics of members of the economic unit as well as their tastes, the environment in which they live, be it physical, social or political. Capabilities have to be satisfied in order to allow people to function in any of the many ways they can choose. But to know that individuals have these capabilities guaranteed to them, we have to know the resource requirements necessary as determined by the environment, their personal characteristics and the material characteristics of goods. Once we know that people have the capabilities guaranteed, what we observe are their functioning. In evaluating these functioning, Sen deliberately avoids a utility metric and thus the problem of aggregating functioning to obtain a similar measure of well-being remains. I come to this thorny issue later.

In his discussion of Sen's Tanner lectures, John Muellbauer offers a conceptualization of Sen's scheme. This is given in Figure 1.

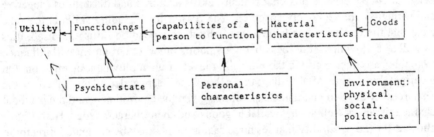

Figure 1   Muellbauer's conceptualization of the capability approach

We see here that the environment and personal characteristics condition the material characteristics/goods required to guarantee capabilities. Once these capabilities are guaranteed, then it is their functioning that are observable data. In Muellbauer's representation, there is a utility function of the functioning. This in turn depends on tastes.

To clarify matters a bit further, I have drawn Figure 2 which illustrates the standard textbook case of a consumer maximizing utility. In this world, functioning consist primarily of consumption of goods and leisure. There is no room for capabilities here because the only enabling element is freedom of choice. The Neoclassical consumer plays a game against nature and is a price taker. As long as there is freedom of choice, s/he can optimize. The only constraint is the resources available. In Neoclassical theory there is no view that any level of resources can be insufficient, or for that matter super-abundant. The individual does the best s/he can given the resources. If an optimum is reached, that is that. The level of utility achieved may be high or low, but since no minimum is specified it can never be

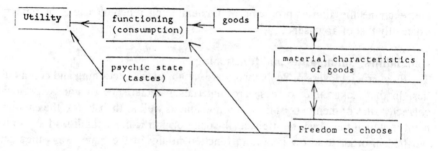

Figure 2   A Neoclassical model without capability

inadequate. If there are restrictions on choice, the level of utility achieved may be suboptimal but that is the only unwelcome outcome in Neoclassical economics.

This is why capabilities never appear in Neoclassical analysis. To clarify this matter and put resources explicitly in the picture, look at Figure 3 which is an adaptation of Muellbauer's picture but reflects, in my view, Sen's model better. Figure 3 is more elaborate that Figure 1 for several reasons. To begin with, in the environment box the (macro) economic environment has been added and in the personal characteristics box endowments, skills acquired and disabilities (negative endowments) are separately specified. The reason for including skills is to make clear that the resources available to the individual depend on skills and disabilities as well as endowments but the economic (among other) environment will influence available resources e.g. via the prevailing level of unemployment or inflation. On the right hand side of the diagram, a box has been added. This specifies the resources required to guarantee capabilities given the environment and the personal characteristics as well as the available goods and their characteristics. Here I have allowed for the possibility that resource requirements may be computed directly in terms of goods (given their prices) or of characteristics of goods (given their shadow prices).

The essence of the argument then is to compare the resources required and the resources available. The environment again enters the scene here via, for example, guaranteeing choice or increasing costs by allowing discrimination by race or gender. If the resources are sufficient to guarantee capabilities, then we can speak of functioning and by implication of a standard of living. If resources are insufficient, then the individual has obviously a truncated set of functioning; hence, the broken line. But in this case, Sen's insistence would be that we don't take either the available resources or the existing environment as given. This is why I have allowed for steps to improve resource position or change the environment. These are feedback processes which endogenize resources and environment taken as 'given' in Neoclassical economics.

The analogy with the poverty literature should be now clear. I interpret Sen as saying that there has to be a set of capabilities which every society should try to guarantee every individual member. Given the environment and the available goods, this generates a minimal resource requirement for each individual given his/her personal characteristics. Thus, in the space of commodities, we have a measure

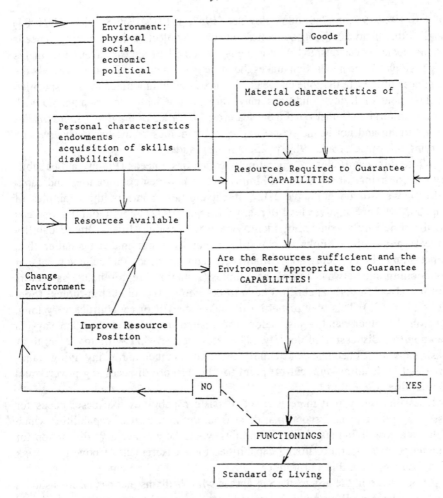

Figure 3 Capabilities and resources

relative to the society and specific to the individual with a certain set of characteristics.

It is only if the resources are sufficient to guarantee capabilities that we can speak of evaluating the functioning to yield a standard of living. If not, something has to be done to ameliorate the situation.

Capabilities: many or few?
Having said this, the task of operationalizing the capabilities approach still remains. It is natural to think of these capabilities as a small number of basic items rather as we think of basic needs. At one stage during the Tanner lecture, Sen quotes Pigou's list, 'the minimum includes some defined quantity and quality of housing accommodation, of medical care, of education, of food, of leisure, of the apparatus of sanitary convenience and safety where work is carried out, and so on',

(Pigou, 1920/1952, p. 759; quoted by Sen, 1987, p. 14). Adam Smith (1776/1904) on the other hand cared not so much about such an objective list of minimum needs as the social consciousness of not being 'ashamed to appear in public'. In his discussion of basic needs, Sen makes the more general point, 'The main issue is the goodness of the life that one can lead. The needs of commodities for any specified achievement of living conditions may vary greatly with various physiological, social, cultural and other contingent features. *The value of the living standard lies in the living* and not in the possessing of commodities which has derivative and varying relevance', (Sen, 1987, p. 25: emphasis added).

While this makes clear a separation between basic needs (Pigou) and capability (of not being ashamed/Adam Smith) and as between commodities and capabilities, we still do not have a list of capabilities. Some of the examples of capabilities that Sen gives lead Bernard Williams (1987) to point out that one can easily trivialize the concept by identifying it with commodities – 'my capability to eat caviar'. Sen thinks of capabilities not as a minimal set smaller than functioning. In his reply to Williams, he said, 'Indeed, the achievements of functioning must always be seen as n-tuples (sometimes representable as vectors but not always), and capabilities have to be seen as *sets* of such n-tuples' (Sen, op. cit., p. 109). This way of putting it makes the list of capabilities very long. But on the other hand – just before the response quoted above, Sen says in relation to a discussion of poverty, 'The relevance of what Williams refers to as basic capabilities becomes particularly clear, not so much in ranking living standards, but in deciding on a cut-off point for the purpose of accessing poverty and deprivation' (Sen, ibid.).

Does this imply that there is a set of basic capabilities like basic needs for assessing poverty and beyond that there is an unlimited set of capabilities which help us assess living standards? While this would be a convenient distinction for our purpose of operationalizing capabilities for measurement of poverty, I think one should explore this a bit further.

At one stage in the argument, Sen agrees with Williams that capabilities should be 'co-realizable'. But should the same set be co-realizable for everyone or should some have a few and others many? I would like to argue very strongly that:

a. the set of capabilities should have only a few elements and that this set is common for all individuals;
b. these capabilities must be co-realizable;
c. the *level* at which the capability can be guaranteed can be different for different societies in as much as this is expressed in terms of commodities/resources (Sen's example of education requiring very little in Tanzania but a lot in UK shows this): the level can go up over time as a society gets richer: thus education in Victorian England was guaranteed at a much more basic resource level than today.
d. the small number of capabilities can support any number of functioning but the number of functioning *actually enjoyed* by anyone will be determined by his/her *actual* resources (by definition exceeding the minimal required for guaranteeing capabilities); thus an improved living standard is measured by the larger

set of actual and possible functionings made possible by the improvement in resources, private as well as public.

These four propositions presume a minimal set in the space of capabilities, allow for an unlimited expansion in the number of functionings and adopt a relativistic position in the space of commodities/resources. They allow us to operationalize capabilities for measuring the poverty level without committing us to separate basic and non-basic capabilities.

Let me give two examples, one informal and the other formal. Suppose we take as one of our capabilities 'the capability to acquire and use knowledge and have access to information'. Obviously, this relates to a number of specific needs, commodities and functioning. Literacy, school attendance, travel for research and training are functionings and expenditure on books and personal computers are examples of the commodity space correlates of this capability. Now take the idea of the Victorian middle classes that a young girl should be able to play the piano. This was regarded as, and is, an *accomplishment*. But does every young lady or every-one for that matter need to be *capable* of playing the piano? I would say no. The capability is the one I gave above. At the minimal level it is met by providing education for literacy and as times change this minimum may be expanded to include computer literacy. Thus the resource requirement to guarantee this capabil-ity will increase over time as the environment (in this case the economic one due to innovations such as computers) changes.

Across different societies at a point of time, the resource cost of guaranteeing literacy will differ. But in any society, illiteracy will mean the failure to guarantee the capability to acquire and use knowledge etc. (even though some knowledge can be imparted without needing literacy).

One the capability has been guaranteed, the number of functioning that this can span is very large. To appreciate and even perform music are functionings and my living standard is high the larger the number of such functionings. But I *don't need to be capable* of playing the piano or the Moog synthesizer or the tabla. This is where Bernard Williams's fear that the notion of capabilities can be trivialized by an infinite expansion in their numbers is relevant.

A formal example can be given by analogy with a well-known functional formu-lation in demand theory. The Klein-Rubin-Stone-Geary utility function is specified in terms of goods and the minimum required amount of each good. Thus if x_i is the amount of ith good and x_i^* is the minimum quantity required, we have

$$U = \sum \alpha_i l_n (x_i - x_i^*) \qquad (1)$$

U is the total utility derived from consumption for the consumer to derive any positive utility at all from consumption, it is required that $x_i > x_i^*$ for each and every i. Thus the vector $\underline{x}^*$ is co-realizable or rather it has to be co-realizable before the functioning (consumption) can be evaluated in utility terms. Failure to co-realize these x_i^*, is tantamount to saying that the functioning is *valueless*; it cannot be evaluated in any positive way. It yields no positive utility and has no welfare connotation. Capabilities are analogous to these x_i^*, although they are most definitely not commodities.

Operationalizing the capabilities approach

Our first task now is to propose a list of capabilities that we can agree are such that no person should be without. The next task would be to see how we can gather relevant information on personal characteristics of individuals so that we can calibrate the resource requirements of each individual to furnish capabilities. We then need to find out what commodity bundles are necessary to be at the individual's command to match the commodity characteristics to the capabilities requirements. We then need to cost these commodities and compare the expenditure to the model values in any society.

The most basic capability must be concerned with keeping alive in a healthy state. The central concern of all societies is to prevent avoidable death, as is seen by the generous response of strangers to those caught in natural disasters – flood, earthquake, droughts. Thus reducing mortality or enhancing life expectancy is a basic goal of any society. It has to furnish the individual with the resources to stay alive. These are likely to include public goods as well as publicly provided goods in lieu of the lack of private income to meet unexpected demands in face of disaster. This would mean, however, that those whose health is already precarious due to previous illness, disability, etc. may need greater resources to keep alive. They are not better off because it may take twice as much to keep them alive as it does ordinary people. It costs more just to stay alive for them (Sawhill (1988) misses this point in her criticism of including health expenditure in a poverty measure).

Thus the resource cost of guaranteeing a capability is a function of personal characteristics. This is the sense in which the ECLAC approach of specifying the requirements of nutrition for pregnant and feeding mothers separately is such an important indicator of society's capacity to provide for its members. Infant mortality and life expectancy at one and five years of age are basic social indicators. To some extent we may not be able to find information on personal characteristics of every individual to compute the resource cost of furnishing such a basic capacity as that of keeping alive. In that case, we might use the statistics of mortality/life expectancy at different ages to proxy for that missing information. Such data on mortality/life expectancy should be as disaggregated as possible by age, gender, location of residence, to be meaningful.

Along with life expectancy, good health/absence of morbidity is the second basic issue. One must be capable of leading a life free of disease, of chronic illness and anything physical/mental that hinders a full productive contribution to society. The costs of providing good health will again depend on the way in which health care is financed and the availability of infrastructural facilities such as hospitals. But all aspects of nutrition as well as other inputs to ensure good health have to be measured.

Having given these two examples of capabilities, let me make bold to propose a list of five capabilities. Although I refer to them sometimes below as basic capabilities, I must emphasize that the view taken here is that there are no non-basic capabilities. This is all that there is to the number of capabilities. These are:

1. capability to stay alive/enjoy prolonged life
2. capability to ensure (biological) reproduction
3. capability for healthy living
4. capability for social interaction
5. capability to have knowledge and freedom of expression and thought.

There is some overlap between these and some may collapse (1) to (3) into a single capability in terms of health and (4) and (5) in terms of social relations. But let me stick to these five for the while. Notice that these are not needs and hence nutrition, warmth, shelter, etc. do not appear here nor do the commodities such as food, housing, education. The space of capabilities consists of a small number of absolute requirements. We can then move to the characteristics space or commodities space but these must be kept separate. But we also need to argue that our five capabilities cover the more important requirements. Let us argue for our list of capabilities.

What then do our five capabilities refer to? First of all, they are built around life, birth and death. In the process of reproducing social relations, a society must guarantee physiological reproduction. A society is after all made up of all the living members of itself and their manifold interactions. Thus the more people can stay alive and the longer they can live must contribute both to individual happiness and society's welfare. This is of course a view in deliberate contrast to the neo-Malthusian view which regards the level as well as the growth of population negatively. But this is surely not valid. One cannot wish to enhance per capita income by reducing the denominator (i.e. letting people die quickly); it has to be by increasing the numerator faster. The economy exists to better people's lives, not the other way around. The desire to extend human life is so basic that one must regard the capability to stay alive and live longer as the most basic of all capabilities.

It is difficult to judge the fulfilment of this capability in each case separately but there are social, aggregate indicators which signal the failure to guarantee this basic capability. The rate of mortality or its reverse the life expectancy at various age levels is one way to judge the provisions of this capability. Interestingly this also has a gender dimension. One concomitant of economic and social progress is the longer life expectancy of women relative to men.

But the continued life of the existing generation is not enough. Death is inevitable and reproduction requires a birth to replace the loss by death. Of course, reproduction takes place at the household level for a variety of motivations but the desire to reproduce the original household is a very strong urge. The capability to reproduce requires various resources especially concerned with the health of women in their reproductive age and of children especially at the young age. The guaranteeing of such capability does not rule out policies for birth control nor the freedom to choose when to bear children and how many children to have. Since in Sen's view capabilities don't restrict but provide the freedom to choose functioning, the freedom to decide when and when not to have children can in no way be denied by the capability to reproduce. Indeed, it implies this choice. Mortality during childbirth, the rate of stillbirth and infant mortality are all sensitive indicators of social and individual deprivation in this case.

These two capabilities have obvious social as well as individual dimensions. They are so basic that often they are not even thought of explicitly. (Much economics talks of infinitely lived consumers who are born adults and often by a process of parthogenesis.) It is better to get these obvious omissions out of the way at the outset.

The third capability is good health. This means health good enough to be able to perform productive work and play a full part in social life. Such productive work can be paid work, voluntary unpaid work outside the home or household work. It also should cover the ability of children and the elderly to be able to pursue education, leisure and other activities. It requires safety at work, in the household or at play.

What are usually called basic needs, indeed everything that Pigou mentions in his definition quoted above, except for education, is covered under our three capabilities. In order to ensure these three capabilities will require food, clothing, shelter, medical care, safety at work. It will also require publicly provided goods such as hospitals, inoculation, ambulance, fire and police services, the provisions of water, electricity, etc. It may almost be true to say that virtually all that is called basic need (again with the exception of education) relating to private consumption goods would be covered by the requirement to satisfy our third capability. It is the first two which add to the public goods requirements.

The other two capabilities could be said to be concerned with non-material or at least non-basic needs. I wish to argue that they are basic. The fourth capability put deliberately in a general way is for social interaction. Townsend in his questionnaire emphasized the requirement of social reciprocity. Living in society involves give and take, entertaining and being able to be entertained. This is an important dimension of socialization of children, of immigrants in a new country and of people for one reason or another not in a 'normal' household. Consider its lack. Jews were restricted from full mobility in many countries until recently and the same is true of many ethnic minorities even today. Legal restrictions on where one can live, what activities are excluded *a priori*, exclusion from certain types of education and education establishments – these all imply a failure to guarantee this capability. Physical mobility is an important part of this capability as is the right to associate with others without hindrance. Adam Smith's statement about shame concerns this capability. Without decent shoes, an 18th century person would not enter into social relations. He or she would be ashamed to be seen in public. This feeling presumes that other needs are satisfied – one is alive and healthy enough to go about, well fed, clothed but may not be well dressed and well shod enough to be able to associate socially. It is social norms and practices of each society which will determine the commodity requirements. Thus it may almost be impossible these days in Britain to have a social conversation if one did not have a TV and watched the soap operas. Lack of a TV set at home would certainly deprive a school-going child of the full ability to participate in communal conversations.

The fifth ability is further along than the previous four in its non-materiality. But education would be absolutely necessary to guarantee it. In daily life whether social, economic or political, there is a basic requirement that one be able to receive and process information. Literacy and perhaps numeracy are basic to this capability. But again in some societies this may have gone up to include capacity to handle a computer keyboard. Handicaps such as dyslexia increase the resource cost of providing this capability. But this capability also implies the resources to be able to buy or acquire access to newspapers, books, radio and TV. It is a vital input to political life. Training and retraining for work is another aspect of this capability.

It may also seem that by insisting on freedom of expression and thought we are merely trying to swim with the recent free-market, libertarian tide. But as Sen has emphasized capabilities incorporate the notion of freedom to choose which set of functioning one will engage in. In making it an explicit capability we recognize that everywhere in the world, lack of political freedom means serious economic deprivation for sizeable minorities if not a majority of the members of a society. This capability presumes all the previous ones but insists that more is needed than being well fed if one has no choice to feed oneself as one likes or more than to be healthy as a slave.

Although the capabilities are linked in some order and it may appear that the earlier ones are more basic than the latter ones, I would wish to argue that all the five are equally and jointly essential. Thus it is often contended that the first three more material capabilities are all that is required for poor countries or poor people and that the other two are luxuries. What will be the case is that as a society gets richer and/or as the number in poverty decline, the capabilities will span an even wider set of possible functionings and correspondingly a richer set of commodities. Take the example I used earlier. The capability of responding positively (whether actively or passively) to artistic stimuli – music, sculpture, painting is not an additional fringe capability. It is better to consider it an aspect of the fourth capability for social interaction and the fifth capability for information gathering and processing. A society will find it possible to devote resources to train this capacity which is latent in everyone to a greater or lesser extent but only after it has satisfied more basic educational urges. A rich person's daughter in Victorian England was regarded as uncultivated if she did not demonstrate this capacity and families devoted considerable resources to acquire such 'accomplishments'. Such a view of accomplishments is not a philistine one. Everyone ought to be able to respond to music. What is philistine is that only the rich can afford the resources to cultivate this capacity, whether or not a natural talent exists among them to profit from such cultivations.

What then determines the extent to which these capabilities are satisfied? What in other words determines the set of alternative functionings which the capability must span? It is here that the relative view of deprivation comes into its own. The norm of expenditure in the commodity space which can be taken to be necessary for guaranteeing the capabilities must be determined by social practice. Only the society in which people live can take a view as to what its members ought to have to lead a decent life or possess a minimum capability to function as members of that society. Barring deliberate discrimination against people on grounds of race, ethnicity, gender, etc., it is perfectly open for us to accept that the society may choose a spartan form of existence as a norm. As the world gets mobile our definition of society gets more and more universal and conflicts are bound to occur between what one country considers its social norm and what another does. This conflict arises most acutely in terms of gender-based issues. What is normal for one society (female circumcision, for example) may be thought to be a gross deprivation by the norms of another society. This raises very tricky questions of culture and politics. Having raised them, I recognize that there is no answer to them. For our purposes we can take a narrow view of society in terms of the economy in the context of which the fiscal burden has to be computed for better provision of capabilities for all. At least at the present the national economy is such a unit. So for the practical purposes of computing poverty measures, we identify the society with the national economy.

Empirical implementation of the capabilities measure

Having specified a list of five capabilities and made repeatedly clear that in the space of commodities, one has to be a relativist, how do we proceed? In particular, how do we bring to bear the social norms, customs and practices in the measurement of minimal resource requirements?

The three approaches at the outset which have all been empirically implemented provide a good starting point here. The PL approach typically takes the average share of food expenditure in total expenditure (or income) as a starting point. This average is taken over all households, not just the poor. In the studies done by ECLAC, for each member of a household calorie and protein norms are specified. These norms are allowed to vary with age, gender, type of physical activity, health status (especially in case of pregnant or breast-feeding mothers). Having then obtained the total requirements for each nutrient for the household, the problem is to see what combinations of commodities satisfy these requirements. The ECLAC approach is to take from an expenditure survey a sample of *all* households a list of frequently bought food items and see what alternative combinations will provide the nutritional requirements. This is then costed at prevailing prices. A minimum cost basket then provides the resource requirements for food. This is then blown up by the reciprocal of the share of the food in total expenditure. This gives the poverty line. Families whose income is below this amount are labelled as poor; those whose income is below the required amount of food alone are labelled as indigent. The PL method in concentrating on energy and nutritional dimensions relates by implication to our first three capabilities. In setting prior norms, it takes these as time and space invariant although specifically related to personal characteristics. But bundles are chosen as *a priori* after studying social practice. The problems relate to the rigid multiplier set by the reciprocal of the share of food in total expenditure and prices. In principle, both of these should vary over time as should the typical commodity bundle. This raises practical issues of intertemporal comparability. (Those are dealt further in my paper, 'Methodological Problems in the Measurement of Poverty' (MPMP) referred to above.)

The DBN approach again as used in ECLAC studies has four questions on housing:

a. the stability of the structure
b. a measure of overcrowding
c. availability of running water

d. availability of sanitary facilities

In addition there are questions on education:

e. level of education of head of household and
f. access to primary schools.

A further question relates to the dependency ratio in the household. For each of these, a norm is specified. If a household fails to meet the norm in any one of the seven dimensions, it is labelled as not having its basic needs satisfied. There is no numerical measure of resources required to meet all these needs though in some of these questions, especially housing, this could be done. (See MPMP.)

The DBN measure is thus very restrictive in terms of relating to social norms and practices. It relates mostly to capability 3 and perhaps capability 1 (unsafe housing can kill) in its housing questions. Its education questions relate to capability 5. It can perhaps be more useful if an estimate of minimal resource requirements for adequate housing could be combined with the minimal food expenditure of the PL method, to obtain a more comprehensive resource requirement. But even then the absence of the social dimension is more worrisome.

Townsend in his well-known study of poverty adopted the method of asking questions on a variety of topics. The questions were grouped under nine headings: (1) Housing and Living Facilities (18 questions) (2) Employment (17 questions) (3) Occupational Facilities and Fringe Benefits (20 questions) (4) Current Monetary Income (33 questions) (5) Savings and Assets (17 questions) (6) Health and Disability (9 questions) (7) Social Services (18 questions) (8) Income in Kind (10 questions) (9) Style of Living (26 questions). As one can see these 168 questions cover individual, household and environmental aspects, work, leisure, consumption, income, transfers and public goods. Much attention, however, was focused on a subset of 12 questions which were taken from the last section on the style of living. These questions related mainly to food consumption, social reciprocity (visiting friends, ability to invite them back), possession of durable consumer goods and quality of housing. The responses to these questions were highly negatively correlated with income. The responses were scored 0 if the answer was the same as the social norm and 1 below. Then these responses were added up for each household. When aggregated across different household types for each income band, they showed a negative slope with respect to income and could even be said to indicate a critical level of income below which the deprivation score rose sharply (Townsend, 1979).

The procedure which Townsend claimed located poverty threshold became the subject of much controversy (See Desai and Shah (1988) and reference therein especially Piachaud (1981)). The problems were many. Firstly, for each questions where the amount could be quantified, e.g. 'How many times have you had a meal this week?', the question was couched in terms of a prior norm, e.g. 'Have you eaten more than x meals this week?' The answer was scored as 0 if meals exceeded x and 1 if not. But the norm was not explained in any precise terms. Secondly, some of the questions were narrowly focused which imposed tastes of the investigator, e.g. 'Have you had a *cooked breakfast?*' Lastly the responses were aggregated giving equal weight to all questions.

Subsequently, Desai and Shah have proposed a procedure which overcomes these objections. They abstract from goods and concentrate on consumption *events*. They then define a person's (household's) deprivation in terms of the difference between the frequency with which a household enjoys the event and the modal frequency of the event. Thus, the norm is defined by the modal frequency. Lastly, they propose that the distance in terms of the various events should be aggregated not with equal weight but with weights proportional to the overall incidence of deprivation in the sample. Thus, if 98 per cent of the sample have a television but two per cent do not have it, the weight should be 50 (1/(1-0.98) but if one per cent have caviar for breakfast and I do not have it, the weight is 1/(1-0.1) = 1.2. Thus the subjective feeling of deprivation as isolation from the community is captured (Desai-Shah, 1988).

The Desai-Shah procedure is limited to events where frequency can be quantified and so may not work with yes/no type of questions – 'Is there running water in the house?' They also do not say anything about what events are necessary for inclusion since their weighting scheme guards against frivolous questions. This is a question which one can address to Townsend's list of questions and tackle the answer in terms of Sen's capabilities idea. It is by combining the ideas in Sen, Townsend and Desai-Shah that we can advance to the next stage in poverty measurement.

As far as the measurement of poverty is concerned, we are interested in guaranteeing that people have certain capabilities guaranteed, i.e. they have the resources required to function in any of the several alternative ways possible. *What they do – their actual functioning* – is, I would like to argue, irrelevant for our purpose. Thus to use the example Sen does, people should have enough to eat i.e. guarantee capabilities (1) and (3). Whether they actually choose to fast to death or not is not our concern. We merely with to guarantee that they do not starve to death.

There is a deeper sense in which actual outcome should be kept out of our calculations. As is well-known, people's expectations and desires are conditioned by their actual resources. But in some cases even their physical requirements adjust to lack of resources. People adjust their activities to the food they get and subsist at much lower levels of nutritional intake than is thought possible. But this does not mean that it costs less to keep the poor alive than the rich but that the poor function at a lower level since they lack the capability to stay alive indulging in a level of activity that the non-poor can afford.

Capabilities thus afford the freedom to function in a variety of ways. Actual functioning are what people do. It is precisely because we wish to avoid the bias caused by adjustment to the felt lack of resources that we avoid looking at actual outcomes to compute the poverty line.

The insistence on ignoring actual outcomes takes the form in actual measurement of poverty of referring to modal behaviour or social norm as a way of determining what the poverty level is. I have said above that in measuring poverty one must keep referring to the non-poor. In practical terms, therefore the connection between goods and capabilities is taken from social practice. It is what it costs 'everyone' to have the capability for healthy living that needs to be measured. Personal characteristics of the individual e.g. physical disability or age or gender may put the cost above or below average but the commodity requirements should be computed using the social norms. Thus the Desai-Shah improvement to the Townsend approach can be adopted.

A capabilities interpretation of the poverty line

Let me now briefly adopt the PL approach to derive a measure of poverty that relates to capabilities. The PL approach, of course, misses out on public goods as well as publicly provided goods and it neglects social dimensions of living. But these questions can be dealt with later in this paper. At this stage I merely wish to show how a capabilities approach would modify or at least reinterpret the poverty line.

Let us begin by using elements of the PL approach as adopted in ECLAC studies. We have five capabilities indicated by K_1, K_2, K_5. Let Z_1 be the protein and Z_2 be calorie. Now suppose Z_{11} is the protein required for keeping alive, i.e. guaranteeing K_1 and in general Z_{ij} is the ith characteristic (nutritional component) required to guarantee the jth capability. Now the nutrition case is linear and we can sum the Z_{ij} to Z_i. To keep matters general however, let us keep the functional form implicit. Finally, let X be the personal characteristics of the a household's members.

Then

$$Z_{iaj} = Z_i (K_j; X_a) \qquad (2)$$

is the ath household's requirement for protein to meet the jth (I have not put in a separate subscript for individual members of a household for obvious reasons) capability. We can sum Z over all j to obtain the household requirements of portions. As personal characteristics change, e.g. health status, Z_{ij} will change but

$$Z_{ia} = \sum Z_{iaj} \qquad (3)$$

is then the household's protein requirements at time t. Now the PL method translates characteristics into commodities by using information on modal social practice. This is equivalent to using a 'technology matrix' connecting goods to characteristics and then a social norm for selecting among the feasible set of goods to arrive at an expenditure function. We can point a 'technology matrix' in a simple way as

$$Q = AZ$$

Where Q is a vector of commodities and A some (rectangular) matrix.

Let E be the ath household's expenditure as food. Then

$$E = E(P_f, Z_1 (K_1, X_a), Z_2 (X_1, X_a)) \qquad (4)$$

Here P_f are the prices of the typical commodity bundle (Qf) chosen from a study of social practice and Z_i are the nutritional requirements. Applying the Engel coefficient to E_{fa} one would arrive at a poverty line specific to the ath household.

The PL method can thus be used to illustrate how we can go from capabilities to characteristics via commodities to expenditure. The step going from characteristics to commodities involves social norms but in view of the sort of consideration Adam Smith was worried about, this may be too physically-oriented a concern. The point then is to ask if food requirements also relate to the other capabilities. Townsend was trying to find implicit connections between food and social reciprocity. The importance of meals during the school day for young children is well-known and hence we get a connection across all capabilities. Our equation (2) is perfectly general in a formal sense but in empirical investigation the details of the connections between food and all the capabilities have to be pursued as fully as possible, i.e. not to stop at specifying food (nutritional requirements for survival alone). The social dimensions of food are as important as its physiological dimensions. This also has been brought out by the many studies of intra-household gender discrimination in feeding. (Thus X_a will have to be separately specified by each member's characteristics.)

On the other hand, the point also is that food is not the only requirement for keeping alive or for ensuring physical reproduction. Other commodities (characteristics) will also be required for ensuring these capabilities. It is the task of the poverty investigation to specify by empirical research the commodity requirements to satisfy the capabilities. Thus the housing needs listed by DBN are related to capabilities K1, K3 and K4 and perhaps K2 as well.

Thus in general, there is no one to one connection between capabilities and commodities. To generate a capability many commodities may be required and one commodity may be relevant to many capabilities. Thus food is relevant for K1 to K4 and literacy may be relevant to all five. We need therefore a more determinate way to proceed to the next stage where we can operationally implement the capabilities notion.

The poverty line example has given us a few pointers. This in the ECLAC method the connection between the first capability to nutrition and food was seemingly straightforward. Even when a commodity served across capabilities, the calorie level was the relevant characteristic and it was additive. But in general we will not have such additivity. But more than that, the 'mapping' from K to Z is not straightforward. The principal reason is that the notion of capabilities is at once much more basic and much more general than the notion of subsistence of even of needs. It is in a sense too vague. This is an advantage in as much as a small set of capabilities can span a large set of functioning. (The analogy with matrix theory is deliberate here.) But at the same time a capability does not readily yield a 'shopping kit' of characteristics, much less a list of commodities.

In fact it may be helpful here to introduce the notion of needs here as intermediary between capabilities and characteristics. My *capability* to lead a long life (K1) (or even a healthy one (K2)) generates a need for satisfying hunger, a need for nourishment, for energy giving intake. But the same capability generates other needs – for parental care (when I am young), for shelter, for companionship (when

I am elderly). These are not just basic needs; basic needs somehow convey a strict one-to-one relationship forward with characteristics/commodities and backward with capabilities.

Needs are varied; indeed as we saw above in relation to Marx's views of needs, it is of their essence to proliferate. One way in which capabilities get satisfied at higher and higher levels as a society gets richer is by the number of needs to guarantee a capability increasing as well. But more important we can attach a number of needs to a capability and then go from needs to characteristics. Needs are much more 'concrete' and detailed than capabilities; needs can proliferate without harming their usefulness as an organizing concept. The same is not true of capabilities; they should be few and not infinitely multipliable.

Figure 4 has been drawn up to illustrate this idea. For ease of exposition, I have taken Pigou's minimal list plus Adam Smith's 'sense of shame' and put them suitably modified in the needs column. Although Pigou does not mention food (taking it for granted in Edwardian England), I have added it among needs. The need to avoid hunger and thirst or the need for food and drink is relevant to capability 1 but also to 2 and 3. The same is true of the need for shelter and for medical care. Convenience, as qualified to (sanitary) convenience by Pigou, but even more generally is not only relevant to health but also to social interaction. Leisure is necessary for K3, K4 and K5.

No doubt the list of needs could be further elaborated; some may prune it down to basic needs and secondary needs. For my purpose it suffices that needs play a role in concretizing capabilities. The connections between needs and characteristics are also multiple but more straightforward. Thus cleanliness (necessary for healthy living) should be a relevant characteristic of food, housing and of medical facilities. For the last capability, the need is for education and information; the characteristics (among many) are diversity, openness and freedom but also reliability.

The characteristics/commodities interrelationships have been dealt with extensively in the literature. It is here that different societies may have different 'technologies' with richer societies proliferating commodities specializing in providing a certain characteristic while in poorer societies commodities are put to versatile uses. The relativism of poverty measures impinges in this dimension although it may also appear in the capabilities/needs mapping.

The list of commodities is also designed to bring out the fact that public and publicly provided goods are important constituents of the 'poverty line'. Too much attention has been paid in the past to consumer expenditure estimates. Public and publicly provided goods are either not included or are typically undercounted. The actual importance of public expenditure in guaranteeing capabilities is therefore understated if not ignored. It is easy then to think of cutting public expenditure 'to ease the burden' and the effect of such measures on poverty is not taken on board but if only private expenditure defines the poverty line.

Thus private expenditure to meet the relevant needs has to be modelled in the context of public goods provision. Our expenditure function has to reflect this. But there is another crucial aspect of this. Public goods are jointly consumed; their availability is a benefit to me even if I do not consume them but others do. Good street lighting is an externality.

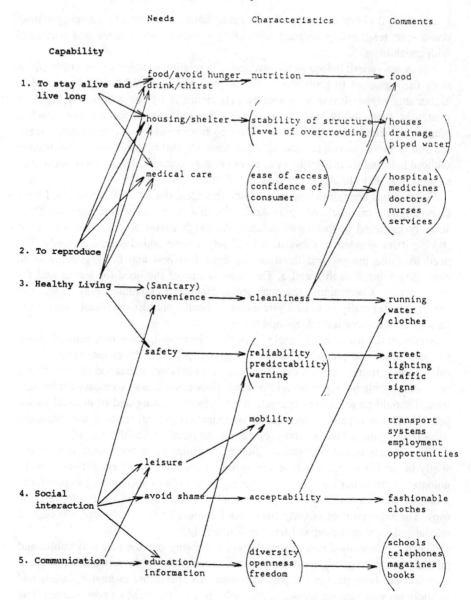

Figure 4

But the same logic should be extended much more radically further. To have people not in poverty is a gain to the non-poor as well as to the poor. Want breeds waste and inefficiency if not crime and violence. No one is safe in the knowledge that some may have to steal, rob or mug to feed themselves. Even with the best provision of policing, street safety is guaranteed more by a well fed population than anything else. Thus it is possible to regard the guaranteeing of other people's capabilities itself as a public good which enters my expenditure function. This while not a part of Sen's text is surely in the spirit of his theory (if not, it should be).

Thus take an individual a with personal characteristics (gender, age, health, status etc) Sa. Let needs be generically labelled N and N(K) being relevant needs so we have:

$$Za = Z(N(K, Sa)) \qquad (5)$$

No additivity is assumed over capabilities or needs. The details of a general formulation such as (5) can only be filled in by empirical work. Now take it that private expenditure is E as before but that public provision is G and that this is not individual specification

$$Ea = E (Za, G(N(K)) \qquad (6)$$

Ea is the amount required to meet a's capabilities. The expenditure function includes the public goods expenditure G. Now (6) is still very much the required expenditure for the isolated individual. Other people's living levels will have influence on a's requirements. To express this let Za' be everyone else's requirements. We expect (6) then to include Za' in the argument:

$$Ea = E (Za, G(N(K),Za')) \qquad (7)$$

In (7) I have put Za', other people's needs inside the public provision expenditure. This is not necessary but realistic. The individual may still have to incur private expenditure (security locks on his/her car to prevent theft) if the public provision is not enough. But in general s/he will expect the public provision to be adequate to insure that Ea is minimal to meet Za without further unnecessary expenditure.

Of course there is an Ea for every a in the society. So there has to be a joint equilibrium defined of all the Ea. That set of equations is trivial to write does but it is a non-trivial task to prove than an equilibrium will exist within the resource constraints.

Ea is deliberately made to look as much like poverty line calculation as possible. But there is a much more explicit *a priori* foundation for it. We have a small number of capabilities. If anything we should ask whether this is small enough. But once we have accepted this list, the difficult task is to implement empirically the Z(N(K Sa)) and Ea(Za,G( )) functions.

What our algebraic exercise does amongst other things is to address the question of valuation which comes up in the course of the discussion of Sen's lectures. Sen recognizes the 'inescapable need for different valuation exercises for adequately pursuing the capabilities approach to the living standard' (Sen, 1987, p. 107). But the space of capabilities is not one where valuations can be carried out. To do so would require ranking them and regarding some as more important than others. Our small number of capabilities comprises a set of co-realizable entities. They stand or fall together. One must take the view that if one of them is not realized, no meaning can be attached to the living standard no matter how far the rest of them are fulfilled: It is not good to be well fed and healthy in prison nor long lived if you are serving a life sentence. There is no freedom to choose in that situation. It is also precisely why slaves do not enjoy standards of living though they may eat a lot and live long.

The valuation in the economic sense is of course carried out in the space of commodities once we are assured that capabilities are guaranteed then different commodity bundles may be offered at different stages of society. This is the sense in which the same capabilities may be fulfilled better and better and over time living standards may go up. It is only conditional on meeting the capabilities of everyone at some minimal level that the economic valuation of commodities, say be relative prices, has any moral validity.

The consequence of this way of approaching the problem of valuation is obvious for a poverty study. If we find that by a society's standards (with all that implies), if some people's capabilities are not guaranteed because of inadequacy of their resources, then *these people have no standard of living*. If, to quote Sen again, 'The value of the living standard lies in the living...' then these deprived people are not living in any except a biological animal sense. This is the point at which the relevance of Marx's notion of needs distinguishing human beings from animals, precisely in their nature of being unbounded becomes clear.

Conclusions

We have so far only scratched the surface. My main purpose in this paper was to show *one* way, in which we can implement a measure of poverty starting from a capabilities approach. If this was accepted as a starting point, then one would need to start more in details of data gathering by methods of household surveys and other sources mainly in the public expenditure side. Such issues cannot be discussed in the abstract. I hope that this approach arouses sufficient interest to begin this second stage of the measurement of poverty.

Bibliography

Desai, M. (1989), 'Methodological Problems of Measurement of Poverty in Latin America.' (LSE unpublished).

Desai, M. (1990), 'Income and Life Time Deprivation: A proposal from an Index of Social Progress.' (LSE unpublished).

Desai, M. and A. Shah (1988), *An Economic Approach to the Measurement of Poverty*. (Oxford Economic Papers, October).

Hawthorne, G. (ed.) (1987), *The Standard of Living: Tanner Lectures of Amartya Sen*, Cambridge: Cambridge University Press.

Heller, A. (1976), *The Theory of Need in Marx*, London: Allison and Busby.

Muellbauer, J. (1987), Comment in Hawthorne (1987).

Piachaud, D. (1981), 'Peter Townsend and the Holy Grail', New Society, Sept. 10.

Pigou, A.C. (1920/52), *The Economics of Welfare*.

Sawhill, E. (1988), 'Poverty in the USA', *Journal of Economic Literature*.

Sen, A. (1981), *Poor, Relatively Speaking*, Oxford Economic Papers.

Sen, A. (1985), *Commodities and Capabilities*, Amsterdam: North Holland.

Sen, A. (1987), 'The Standard of Living', in Hawthorne (1987)

Smith, A. (1776/1904), *The Wealth of Nations*. Cannan edition. London: Methuen.

Soper, K. (1981), *On Human Needs: Open and Closed Theories on a Marxist Perspective*, Brighton, Sussex: Harvester.

Sprinborg, Patricia (1981), *The Problem of Human Needs and the Critique of Civilisation*, London: Allen and Unwin.

Townsend, P. (1979), *Poverty in the UK*, Harmondsworth: Penguin.

Williams, B. (1987), Comments in Hawthorne (1987).

[14]

Methodological problems in the measurement of poverty in Latin America

Introduction

The problem of poverty has attracted increasing attention in recent years, nowhere has this been more so than in Latin America. After a reasonable experience of growth (which did not do much to reduce the absolute numbers of poor anyway) during the 1960s and 1970s, there has been a sharp reversal in the 1980s. Overall growth rate in per capita terms has been negative for many countries of the region. As they have tried to cope with demands put to them for structural adjustment, the main cutback has been in the real value of transfer payments and of the subsidies on publicly provided goods and services. There is a widespread feeling that this has exacerbated an already precarious situation. While once there was growth without equity, now there is stagnation with a deliberate bias against equity. One way to check whether such a feeling is justified would be to look at the poverty data. There has been a lot of effort in this direction in recent years, most notably by the Economic Commission for Latin America and the Caribbean (ECLAC, CEPAL in Spanish). The purpose of this paper is to examine the methodological problems encountered in measuring poverty. The focus is on Latin American efforts in this direction. For the present, our focus is on the official efforts made in this respect.

Two methods of poverty measurement

There seem to be at the present in Latin America two methods for measuring poverty – the Dissatisfaction of Basic Needs (DBN) (*Necesidades basicas insatisfechas* (NBI) in Spanish) method and the Poverty Line (PL) (*Linea de Pobreza* (LP) in Spanish). The former is a method that concentrates on overcrowding in housing, lack of water and sanitary services, non-attendance at school by children, high dependency ratio, low educational attainment of the head of household and precariousness of dwelling structure. If a household fails to meet the minimum standard laid down in any one of these, the household is labelled as having its basic needs not satisfied and hence poor.

The Poverty Line method starts with a nutritional norm in terms of calories, proteins and other nutrients. These norms are differentiated by age, gender and type of work. Ideally therefore for each household the nutritional norm can be different. The nutritional norm then leads to a basic basket (BB) being defined and costed. The cost of the BB then represents an indigence line and some multiple of the cost (2.0 in most cases) is regarded as defining the poverty line. If a family's income falls below this, the family is labelled as poor.

Even from this brief description, it should be obvious that each method has conceptual as well as measurement problems. We shall come to these later. But

205

Table 1   Estimates of poverty for Greater Buenos Aires by the two methods

	PL	DBN	Poor By both methods	Not Non Poor By both methods
1974	3.2	18.1	1.8	19.6
1975	6.7	18.1	3.0	
1976	21.9	15.8	6.9	30.8
1980	7.9	13.5	3.4	
1982	23.6 (22.1)[1]	11.7	6.4	28.9
1983	14.2	15.8	–	

Note: [1]Estimates differ in two of the sources I have read. Beccaria (1984) gives the higher estimate.

Sources: Beccaria, 1984; Boltvinnik, 1989a

they also display a lack of comparability over time within and between themselves. Available accounts argue that the PL method's estimates of the proportion of households who are poor fluctuate quite widely. (See Table 1.)

The rise in the poverty proportions by the PL method in 1976 and again in 1982 seems odd, but *results for other countries especially India would lead one to believe that the higher figures are much closer to the truth than the lower ones*. It is these which are in agreement with those given by the DBN method. The latter shows a downward trend in the proportion of the poor until 1981 and then a sharp rise but given the problems caused by structural adjustments to the burden of debt repayment, this is not surprising.

It has been recognized that the methods measure different things – private (non-durable) consumption in one case (PL) and the quality of durable goods, public goods and the current and future human capital potential of the household in the other. The PL method is very sensitive to the inclusion or non-inclusion of non-food items in the BB especially fuel costs. (The steep rise in 1976 and 1982 *may* be due to the feeding through of higher fuel costs with a two-year lag following the rise in oil prices. This is, however, a speculation which needs to be checked.) The DBN method picks up housing deprivation – overcrowding, precarious structures, lack of running water and facilities for removal of nightsoil. Housing very often lags behind in the course of economic progress as it is a highly capital intensive good. (The Soviet Union is a frequently cited example but even in the UK, housing conditions have improved dramatically only since the 1950s.) Ideally DBN should give an upper bound to the poverty estimate while PL may give a lower bound.[1] This is especially so since DBN has a binary/qualitative way of classifying households. Failure to meet any one of the criteria is sufficient to be labelled poor. There is no weighting of the different criteria.

It is clear that these two methods are complementary but having said that, even together they do not exhaust the possibilities for identifying poverty. Their inter-

---

1. This is on the crude argument that housing is income elastic and food expenditure is income inelastic.

Table 2   Contingency tables for the two methods

	1974			DBN 1976			1982		
%	Poor	Non Poor	Total	Poor	Non Poor	Total	Poor	Non Poor	Total
Poor	1.8	1.4	3.2	6.9	15.0	21.9	6.4	17.2	23.6
Non Poor	16.4	80.4	96.8	8.8	69.2	78.1	5.2	71.1	76.4
Total	18.1	81.8	–	15.8	84.2	–	11.7	88.3	–

Source: same as in Table 1

section is small but moves as PL does (see table 2). It would be more interesting to measure their union i.e. all families which were labelled poor by either criterion. One could then look at the characteristics of the household that fell into this set. Notice that this set goes up from 21.3 per cent in 1974 to 37.7 per cent in 1976 and down to 35.3 per cent in 1982. A range of 20 to 30 per cent in poverty in an urban area does not seem to be too far-fetched.

There are two totally different ways of proceeding at this stage. One is to suggest ways in which each method can be improved *given its conceptual basis*. Thus we could concentrate on statistical measurement problems. This can help to improve the intertemporal or mutual comparability of the two series. This is, however, a limited task. It is much more important to re–examine the conceptual basis of the two series and propose a more comprehensive alternative. I will do this in a later section.

The Poverty Line method
In suggesting ways of improving the method it is helpful to formalize matters a little. Let goods be indicated by x_i, characteristics of goods by z_k, prices of goods by p_i and (shadow) prices of characteristics by q_k. Stocks including those of human capital will be indicated by capital letters and their corresponding flows by lower case letters. Income will be denoted by y, household by j.

The PL method consists of

a. Specifying required levels of energy by age, sex, height, weight. Distinction is especially made about pregnant or lactating women. These were then converted into protein and calorie requirements. Let z_1^* and z_2^* be the protein and calorie requirements. Given the characteristics of a household – age, sex composition etc. and particular contingent circumstances – pregnancy, in employment or not, type of job etc., these will be household and time specific i.e. z_{1jt}^*, z_{2jt}^* etc.

b. Convert z_{1jt}^*, z_{2jt}^* into normative food baskets. Ideally, one should have information on cultural and taste factors for each household i.e. the household's production function for generating energy via proteins/calories from the food it eats. The *first* problem here is that households may differ in the efficiency with which they do this food/energy conversion. The *second* problem is that different households may choose different specific goods in their production function, although in practice cultural patterns restrict actual choices to a few goods. Thus uniqueness of the goods vector x_{ij}^* which yield the jth household z_{1j}^*, z_{2j}^* may not hold.

The empirical approach seems to have been to sample all households and choose a reference stratum whose expenditure on food was (a) unconstrained in any significant way by lack of resources, (b) was representative, and (c) covered the nutritional requirements. From the expenditure of these households, commodities were identified which were frequently bought. Let the expenditure on good i be e_i. Information was thus available on, let us say, the expenditure of the modal household $\tilde{e}_{ij}$. From this vector $\tilde{e}_{ij}$ were derived the simplified quantities by deflating by prices *independently obtained and assumed to be common to all households*. Formalizing this may clarify the problems involved. Let the vector of nutritional characteristics $(z_1. z_2)$ be z_n. Let the total expenditure of the modal household be $\tilde{e}_j$. The method is to confine oneself to food items and compute the quantities of food consumed by the modal household by deflating $\tilde{e}_{fji}$ by where f denotes food. Thus

$$X_{fij} = (\tilde{e}_{fij/pfi}) \qquad (1)$$

Now among the X_{fij} we pick the most frequently used goods $\tilde{X}_{fi}$, thus neglecting esoteric goods. We are assumed to know the technology matrix of converting food into nutrition, given as *common to all households*. Let this be denoted

$$z = A\tilde{X}_f \qquad (2)$$

where A is a rectangular matrix of constants. We then calculate the minimum expenditure required to achieve z_j^* i.e. calculate the expenditure function

$$\bar{e}_{fj} = e(\bar{p}_i ; z_j^*) \qquad (3)$$

using (2) and some further restriction on how much calorie can come from protein, from fats etc. ($\bar{p}_i$ are the prices of the $\bar{X}_f$ goods). Now if a household's actual income $y_j < \bar{e}_{fj}$ then it is labelled as *indigent*. Otherwise, the poverty line is calculated as

$$\bar{y} = \bar{e}_{fj} / \bar{\lambda}_j \qquad (4)$$

where $\bar{\lambda}_j$ is the share of food in total expenditure of the modal household i.e.

$$\bar{\lambda}_j = \bar{e}_{fji} / \bar{y}_j \qquad (5)$$

While typically $\bar{\lambda}_j$ is taken to be 0.5, estimates have ranged from 0.303 (Caracas) to 0.529 (Lima). The 'multiplier', $\bar{\lambda}_j^{-1}$, is a matter of some debate among the experts involved in the measurement of poverty (Boltvinnik, 1989b).

Once the poverty line calculation is set out as above, its logic and the problems it may run into are clear. But before I come to the problem, let us note that the attractive part of the measure is that it defines the poor with reference to the modal i.e. non-poor behaviour. The argument for measuring poverty with reference to normal community behaviour is very strong and I shall use it again below. But having said that, note also that given the quantitative nature of the information generated, the PL measure is only a head-count measure. It merely enumerates those households with income below y_j. It does not then go on to retrieve the head-count measure by measuring the intensity of poverty among the poor. Thus the Sen measure, for example, combines head-count with the gini coefficient of income distribution *among the poor* (Sen, 1976, 1981). It should be a straightforward task to compute the Sen measure. This will tell us both how many poor there are and how poor they are. (Other ways of combining poverty gap data at household levels into a scalar index have been proposed by Foster et al. 1984; Watts; Clark. See Atkinson, 1989, Chapters 1–2 for a critical review.)

The problems with a measurement such as $\bar{y}_j$ can arise at any of the many steps which go into its construction. I have already pointed out that the production function for converting goods into nutrition may be household specific and almost certainly the goods may differ by region (rural/urban) if not by household. But this is not so important since in this measure the idea is to estimate relative poverty – relative to normal community practice. Thus the goods that 'everyone' eats should be potentially purchasable by the poor; the poor should not have 'poor' foodstuffs which they have to be satisfied with. The issue is not what they actually eat and the amount of nutrition they actually derive. The measure is normative and the norms are defined by community practice.

The more serious problem is in the assumption that the prices are common across households. American studies have found that 'the poor pay more'. Either due to lack of storage facilities or of transport to go and bulk buy, the poor shop in neighbourhoods where quality is low and prices high. Thus in equation (1) even if the prices p_{fi} were the correct ones in equation (3), the $\tilde{p}_i$ need not be the relevant one for poor households. This will typically bias $\bar{e}$ *downwards*.

Similar remarks can be made about the appropriate subset $\tilde{X}_f$ to choose and whether the vector Z of nutritional characteristics should be extended. Indeed, a crucial criticism is the necessity of confining one's poverty criterion to nutritional adequacy as such. This leads to a concentration on a subset of food items and neglect of non-food items.

The most serious consequence of this arises in taking $\tilde{\lambda}_j$ the share of food expenditure as fixed. When updating $\bar{y}_j$, typically the vector $\tilde{X}_{fi}$ is often taken as fixed from previous surveys as is z^*. The only variable element is the price vector. (Ideally z_j^* – the household's $\tilde{p}_i$ requirements – should also be taken as variable.)

Thus the typical practice would be to 'blow up' the original measure by the overall price index, i.e.

$$\bar{e}_{fjt} = (P_{ft} / P_{fo}) \, \bar{e}_{fjo} \tag{6}$$

Where P_{ft} is an index in year t, P_{fo} in the initial year. Further keeping λ_j unchanged we have

$$\bar{y}_{jt} = \bar{e}_{fjt} / \bar{\lambda}_{jo} \tag{7}$$

The correct, if somewhat expensive, measure is

$$\bar{e}_{fjt} = e \, (\bar{P}it; z_{jt}^*) \tag{8}$$

and

$$\bar{y}_{jt} = \bar{e}_{fjt} / \bar{\lambda}_{jt} \tag{9}$$

Of course it is difficult to update the list of typical commodities $\tilde{x}$ and obtain their prices p_{it} as it is to obtain estimates of the share $\bar{\lambda}_{jt}$. The extent and direction of bias caused by these simplifications can be calculated under different assumptions about the degree of substitutability within the vector of food items and as between food and non-food items. If the P_{ft} index is updated in the light of recent budget data, then the first problem will not be serious. Any substitution possibility within the food items will be reflected in changing weights of the different items. As for the latter, one can only try out different parameter values for the elasticity of substitution and examine the hypothetical impact of differential rates of growth of prices of food and non-food items.

The relevance of these problems is seen when we compare the variability of the Poverty Line as calculated from different data sources. Thus, the Colombian statistical office DANE, estimates the poverty line in 15 Colombian Cities as

PL	1984	$6 370
PL	1984/base 1973	$7 835
PL	1984/base 1970	$4 895

Source: DANE (1988)

The first two come from a common source, DANE, and the last one is an updating of Altimir's 1970 estimates with 1984 prices. Thus for 1984, the PL range is nearly $3 000, roughly 50 per cent of the midpoint estimate around $6 300. There is no way of judging which is the correct or even the plausible estimate.

DBN method
By comparison with the PL method, the DBN method has fewer problems of updating. The idea here is to fix certain norms and measure actual data against them. Some of these norms are qualitative and the measurement of actual data involves all or nothing statements. The problems with DBN are first that there is no attempt to judge the relative importance of these different needs; in some sense,

they are all equally basic. A second problem is that there is no attempt to put any price tag on them. Thirdly, they are disparate in as much as they refer to housing and environmental deprivation on the one hand and indicators of present and future earning power on the other. A little bit of formalization may help here.

Let N_j be household size and A_j number of rooms in the dwelling so that N_j/A_j is a measure number of people per room. Let N_{ij} be dependents so that $N_{ij}/(N_j - N_{ij})$ is a measure of dependency. E_j can be the number of years of education of the head of the household. Other measures are qualitative. The solidity/precariousness of dwelling structures, the comfort (availability of water), salubriousness (lavatory facilities) and school attendance by the children are all one/zero variables.

Unlike the PL method, we are confined here to the space of characteristics rather than commodities. In order to translate this measure to the commodity space, we may have to seek additional information. To draw a parallel with the PL method, we could ask what the rental was for a house with at least one room for three people with water and sanitary facilities which was solidly built. If by hedonic regression we could attach a separate average rent coefficient to these characteristics in the reference population, then we could compute the cost of non-deprivation in housing. This is equivalent to attaching a shadow price q_i to the ith characteristic.

The existing DBN measure can then be described as follows. Let overcrowding, precariousness of structure, water availability and sanitary facility be labelled z_3, z_4, z_5, z_6. They are calculated as follows:

$$z_3 = 1 \text{ if } N_j/A_j > 3$$
$$= 0 \text{ otherwise.}$$

The other three are qualitative. We score 1 if there is deprivation, 0 if not. Then the dependency variable can be labelled z_7 so that

$$z_7 = 1 \text{ if } N_i/(N - N_i) \geq 0.4$$
$$= 0 \text{ otherwise.}$$

Similarly, for z_8 education of head of household and z_9 for non-attendance of school by children. The DBN measure then is some 0/1 variable h_j^* such that

$$h_j^* = \max (z_3, \dots z_9) \tag{10}$$

A household is deprived if $h_j^* = 1$.

Now the housing deprivation variable can be given a hedonic price measure. Thus the expenditure required for non-deprivation would be

$$\sum_{i=3}^{6} q_i = \bar{e}_{hj}$$

where $\bar{e}_{hj}$ expenditure (rent) for housing. The other three are not so easy to translate into expenditure. Dependency ratios affect consumption/expenditure per capita adversely and if one can only find the equivalent expenditure in the modal house-hold with similar size, that may be enough. The other two variables are tricky. Low education indicates low earning capacity and non-attendance at school may indicate environmental deprivation (no schools nearby), high opportunity costs (needed to contribute to household income) or a low subjective estimate of the benefits of education. In any case, it will affect the possibility of future deprivation of the child not attending school.

Another way to use the DBN data would of course be to add the 1/0 score up. Thus instead of h_j^* as in Equation (10), we could have

$$d_j^* = \sum_{i=1}^{7} z_{2+i,j} \tag{14}$$

This is the method Townsend (1979) used. But there is an improvement that can be made on this by using an aggregation suggested for the Townsend data – Desai and Shah, 1988. This is to weigh each deprivation by the social incidence of non-deprivation in that dimension i.e.

$$dd_j^* = \sum \theta_i \, z_{2+i,j} \tag{15}$$

where $\theta_i = \# \, (z_{2+i} = 0)/\#$ in sample.

The idea here is as follows. θ_i measures the proportion non-deprived in the population. One feels more deprived if one is in a minority of the deprived rather than if many others are in a similar condition. Thus the θ_i's are weights to convey the subjective 'feeling' of deprivation in the ith dimension, while the z_{2+i} are the objective incidence of that particular deprivation. The dd_j deprivation score for the jth household then is a composite subjective/objective measure of deprivation.

A comparison and synthesis
There are two ways of pooling the information in the DBN method and PL method. The first is as follows: add up the food expenditure $\bar{e}_{fj}$ and the housing expenditure $\bar{e}_{hj}$ defined in (11) above. Calculate the share of food and housing expenditure in the total income of the reference group, say, $\bar{m}_j$ then we have

$$\bar{e}_{1j} = \bar{e}_{fj} + \bar{e}_{hj} \tag{12}$$

and

$$\bar{y}_{1j} = \bar{e}_{1j} / \bar{m}_j \tag{13}$$

Now $\bar{y}_{1j}$ is a more comprehensive measure than either PL or DBN since it includes food as well as housing and may capture inadequacy of income better than the PL measure alone. It would certainly be better to use $\bar{e}_{1j}$ as a measure of indigence rather than $\bar{e}_{fj}$.

By analogy one could reduce the PL method to the DBN one by obtaining data on the *actual* food consumption of households and checking the calorie/protein content. Then we can say that a household is labelled poor if

$$z_{1j} < z_{1j}^* \qquad \text{or}$$
$$z_{1j} < z_{2j}^*$$

i.e. if its protein or calorie intake is inadequate. By adding these two characteristics to those under h_j^* in Equation (10), we establish a parallel with the synthetic measure of (12) and (13).

Thus we can either translate the 0/1 housing deprivation scores of the DBN variable into an expenditure measure analogous to the PL measure or obtain additional data on actual food consumption in the PL approach and convert them into 0/1 variables as in the DBN method. If we could do both it would be an almost foolproof way of checking the reliability of the two approaches and improving their comparability. This however may require a major effort. There is another way of pooling the information in the two approaches. This is to look at the small data set where households were surveyed by both methods. We can exploit this common source in the following way.

The PL method gives us a measure of the poverty gap (G_j) for each household. This is defined as $(\bar{y}_j - y_j)/\bar{y}_j$. It is obviously defined in the (0,1) interval and is hence suitable for treatment by logit/probit methods. There are then two ways of using the common data set:

a. A Single Equation Approach: Take G_j as the dependent variable and the DBN variables $z_3 \ldots z_9$ as independent variables. There may be other exogenous variables measuring the household characteristics say Q. We then try

$$G_j = (1 + \exp(zB + QC))^{-1} \qquad (16)$$

where B and C are coefficient vectors of z and Q respectively. But some of the z variables are alternative indicators of poverty e.g. $z_3, \ldots z_6$ while others are measures of current or future earning capacity. The interpretations of B vector is thus a troublesome problem.

b. A Simultaneous Equations Approach: Treat G_j along with the housing deprivation variables as well as actual income y_i as jointly dependent variables. The exogenous variables would be z_7, z_8 and z_9 plus the vector Q. We then specify in the normal fashion

$$AY + \Gamma X = U \qquad (17)$$

where $Y = (G_j, z_{3j}, \ldots, z_{6j}, y_j)$ and $X = (z_{7j}, z_{8j}, z_{9j}, Q_j)$ are respectively the endogenous and exogenous variables and A, Γ their coefficient matrices. What will this tell us? First, we would like to study the pattern of A. Does housing deprivation, for example, affect income adversely? Is there a strong positive correlation between G_j and the housing variables or are they offering us separate, additive bits of information? But the Γ matrix may also begin to tell us about the determinants of poverty. If we can get interesting results from this pooling, we would gain much insight into the problem of poverty.

Conclusion

The aim of this paper has been to discuss the problems created by the two alternative approaches to the measurement of poverty. While pointing out their shortcomings, I have also attempted to suggest ways of making them comparable as well as of pooling the information contained in them. There is a further aspect that is worth pointing out. It is clear that there is a basic similarity between them. In the characteristics space – nutrition, housing, comfort etc., there is an absolute *a priori* norm which can be laid down. Such a norm can be different depending on household composition but for a given type of person it is constant. In the commodity space we translate this absolute norm into a relative one. This is done explicitly in the PL method but as I showed above it can be done in the DBN method by a simple extension. It is a possible thus to bring the two measures together and examine their union rather than their intersection. But having said that, the question remains whether the particular set of characteristics chosen has anything special to recommend it. Do food, housing deprivation and access to educational facilities exhaust the possible characteristics we need to look at? Are there general criteria which would tell us what to look for or is our investigation to be determined by data availability? It is these larger questions which I examine in another paper.

Bibliography

(More items are listed here than are referred to directly in the text.)

Atkinson (1989), *Poverty and Social Security*

Altimir, O. (1979), *La Dimension de la Pobreza en America Latina*, ECLAC.

Beccavia, L. (1984), *Sobre La Pobreza en Argentina*, ECLAC.

Boltvinnik, J. (1989a), *Alternative Methods for the Measurement of Poverty Incidence*, Bogota, Columbia: UNDP, unpublished.

Boltvinnik, J. (1989b), *Notes on the Methodology Applied by ECLAC to Estimate Poverty Incidence*, Bogota, Columbia: UNDP, unpublished.

Boltvinnik, J. (1989c), *Notas Sobre El Tranbajo de Actualizacion y Elaboracion de Informacion Sobre La Dimension de la Pobreza en Ocha Paises de America Latina*, Bogota, Columbia: UNDP; unpublished.

DANE, (1988), *La Pobreza en Latina America*, Bogota, Colombia.

Desai, M. (1989), *Poverty and Capability: Towards an Empirically Implementable Measure*, LSE; unpublished.

Desai, M. and A. Shah (1988,) *An Econometric Approach to the Measurement of Poverty*, Oxford Economic Papers, October.

ECLAC (CEPAL) (1988), *Determinacion de Las Necesidades de Energia y Proteinas para la Poblacion de Nueve Paises Latino americanas* Santiago, Chile unpublished.

Katzman, R. (1989), 'La Heterogenesdad de la Pobreza: El caso de Montevideo', *Revista de la CEPAL*, no. 37.

Sen, A. (1976), 'Poverty: An Ordinal Approach to Measurement,' *Econometrics*, March.

Sen, A. (1981), *Poverty and Famine*, Oxford: Clarendon Press.

Townsend, P. (1979), *Poverty in the U.K.* Harmondsworth: Penguin.

Name index

Economists of the Twentieth Century

Monetarism and Macroeconomic Policy
Thomas Mayer

Studies in Fiscal Federalism
Wallace E. Oates

The World Economy in Perspective
Essays in International Trade and European Integration
Herbert Giersch

Towards a New Economics
Critical Essays on Ecology, Distribution and Other Themes
Kenneth E. Boulding

Studies in Positive and Normative Economics
Martin J. Bailey

The Collected Essays of Richard E. Quandt (2 volumes)
Richard E. Quandt

International Trade Theory and Policy
Selected Essays of W. Max Corden
W. Max Corden

Organization and Technology in Capitalist Development
William Lazonick

Studies in Human Capital
Collected Essays of Jacob Mincer, Volume 1
Jacob Mincer

Studies in Labor Supply
Collected Essays of Jacob Mincer, Volume 2
Jacob Mincer

Macroeconomics and Economic Policy
The Selected Essays of Assar Lindbeck, Volume I
Assar Lindbeck

The Welfare State
The Selected Essays of Assar Lindbeck, Volume II
Assar Lindbeck

Classical Economics, Public Expenditure and Growth
Walter Eltis

Money, Interest Rates and Inflation
Frederic S. Mishkin

The Public Choice Approach to Politics
Dennis C. Mueller

The Liberal Economic Order
Volume I Essays on International Economics
Volume II Money, Cycles and Related Themes
Gottfried Haberler
Edited by Anthony Y.C. Koo

Economic Growth and Business Cycles
Prices and the Process of Cyclical Development
Paolo Sylos Labini

International Adjustment, Money and Trade
Theory and Measurement for Economic Policy, Volume I
Herbert G. Grubel

International Capital and Service Flows
Theory and Measurement for Economic Policy, Volume II
Herbert G. Grubel

Unintended Effects of Government Policies
Theory and Measurement for Economic Policy, Volume III
Herbert G. Grubel

The Economics of Competitive Enterprise
Selected Essays of P.W.S. Andrews
Edited by Frederic S. Lee and Peter E. Earl

The Repressed Economy
Causes, Consequences, Reform
Deepak Lal

Economic Theory and Market Socialism
Selected Essays of Oskar Lange
Edited by Tadeusz Kowalik

Trade, Development and Political Economy
Selected Essays of Ronald Findlay
Ronald Findlay

General Equilibrium Theory
The Collected Essays of Takashi Negishi, Volume I
Takashi Negishi

The History of Economics
The Collected Essays of Takashi Negishi, Volume II
Takashi Negishi

Studies in Econometric Theory
The Collected Essays of Takeshi Amemiya
Takeshi Amemiya

Exchange Rates and the Monetary System
Selected Essays of Peter B. Kenen
Peter B. Kenen

Econometric Methods and Applications (2 volumes)
G.S. Maddala

National Accounting and Economic Theory
The Collected Papers of Dan Usher, Volume I
Dan Usher

Welfare Economics and Public Finance
The Collected Papers of Dan Usher, Volume II
Dan Usher

Economic Theory and Capitalist Society
The Selected Essays of Shigeto Tsuru, Volume I
Shigeto Tsuru

Methodology, Money and the Firm
The Collected Essays of D.P. O'Brien (2 volumes)
D.P. O'Brien

Economic Theory and Financial Policy
The Selected Essays of Jacques J. Polak (2 volumes)
Jacques J. Polak

Sturdy Econometrics
Edward E. Leamer

The Emergence of Economic Ideas
Essays in the History of Economics
Nathan Rosenberg

Productivity Change, Public Goods and Transaction Costs
Essays at the Boundaries of Microeconomics
Yoram Barzel

Reflections on Economic Development
The Selected Essays of Michael P. Todaro
Michael P. Todaro

The Economic Development of Modern Japan
The Selected Essays of Shigeto Tsuru, Volume II
Shigeto Tsuru

Money, Credit and Policy
Allan H. Meltzer

Macroeconomics and Monetary Theory
The Selected Essays of Meghnad Desai, Volume I
Meghnad Desai

Poverty, Famine and Economic Development
The Selected Essays of Meghnad Desai, Volume II
Meghnad Desai

Explaining the Economic Performance of Nations
Essays in Time and Space
Angus Maddison

Economic Doctrine and Method
The Selected Papers of R.W. Clower
Robert W. Clower

Economic Theory and Reality
Selected Essays on their Disparity and Reconciliation
Tibor Scitovsky

Doing Economic Research
Essays on the Applied Methodology of Economics
Thomas Mayer

Institutions and Development Strategies
The Selected Essays of Irma Adelman, Volume I
Irma Adelman

Dynamics and Income Distribution
The Selected Essays of Irma Adelman, Volume II
Irma Adelman

The Economics of Growth and Development
The Selected Essays of A.P. Thirlwall
A.P. Thirlwall

Theoretical and Applied Econometrics
The Selected Papers of Phoebus J. Dhrymes
Phoebus J. Dhrymes

Innovation, Technology and the Economy
The Selected Essays of Edwin Mansfield (2 volumes)
Edwin Mansfield

Capitalism, Socialism and Post-Keynesianism
The Selected Essays of G.C. Harcourt
G.C. Harcourt